FRENCH THEATRE SINCE 1830

Frontispiece: Paris Street Scene by Steinlen. Illustration from *Gil Blas* 23 December 1894

FRENCH THEATRE
SINCE 1830

Harold Hobson

JOHN CALDER · LONDON
RIVERRUN PRESS · DALLAS

First published in Great Britain 1978 by
John Calder (Publishers) Ltd.
18 Brewer Street, London W1R 4AS

First published in the U.S.A. 1979 by
Riverrun Press Inc.,
4951 Top Line Drive, Dallas, Texas 75247

All photographs courtesy of H. Roger-Viollet unless
otherwise indicated

Typeset in 11pt Baskerville solid by Gloucester Typesetting Co. Ltd.

Printed by M. & A. Thomson Litho Ltd., East Kilbride.
Bound by Hunter & Foulis Ltd., Edinburgh.

CONTENTS

LIST OF ILLUSTRATIONS

Other books by the same author

The First Three Years of the War
The Devil in Woodford Wells (novel)
Theatre
Theatre II
Verdict at Midnight
The Theatre Now
The French Theatre of Today
The International Theatre Annual 1956–1960 (Ed.)
Ralph Richardson
The Pearl of Days; an intimate memoir of The Sunday Times
        (with P. Knightley and L. Russell)

TO MY WIFE
in love and gratitude,
now and always

CHAPTER ONE

The Then and the Now

Every work of art that can claim any sort of success gives pleasure and satisfaction, in varying degree, of two separate kinds. The first sort of satisfaction is historical: it comes of being able to place the particular work under consideration in its connection with what has gone before, and with what is to come after; to see it as a link in the long chain that stretches from antiquity to our own day. This, for example, is in painting a great part of the pleasure of *Les Demoiselles d'Avignon*: in that picture Picasso introduced Africa into European art; and in the theatre of the last hundred years it explains the importance of Jarry's *Ubu Roi*.

The other kind of satisfaction is absolute: it is independent of historical continuity; it exists in and of itself, and has no necessary connection with anything else. The value and interest of *Ubu Roi* would be diminished if there were no Beckett and no Ionesco. It belongs to the realm of art in which things are of more significance for what they lead to than for what they are. But the pleasure to be got from the demented stars which Van Gogh makes glitter over the darkness of Provence would not be in any way affected if there were no Picasso nor Braque. To this order of value there belong in the late nineteenth century *Pelléas et Mélisande*, *Le Pain de ménage*, *Le Plaisir de rompre*, and an occasional *tirade* in Dumas *fils*; in the twentieth, *Partage de midi*, *Le Paquebot Tenacity*, *La Valse des Toréadors*, *En Attendant Godot*, *La Dernière bande*, *Le Square*, *Chin-Chin*, *L'Amante anglaise*, and a couple of speeches in Giraudoux, a dramatist otherwise highly criticizable.

The nineteenth century should not be seen merely, nor even chiefly, as an introduction to the twentieth. It is a house, not a vestibule. History is about what was important at the time, as well as about what is important to us now. The nineteenth cen-

tury's best work was done in symbolism, naturalism, and melodrama, that is, in theatrical forms which have had little or no
influence on the principal dramatic achievements of later days,
apart from an occasional production like Peter Stein's *Summerfolk*.[1] The idiom of *Ubu Roi* (though, contrary to the general
impression, it shies at using the word *merdre*), is considerably
closer to that of the plays most in fashion after *Look Back in
Anger* and *Huis Clos*, Rita Renoir and *Oh! Calcutta!*, than is the
Denise of Dumas *fils*, a melodrama about a betrayed maiden, an
upright hero, and a villainous seducer. Yet *Denise* contains one
long, whiplash speech mounting by a tremendous crescendo to
a shattering climax which is exciting to read even today, and
must have been overwhelming when it was delivered by
Coquelin. On the other hand, the coarseness and crudity of
Ubu Roi are in themselves repellent, receiving only an acci-
dental merit through the backward light thrown on them by
subsequent and better works.

Nevertheless, though the nineteenth century is to be valued
for itself rather than for its foreshadowing of what was to come
later, the seeds are to be found in it of the things which became
the most salient characteristics of the twentieth: surrealism,
commitment, social philosophy, and an increasing preoccupation with the working class. It built up a theatre which, after
the middle of the century, began to rouse dissatisfaction in some
sections of artistic opinion, but which was also both powerful
and prosperous. In the eighteen-fifties young men of promise
increasingly turned their attention to the theatre as the most
effective method of expression open to them, just as did the
leading French authors in the golden period between Sartre's
Les Mains sales in 1948 and Samuel Beckett's *En Attendant Godot*
a few years later.

In 1851 Edmond and Jules de Goncourt published their first
novel, *En 18—*. It came out unfortunately on the day of the
coup d'état which changed France from a republic into the empire
of Napoleon III, and in all the political excitement it naturally
attracted little attention. But the most famous of living drama
critics, Jules Janin, spoke of it favourably, and when the young
men went round to thank him for his kindness he told them that
if they wanted to get anywhere they must write for the theatre.

---

1. National Theatre: *Summerfolk* (by Maxim Gorki), directed by Peter
   Stein for Berlin, seen in London, March, 1977.

It happened that the same idea had already occurred to them, and they had in their pockets a little revue in which at the end of the year a man and a woman sat on either side of the fire and talked about the events of the previous twelve months. They hoped to get this modern notion of actuality produced by the Comédie Française on the night of December 31, that is in about ten days' time from their visit to Janin. On leaving Janin they rushed off to the house of Mme Allan, one of the Comédie's most celebrated actresses. It was rather as if two unknown young men today tried to get into the home of Laurence Olivier or Ralph Richardson. But the Goncourts were unexpectedly successful.

They found Madame Allan dressing in front of a mirror with three glasses that enabled her to see herself from every side, a fact that made a deep impression on them. She liked their little play, and said that she would act in it within the very tight time limit they had set. They were interested to observe that she spoke in a rough, raw voice quite different from the noble tones she emitted on the boards of the National Theatre.

The management of the theatre, however, was less agreeable than Mme Allan, and refused to put on the play at such short notice. But their first acquaintance with the stage did not discourage the Goncourts, and in later years, after the death of his brother, Edmond exercised a considerable influence on the development of the drama. Though this incident for the time being came to nothing, it shows both that the French theatre in 1851 was regarded by the young as important, and that some at least of its actresses were enterprising and generous.

For the next seventy or eighty years the theatre was the principal source of Parisian entertainment. Briefly after 1851 the Goncourts became dramatic critics, and managed almost immediately to get themselves prosecuted for indecency in revealing that the actress Rachel had been sent a nude picture by another actress, to whom she replied imprudently.[2] This considerably disturbed them, but it did not prevent them from devoting to the theatre the same kind of social observation out of which they later constructed their plays and novels.

They adopted a statistical approach, and found that there were twenty theatres in Paris, and seven more in the suburbs.

---

2. DE GONCOURT, Edmond et Jules: *Journal* (*Texte intégral établi et annoté par Robert Ricatte*), Fasquelle, Flammarion, 1956.

The central Paris theatres employed 425 actors and 357 actresses. If the higher personnel of the theatres were included, this meant that 1,028 people owed their daily bread to the Parisian theatrical industry. This is to be compared with the figure of approximately one thousand actors, actresses, directors and stage managers who on any one night in the 1970s are sufficient to keep the whole of the theatres in the West End of London in full working order.

The Goncourts enlarged the scope of their inquiries to include the provinces, which raised the total of people employed from 1,028 to 2,788. But this was not enough in itself to give a full picture of the economic activity of the theatre in France at the middle of the nineteenth century.

> 'Si maintenant nous ajoutons à ces 2,788 individus les musiciens de l'orchestre, les machinistes, costumiers, décorateurs, auteurs dramatiques, compositeurs, chorégraphes, ouvreuses de loges et autres employés, les journalistes, les vendeurs et distributeurs de journaux de théâtre, les médecins, architectes etc, les pompiers et autres agents de sûreté publique, les agents dramatiques et le dixième des hôpitaux, qui représente un certain nombre d'individus nourris, logés, chauffés, soignés et guéris, ou enterrés, nous arrivons à ce résultat qu'il y a en France, en y comprenant les mille et onze professions qui se rattache à l'industrie des théâtres, plus de 10,000 personnes qui glanent sur les planches la vie de chaque jour.'[3]

The Goncourts were impressed by the sheer size of the French theatrical industry, and in an unwonted burst of imagination calculated that if all these people held each others' hands, they would form a circle 5,000 metres in diameter, and 16,000 in perimeter.

---

3. If to these 2,788 people we add the members of the orchestra, the machinists, dressers, designers, composers, choreographers, attendants and other employees, journalists, programme producers and sellers, doctors, architects etc., firemen, and other public safety officials, dramatic agents, and a proportion of hospitals, which contain a certain number of theatre people fed, lodged, warmed, looked after and cured or buried, we reach this result: that in Paris, including the thousand and eleven professions connected with the theatre, more than ten thousand people work on the stage each day.

Since all these people were kept constantly in employment, and runs were much shorter a hundred years ago than they are today; since moreover it was the custom to include three separate pieces in each evening's entertainment, the number of productions was prodigious. In Paris in 1851 there were 259 new plays, and 646 revivals. Eugène Scribe alone wrote 43 of these *chefs-d'oeuvre*. On any one night the Paris theatres could accommodate 32,208 people. Altogether during the year 7,100 performances were given. At three plays per performance this gives a total of 21,308, an average of just over 23 performances for each piece. The receipts were 7,100,000 francs, of which the authors received one-tenth.

The theatre remained the chief element in Parisian entertainment until after the First World War. As late as 1921, when Feuillade's *Fantomas*, *The Birth of a Nation*, *Intolerance*, Charlie Chaplin, Max Linder, Mary Pickford, and Douglas Fairbanks were already world-famous, the receipts of the Paris theatres exceeded those of the cinemas by 104 million francs to 75 millions. Ten years later the cinema had crept slightly ahead, leading by 230 millions to 206 millions. In 1939 theatre receipts had fallen catastrophically to 69 millions, whilst the cinemas achieved the triumphant figure of 373 millions. But by 1948 the theatre had begun to recover. Theatre receipts had grown 25 times since 1939, whilst those of the cinemas had risen only 18 times. The critic Francis Ambrière calculated that, for every two people who went to the theatre in 1939, there were five theatregoers in 1948. This of course was at a time when the reputation of the modern Paris stage was at its height, with Jean Anouilh, André Roussin, Jean-Paul Sartre, Edwige Feuillère, Jean-Louis Barrault, and Madeleine Renaud becoming figures of European renown. Some of the finest French dramatists, notably Samuel Beckett and Marguerite Duras, have emerged since Ambrière made his optimistic calculations. But they are of a kind to appeal chiefly to an élite. In the sixties and seventies the popularity of the great boulevard theatres declined. The theatre in Paris had developed an acute social conscience, and in doing so had become dispersed and fragmented into café-theatres and suburban arenas. The boulevard struggles on, but its vitality steadily diminishes.

1. 'La belle Otéro' above and Colette Willy below as stars of the popular music hall which financially threatened legitimate theatre in the first years of the twentieth century. Illustrations by A. E. Marty in *Comoedia Illustré* 5 January 1913

CHAPTER TWO

Quality and Class Divisions

Though economic prosperity often coincides with artistic merit, there is no necessary reason why it should do so. In the 1860s Barbey d'Aurévilly, who had as trenchant an attack, as fierce a fire in his belly as any drama critic of the time, argued uncompromisingly that the popularity of the theatre meant that it appealed to the masses, and that mass audiences were incapable of appreciating artistic standards that would be acceptable to intelligent and educated people.

This attitude was confirmed by another leader of theatrical opinion, Jules Janin (1804–74), the critic of *Le Journal des débats*. It is odd that Janin should have advised the young Goncourts to write for the theatre, since he spent a great deal of his time and considerable eloquence in denouncing whatever the theatre had to offer. His reviews are strange affairs; they are written at a high pitch of emotion; they rarely mention the names of the players or say anything about their performances; Janin sometimes omits even to give the title of the play he is reviewing. But he has a quality which makes him both very antiquated and extremely modern. He judged the plays he saw from an almost exclusively political angle; in the theatre of John Osborne's *Look Back in Anger* or Aline Mnouchkine's *1789* this seems natural enough. What removes him from present sympathies is that his politics were those of the *ancien régime*.

To Janin the romantic drama of Alexandre Dumas *père* (1803–70) and of Alfred de Vigny (1797–1863), as well as of lesser writers like Félix Pyat and A. Luchet, exemplified all the evil of an age that offended his deeply traditional soul: and this simply because it was peoples' drama. He appears to have thought that between the production of Dumas *père*'s *Henri III et sa cour* in 1829 and the *coup d'état* of 1851, the nature of the

7

drama was dictated by the tastes of the poorest members of the audience. These demanded violence, torture, melodrama, unnatural vice, and absurdly romantic bombast.

He is especially hard on one of the most famous plays of the century, Dumas's *Antony* (1831). Dumas's object in this play was to denounce prejudice against bastards (he had one of his own, the future author of *La Dame aux camélias*). Antony, says Janin, talks like a hero of Diderot's: 'My birth is shameful in the eyes of men,' to which his mistress, Mme d'Hervey, sententiously replies, 'Our birth is beyond our control, but our virtues are our own.' Janin then chooses to claim that this is banging a very old drum. It is difficult to explain, he asserted, by what process of reasoning this young man Dumas has been able to persuade himself that as late as 1831 it is worth anyone's while to attack the medieval prejudice of birth, when nobody thinks about it any more, and to fight so fiercely for a principle which everybody adopted long ago: namely, social equality. It would have surprised Janin if he had known that the advanced drama of a

2.   A Paris Theatre in 1837 by Pruche. Photograph by courtesy of Harlingue-Viollet

hundred and fifty years later would still be debating the same question, before audiences with the same very similar tastes for violence, cruelty, and hatred as he himself professed to abhor.

The ending of *Antony* is one of the most celebrated in French drama. Antony's mistress, Mme d'Hervey, hears her husband's footsteps approaching the room where they are both hidden. M. d'Hervey has unexpectedly returned from Strasbourg to Paris. Antony sensibly suggests that both he and the lady should clear out as quickly as possible. 'Oh no,' she cries, 'I must keep my reputation.' This is precisely what Antony, by somewhat drastic measures, enables her to do. As M. d'Hervey comes up the stairs, Antony stabs her to the heart, flings open the door, and says magnificently, 'I killed her with this dagger. She resisted me.' Janin remarks reasonably enough that this was a curious way of preserving a lady's reputation. It was made all the more absurd by the fact that Mme Dorval as Mme d'Hervey sat bolt upright in her chair, and died without a tremor. Yet it was this play that made Mme Dorval famous. It was a culminating point in Dumas's career, and bred a whole progeny of dark, romantic heroes. It was in fact a prime example of the modern drama after *Henri III et sa cour* and *Hernani* had shattered the classical conceptions of playwriting, and the ordinary public in the cheaper seats were wild with enthusiasm.

Janin constantly complained that the influence of this public brought a spirit of demagoguery into the theatre. If an archbishop is a character in a play then he must be a lecher, and even (at a time, too, when fires were mysteriously breaking out all over France) an encourager of arson: if a king, even though he were as brave as François I, he must be shown as a coward, fainting at the sight of a drawn sword. This is an incident in Pyat's and Luchet's *Ango*, a play about a celebrated merchant of Dieppe who built a magnificent house in Varengeville, not far from the picturesque church overlooking the sea in which Georges Porto-Riche and Braque are buried.

Janin was particularly distressed that the new drama was, amongst other things, a drama of social criticism. He called Alfred de Vigny's *Chatterton* a dangerous play because it ascribed to the inhumanity of what we now call the system the death of a sham poet whom Janin regarded as nothing better than a layabout. In his passionate denunciation of the play he expressed the cardinal principle of his thought in the words: 'Society should do nothing for those who have done nothing for society.' Is it, he exclaims elsewhere, contemplating the gloomy fate of a drama critic, is it pleasant to be chained alive to this corpse that is called 'le drame moderne'? Isn't it enough to suffer and follow its blasphemies and deliriums without having to remember them for twenty-four hours so as to describe in detail a mass of crimes and infamies? Yet it was for this place of crime and infamy that Janin advised the Goncourts to write.

There was however one critic who agreed with the popular verdict on the new drama. This was Francisque Sarcey. 'I always come back to this point,' wrote Sarcey, 'there are plenty of people (and it is these who pay for their seats) who come to the theatre with the firm intention of seeing and hearing, not a psychological study, not a dissertation on history, not a philosophic discussion . . . but quite simply a drama, a piece of theatre.' It was from this attitude that he judged the conclusion of *Antony*. 'Antony's dénoument,' he said, 'has become legendary . . . Of all dénouments, past, present, and to come, that of *Antony* is the most dazzling, the most unexpected, the most logical, the swiftest; it is an invention of genius.'

There is however one thing to be remembered. Janin saw *Antony* whilst it was new, and condemned it. Sarcey did not condemn it, but he did not see it till 1884, when it was already old-fashioned. Thus, right at the beginning of this study, we encounter a question which will never be far from its enquiries. Drama critics are assumed, rightly or wrongly, to be more closely acquainted with the theatre of the past and its legacy than ordinary playgoers are expected to be. But because of this are they better judges than others of new, radical departures in drama?

Actually, by the standards of the twentieth century, whether of the naturalistic drama of Galsworthy, the political drama of Trevor Griffiths, or the elliptical drama of Marguerite Duras or Harold Pinter, Janin was right about *Antony*, and Sarcey wrong. That this should be so casts a disturbing question mark over drama criticism in general. For the right decision was reached, and what is more, reached instantly, by the man who took the less serious view of his profession and its responsibilities.

It is interesting to speculate about Janin's sincerity in his judgment of the plays he saw, and his denunciations of the influence of popular taste upon the quality of the theatre. Sarcey (1827–99), who after Janin's death succeeded him as the most powerful of Parisian critics, gravely doubted Janin's integrity the first time he read any of his reviews. An obituary article is conventionally the place for praise and appreciation. But when Sarcey wrote about Janin on the morrow of his death, though he admitted that the man might have had some personal charm, he painted a very black picture of his attitude to the theatre and of his aesthetic morality. In doing so he set out one of the first examinations ever made by a practising critic of the principles that should govern his conduct. All the arguments are on Sarcey's side. His is the true doctrine. He carried it out conscientiously and with ability. It is disturbing to find that it is the charlatan who got things right.

When Sarcey came to Paris from the country in 1859, chance led him to read one of Janin's reviews. He knew that Janin had been for many years' le sacré roi' of French critics, and he was thrown into a state of great mental commotion by what he read. That this was the kind of stuff that Parisians admired bewildered him. He found that Janin wrote about almost anything except what he was supposed to be writing about. He used his ostensible subject-matter—the play and the players—merely to display his own, generally irrelevant, brilliance; and when he deigned to say what a play was about he told the story with a dazzling flippancy designed to make it appear ridiculous, and to demonstrate his own superiority.

Astonishment and stupefaction, said Sarcey, were words too pale to express what he felt. He compared himself to a man who had fallen out of a fourth storey window without killing himself, and gingerly fingered his limbs to make sure that he was all right. The odd thing is that Janin would probably have accepted Sarcey's description of his aims. More than once he came near to thus stating them himself. The critic, he declared, must always make the public think of himself and not of the play or the actors. He exemplified this in one of the strangest boasts ever made by a drama critic.

He said that he had once as a joke actually invented a great actor. The man had not been a great actor at all, but Janin made *le tout Paris* think that he was. The theatre where this man played was a dreadful hole, said Janin a generation after he had deceived his readers; everything in it was repulsive, the air was poisoned, the violins out of tune, and the public came only to rejoice in seeing its hero kicked in the backside. Janin congratulated himself on having hoaxed all fashionable Paris into flocking to this disreputable hovel, and applauding as a great actor the miserable mime whom he despised. In fact Janin did not merely influence his own contemporaries in this matter. The fame which he conferred on the wretched man has persisted right into the middle of the twentieth century. For his name was Deburau, the same Deburau whom Jean-Louis Barrault played with unforgettable wistfulness in *Les Enfants du paradis*.

It is better at this point to call in an independent witness. Edmond Got (1822–1901) was one of the most reliable sociétaires of the Comédie Française during the nineteenth century. He was a man of very sound sense who could see when his colleagues were acting badly and he himself was acting well. He also had the rarer gift of seeing when they were acting well and he was acting badly. He was a leading exponent of the drama of 'le bon sens', as Sarcey was of the same thing in criticism. But his judgment did not confirm Sarcey, but Janin. When he was very young, Got saw *Antony* in its first production with Bocage and Madame Dorval. He was so carried away that the next night he absconded from school to see it again. A few years later in 1842 he saw the same production with the same players at the Odéon. When the curtain rose the theatre was half empty. But after three acts he could no longer stand it, and left. How taste changes, he exclaimed.

The changing atmosphere of the times in which he lived was something of which, as a young man, Edmond Got was almost exaggeratedly conscious. His constant theme in his early days as a pensionnaire is that the old world was dying; with railway trains and the telegraph he prophesies that it will be re-born. For better? For worse? Got had his doubts. He was learned in the classical languages, and in his days of youthful poverty he made a little extra money by translating the Greek Fathers on commission. When everyone is educated, and follows a liberal profession, who will be found to make their boots? Got was worried by such questions as this. He was even more worried when during the revolution of 1848, which briefly established a republic, he saw a man carrying a banner which bore the words, 'For the victors, loot: for the others, the stake.'

Scornful as he was of the revolutionaries' demand for such things as the right to work, Got perceived, and seems even to have been pleased, that in response to the ferment of the age the theatre itself must change. He had no sympathy with the 1848 revolution which threw out Louis-Phillipe; but he had

even less with the Comédie Française when throughout the
tumult it continued to play the old and in his opinion faded
repertory founded on Molière and Scribe. What can such plays
have to say to the world in which we live, he demanded. He was
a striking example of the fact that a man can be in the forefront
of the avant garde of his time and yet a reactionary. He was out
of sympathy with his age, but he insisted that plays should be
relevant to it.

He was immediately responsive to any breath of change in
the air. He noted that the importance of the director was
increasing. The director is the man who supplies the sauce for
the dish. A time will come, said Got, when the sauce will be
more important than the fish: as indeed it did a hundred years
later when Jouvet and Peter Brook and Patrice Chéreau and
Peter Stein arrived. Got recognised a new talent with surprising
speed. In 1844 Got saw two plays at the Odéon by old school-
fellows: one was *Antigone*, by Auguste Vacquerie and Paul
Meurice; the other, *La Cigué*, by the twenty-four year old Emile
Augier. *Antigone* was a skilful adaptation from Sophocles, nothing more. But *La Cigué* roused Got to enthusiasm. It revealed a
temperament and had a real value for the future. It confirmed
Got's conviction that change was in the air. He declared that it
was time for a new generation to surge into the theatre. Second
class dramatists, with Scribe himself, their great chief, will soon
have passed from fashion, he said. It is not always that a new
dramatist destined to be one of the great names of the future is
so swiftly recognised.

About Deburau, Got was more circumspect than Janin either
in his enthusiasm or his repudiation. When Deburau died—
long before Janin recanted or prevaricated—Got said that
Janin and others had probably exaggerated his talent. Nevertheless he was far from underrating him. In 1843—Janin did
not explain away his first opinion until many years later—Got
drew up a list of those performances which, he said, he could
never forget. In the highest rank he placed Mlle Mars in *Le
Misanthrope* and *Tartuffe*; Madame Dorval in *Chatterton*, which
Janin so much hated; Mlle Rachel in *Andromaque*; and Frédérick
Lemaître in *Robert Macaire*. But he placed Deburau at Les
Funambules in *Le Muet d'Ispahan* and *Le Billet de 1000 francs* also
very high, only a little below the greatest. Further he included
Deburau amongst 'les grands artistes qui—à tort ou à raison—

3. Théâtre des Funambules, Boulevard du Crime by Gustave Doré. Photograph by courtesy of Collection Viollet

. . . fouettent le sang de la foule',[1] though he seems to have done this with some misgiving. He puts down the names of Rachel, Lemaître, and Dorval without hesitation: and then adds doubtfully 'even Deburau, since what we are thinking about is popularity.'

In the light of all this it is more than likely that when he first saw him Janin genuinely considered Deburau to be as great an actor as he said he was, and was quite sincere in the laudatory review that made *le tout Paris* flock to the Boulevard du Crime. But thirty years later, when tastes had changed, he may have

---

1.   . . . the great artistes—who rightly or wrongly—. . . whip up the blood of the crowds.

felt it advisable to pretend that his earlier review had been a joke. This, of course, is dishonourable behaviour, and critics should have a sharper sense of their responsibilities. But good aesthetic judgment is not necessarily allied to moral rectitude. Got gives a remarkable instance of this. He recognised that critics have an enormous influence; but in his opinion they were venal and dishonest. The most despicable of them all was a man called Charles Maurice. Maurice gave favourable reviews only to actors who either flattered him or bribed him. Got did neither. Maurice, meeting him one day in the corridors of the Comédie Française just before Got was about to go on to the stage, told him that he was an insolent young upstart for not visiting him to pay homage. Thereafter his reviews savagely abused Got's performances. But Got mentions this point only to add that there was no one whose exposure of his weaknesses had so benefited him.

Got completely confirmed Janin's view, or alleged view, that proletarian influence on the theatre was considerable. In fact, even before the monarchy fell in 1848, he found evidence of it everywhere. Dickens himself was thought lacking in democratic outlook. *Nicholas Nickleby* was condemned in some quarters because it did not accord with the republican programme for the education of the masses. The reception given at the Comédie Française to a performance of *George Dandin* particularly struck him. In 1841 Molière himself was called in question for his political and social outlook. Gentility had then lost so much of its prestige that even a fine actor like Provost could not make the humiliation of the worthy Dandin before the aristocrats acceptable to the public. Dandin's being forced to go humbly on his knee aroused particular hostility. Incidents such as this made a mark on Got's mind that was never afterwards effaced. The Second Empire and the Third Republic which followed the *coup d'état* of 1851 were periods of luxury, splendour, and great national economic prosperity. There was an outburst of patriotic songs on the light opera stage. But looming behind all this Got could see the spectre of revolution. His constant refrain in his diaries is that the world as he knew it was coming to an end. He heard its death knell sounded when Napoleon III legalised strikes. Strikes may not, he said, mean much at present. But they are a weapon which will some day destroy the civilization and prosperity of the West.

Yet the paradox remains. Whilst the theatre presented swashbuckling kings, dashing aristocrats, and dark, romantic heroes to whom honour was dearer than life—especially than the life of others—the people flocked to it. When it began to reflect ordinary life, and deal seriously with moral problems, they stayed away, and left it to the middle and upper classes. It must be admitted that these did not make at all a bad thing of it.

Janin expressed a very influential view. In his *Avant-Propos* to *Le Demi-Monde*, which was played for the first time at the Gymnase on 20 March, 1855, Dumas *fils* also declared that the theatre was not for the working class. It should be directed at men and women of brains and breeding. In the 1860s in Paris as in the 1960s in London there was a strong feeling that the theatre needed a new audience. But with this difference. In the 1960s the urge was to bring, or even force, the working class into the theatre; in the 1860s the urge was to drive them out. By virtue of spectacularly raising the level of theatrical achievement, the earlier movement succeeded better than the later.

Its most effective instrument for driving the workers out of the theatre, and substituting for them an audience entirely composed of the educated and progressive middle class, was Edmond de Goncourt's conviction, that the stage should deal with the ordinary problems of working people, and deal with them, moreover, in a realistic and unsensational way. So long as plays confined themselves to the intrigues of ballrooms and palaces, to duels, adultery, and gambling, the theatre attracted popular audiences. When it began to concern itself seriously with the harsh conditions and sordid temptations of life in domestic service, the popular element in audiences rapidly diminished. The social standing of audiences rose as the social standing of characters in plays fell. The fact that the plays about the underprivileged were a vast improvement on those about courtiers and courtisans seems to have hastened the flight of the working class from the theatre.

It is a mistake to think that the plays which Dumas *fils*, for example, wrote about the rich were frivolous and devoid of merit. The author of *La Dame aux camélias*, *Le Demi-Monde*, *Les Idées de Madame Aubray*, and *Denise* was sincerely and seriously troubled by questions of morality. He was alarmed by the increasing power of courtisans in French society and politics, and wished to see it diminished. At the same time he pleaded incessantly for women to be judged by the same standards as men, or rather, for men to be judged by the same standards as

4. A première in the Théâtre Montmartre by André Deramberg depicting the working class audience disliked by the critics of 1860. Photograph by courtesy of N. D. Roger Viollet

women, and for thus advancing the ideal of sex equality he was roundly condemned by Sarcey. He believed that a woman who has fallen is in no degree morally worse than a man in the same situation.

This is his central thesis in *Denise*, the play which contains the speech I have already praised. Fernand, the heartless seducer of the guileless heroine, unfolds his lax views on morality to a certain Thouvenin, played by the great Coquelin, who probably accepted the part because it provided him with this enormous

5. *La Dame aux camélias* by Dumas *fils* with Edwige Feuillère and Jacques Berthier

outburst, rushing with ever accelerating speed towards a climax that sweeps through the air like the blow of a well-aimed dagger.

Fernand has just said that the only thing that matters in life is vividness of sensation; he wishes to burn with a hard, gem-like flame no matter what the flame consumes and destroys. At this point Thouvenin, who has hitherto listened more or less

patiently, can contain himself no longer. He breaks out: 'Ah!
Je comprends ça! Ainsi un de mes amis, qui était mouchard . . .'
'Mouchard!' exclaims Fernand, in surprise that so eminently
respectable a man as Thouvenin should have associated with
informers.

'Oui,' says Thouvenin undisturbed.

'Vous avez de jolis amis,' replies Fernand sarcastically, at
which point the flood of Thouvenin's scornful and bitter contempt pours out in a cataract of destructive eloquence.

THOUVENIN. Et je les choisis encore. Eh bien, mon ami me
    disait comme vous, en un moment d'expansion, qu'il avait
    dans cette carrière, encore plus discréditée, mais bien plus
    émouvante que celle de séducteur, qu'il avait, lui aussi,
    éprouvé des voluptés d'une finesse inexprimable. Il me
    disait que, quand il serrait la main d'un camarade, d'un
    ami, qu'il le faisait parler, qu'il entrait dans sa confiance,
    qu'il surprenait ses secrets, qu'il allait le dénoncer, qu'il le
    voyait surveillé, arrêté, emprisonné, déporté, sans que
    l'autre le soupçonnât une minute; quand il allait ensuite
    le visiter dans sa prison, qu'il assistait à ses dernières
    entrevues avec sa femme et ses enfants, qu'il faisait semblant
    de pleurer avec lui, qu'il recevait les dernières confidences
    et les dernières recommandations de ce malheureux qui ne
    se doutait de rien, mon ami me disait qu'il avait là des
    sensations auprès desquelles les vôtres doivent être de
    simples balivernes. Cependant—[and at this point
    Thouvenin pauses to make certain of his annihilating
    peroration]—cependant, la plus grande sensation qu'il ait
    eu, je crois, il est vrai qu'il a été la dernière, c'est la nuit où
    il s'est trouvé pris, dans une rue obscure et déserte en
    apparence, entre quatre gaillards qui l'attendaient dans
    l'ombre et qui l'ont assommé. Il a du avoir là quelque
    minutes—supérieures—qui vous manquent encore, mais
    que je vous souhaite de tous mes voeux.[2]

---

2. Ah! I understand that. One of my friends, who was an informer . . .
    Informer!
    Yes.
    You have a very select acquaintance.
    I choose it carefully. Well, one day my friend, in a moment of ela-
    tion like you, confided to me that he had in his career, which is even
    more discreditable, but far more exciting, than that of a seducer, that

There is no whiplash ending to any play in the French theatre comparable with this of Dumas's until the 'damnation éternelle' that concludes the final *tirade* in Jean Giraudoux's *Pour Lucrèce* more than sixty years later.

Dumas's achievement is not to be dispised even if, in his melodramatic, contrived, and sentimental plays, he wrote little but this speech that is capable of arousing an echo today. It is easy to exaggerate how much of past literature, outside national theatres and universities, is still alive. In a poem, even in a famous poem, said George Moore, we generally remember only a single stanza, and of that stanza very often only a single line remains' in the memory.

> Le clair de lune bleu qui baigne l'horizon . . .[3]

was all that Moore could recall of one of Hugo's most celebrated poems, 'La Fête chez Thérèse'. Nor was Moore alone in his opinion, Villiers de l'Isle Adam maintained that no poem should be longer than a solitary line.

> O pasteur, Hespérus à l'occident s'allume.[4]

'The sweet, sad serenity of the evening air is contained in this verse,' said Moore, and asked, 'Why add to it?' If Dumas *fils* gives us only this one speech of Thouvenin's that is worth

---

he also had experienced pleasures of inexpressible delicacy. He told me that, when he shook a comrade, a friend, by the hand, when he made him talk, when he entered into his confidence, when he discovered his secrets, when he went to denounce him, when he saw him followed, arrested, imprisoned, convicted, without the other having the slightest suspicion; then when he went to visit him in prison, when he was present at his last interview with his wife and children, when he pretended to weep with him, when he received the last confidences and instructions of this unhappy man who guessed nothing, then my friend told me that he had sensations in comparison with which yours are simply milk and water. However . . . however, the biggest sensation he ever had and it's true that it was the last—was one night when he found himself caught in an obscure and apparently deserted street, by four ruffians who were waiting for him in the shadows, and who assassinated him. He must then have had several—superior—moments which at present are lacking to you, but which I hope with all my heart that you will soon encounter.

3. The moonlight bathes the horizon.
4. Shepherd, Hesperus rises in the west.

remembering, and that we remember, he has not done badly by us, nor we by him.

Dumas knew the hardship and misery endured by a girl who has been seduced and deserted, as his own mother had been. But though in *Denise* in general, and in Thouvenin's speech in particular, he was writing of things with which he was personally involved, and from which he had himself suffered, the continuing vitality of what Thouvenin says is due less to the sincerity behind it than to its style, which, in the convention of rhetoric to which the French stage takes more kindly than the English, is masterly.

There was frequently an inconsistency between what Dumas said, and what he did. Sometimes he behaved better than his words. He called Zola 'a filthy foreigner', but vigorously supported his claim to enter the Académie Française. Sometimes he behaved worse. Despite the highmindedness of his moral preaching, his own marital betrayals were often the subject of discussion at the dinner tables of his friends, so much so, in fact, that on one occasion his second wife exclaimed in exasperation, 'O God, just let me live long enough to see M. Dumas in his coffin.' She was even said to offer up a prayer to this effect. The prayer was not answered; Dumas outlived her. To the indignation of his daughters he then married a lady whom he had forbidden to be introduced to them, on the ground that she had been divorced, and was therefore probably immoral.

But if Dumas's sincerity may be questionable, his style is not. There was something impregnable about it. It was constructed so that every bolt and rivet fitted perfectly. Alphonse Daudet, in commenting on Dumas's speech on his reception into the French Academy, referred to 'ces formules serrées, concises, énoncées en petites phrases qui se succèdent en s'entrechoquant avec des . . . duretés métalliques.'[5] They are nowhere better exemplified than in *Denise*.

Dumas deserved to live because of a single speech. Ten years later there came a play which went one better, since it actually lived because of a single word. In the 1890s there were three plays, Maurice Maeterlinck's *Pelléas et Mélisande*, Edmond de Goncourt's *La Fille Elisa*, and Alfred Jarry's *Ubu Roi* which broke the theatrical conventions of their time. All three created

---

5. These tight, concise expressions, set in little phrases which interlock like parts of a machine.

a considerable stir. Goncourt was pained by the vilification which *La Fille Elisa*, like most of his other works, brought upon him. *Pelléas et Mélisande* was made an object of fun (rather amusing if wholly imperceptive fun) by Francisque Sarcey. *Ubu Roi* caused dismay nearly everywhere except in its author. That a play should begin with one of the characters saying 'Merdre', which is how *Ubu Roi* opens, was a sensational affront to all the linguistic habits of the age, and it did not secure general approval until the 1960s, when *Ubu Roi* became a banner-leader in the cult of making free use of all the resources of language.

The play made a further departure by presenting caricatures instead of characters, and it made changes in substance as well as in style. It represented the bourgeoisie not as a class requiring, and capable of improvement, as in Dumas, but as wholly acquisitive and vile. It was, accidentally, the first uncompromisingly revolutionary drama, for it was inspired less by political and sociological conviction than by private hatred and contempt for a master by whom Jarry was taught at school. Jarry was born at Laval in 1873, and died in 1907 in Paris.

Ubu Roi was first performed on 10 December 1896, in the Nouveau Théâtre, under the direction of Aurélien-Marie Lugné-Poe for the Théâtre de l'Oeuvre, and its scenes, which take place in Poland ('that is,' said Jarry, 'nowhere'), were designed by Pierre Bonnard, Toulouse-Lautrec, and others. Père Ubu was played by Firmin Gémier, who thus became the first actor to speak the 'mot de Cambronne' out loud on the French stage, however many other players may have muttered it under their breath. Jarry was nervous; he was also anxious to make his play understood. He made a speech to the audience, apologised for the small scenic resources of the Théâtre de l'Oeuvre, said that his main object had been to get Gémier as his principal player, and that everybody had sat up the night before painting cardboard horses. He also distributed programme notes in which he pointed out (unnecessarily, one would have thought) that Ubu was an 'être ignoble', in which he resembled everyone else.

His nervousness was justified. Vallette, the editor of *Le Mercure de France*, considered the play droll, and his wife, Rachilde, the author of a celebrated ambiguous novel, *Monsieur Vénus*, shouted 'Be quiet' to those in the audience who booed it. But the overwhelming opinion of the house was against the play

6. Sarah Bernhardt as Theodora (Théâtre de la Porte St. Martin 1890). Photograph by courtesy of Collection Viollet

from the very beginning. Even Jarry's friends had little faith in it, and hid their heads in embarrassment. They were disconcerted by its comic-book technique, its grotesque masks, and the placards with which, anticipating Brecht, Jarry indicated the scene of the action. Jules Renard, himself the author of two of the few plays—*Le Pain de ménage* and *Le Plaisir de rompre*—which were still genuinely alive three-quarters of a century later, was deeply upset by it.

Renard had gone to the theatre in a relatively exuberant mood, for it had been one of the happiest days of his life. He had visited Sarah Bernhardt, and she had kissed him on both cheeks. This made him feel that he had been admitted into the highest Parisian circles. Edmond Rostand, the author of *Cyrano de Bergerac*, had been with him, and they had both been touched by Bernhardt's affection. They remained touched, melted, until the evening.

But Renard's good humour did not last long. From the middle of the first act he felt it was going to be a disaster. It alarmed him to notice that as soon as Gémier uttered the word 'Merdre' someone in the audience replied 'Mangre'.

Everything that evening filled Renard with gloom, and he wrote in his *Journal* that if Jarry did not confess the next day that he had been making fun of the audience he would never recover from the blow to his reputation. Years later, in London, people said the same thing about Beckett and Pinter. Renard had read the play, and claimed to have perceived that there was a falling away at the end, but, he said, 'I was not prepared for this total collapse.'

Jarry did not take Renard's advice, nor apologise to the public. He wrote other Ubu plays, and an Ubu Almanach. Never did he show the slightest regret for what he had done. He opens *Ubu Enchaîné* with a spirited recollection of the shock he had caused with the first word of *Ubu Roi*. *Ubu Enchaîné* begins:

> *Acte Premier. Scène première. Père Ubu, Mère Ubu.*
> *Père Ubu s'avance et ne dit rien.*
>
> MÈRE UBU. Quoi! tu ne dis rien, Père Ubu. As-tu donc oublié le mot?
> PÈRE UBU. Mère . . . Ubu. Je ne veux plus prononcer le mot, il m'a valu trop de désagréments.[6]

Perhaps Jarry's spirits were kept up, like those of many an

author after a stormy first night, by the words of a judicious critic, in this instance Catulle Mendès, the poet and lover of the actress Marguerite Moreno, to whom Colette some years later wrote a memorable series of letters. Mendès admitted the booing, and the play's crudity. Nevertheless, he said justly, amongst the hubbub and opprobrium, le Père Ubu exists, composed of Punch, an enormous parody of Macbeth and Napoleon, and a souteneur; he exists, and now will always exist; you will never forget him. There is nothing surprising in the filthy language. There are times when, the pavements cracking, the sewers like volcanoes explode and ejaculate; and he noted that Gémier, under the crushing weight of a farcical role that is quite unfunny, and made no one laugh, was excellent in standing up to the insults of the audience, and in faithfulness to the author.

The reputation, though not the value, of the French drama fell more or less rapidly after the period when it was a truly popular entertainment. Whereas in the middle of the century Janin had advised the Goncourts that men who wished to make literary headway must write for the theatre, Jules Lemaître the critic in 1898 accepted as an axiom that the best writers would confine themselves to history, novels, and criticism, leaving the theatre alone.

In saying this he had failed to estimate the importance of two new authors, both of them men who wrote for small and élitist audiences. These were Jules Renard, who so signally failed to appreciate *Ubu Roi*, and Maurice Maeterlinck. They did not actually raise the reputation of the Paris theatre because, with certain exceptions—in the case of Maeterlinck, Octave Mirbeau, who compared him favourably with Shakespeare—few people outside an affected group of intellectuals recognised their merits. Their achievement, however, is more apparent today than it was when their plays were produced for the first time. It is now clear that they each did something which had not yet been accomplished in the theatre. Maeterlinck, in *La Princesse Maleine* and *Pelléas et Mélisande*, demonstrated three things not

---

6. *Act 1. Scene one. Père Ubu, Mère Ubu.*
       Père Ubu walks forward and is silent.
  MÈRE UBU. What! You're not saying anything, Père Ubu. Does this mean you have forgotten the word?
  PÈRE UBU. Mère . . . Ubu. I don't want to say the word. It caused too much trouble last time.

properly appreciated before; that the proper way to write poetic drama is to use unpoetic speech, that moral perversion can produce scenes of high dramatic tension, and that the most effective way of saying something is to say something else.

Renard's achievement was less paradoxical, but equally important. He understood, or at least practised, naturalism better than its titular prophets. Edmond de Goncourt thought that naturalism meant reproducing the misery of servant girls who succeeded in producing bastard children without their employers even noticing that they were *enceinte*. This feat, by the way, is not impossible. Goncourt prided himself on the minuteness of his observation, yet he had a resident maid of long standing who became the mother of two children whose existence he never guessed until after the girl was dead, although she rarely left his house.

Now a play like *Germinie Lacerteux*, which is based on this incident, is notable for introducing into literature and the theatre working class characters with problems and difficulties that are just as compelling as those of the more fortunate members of society. But it is naturalism only if naturalism is anything that exclusively concerns itself with the dramatic darknesses of life amongst the wage-earning classes. The same can be said of Zola, who apparently thought that courtesans and actresses inevitably had their beauty ruined by syphilis. It is really the romantic agony transposed down the social scale. It serves a useful purpose, but it is not naturalism. The naturalism of Renard however is the real thing. It is the reproduction of the audible and visible surfaces, not of exceptional misfortunes, but of quite ordinary life.

What Zola and the Goncourts did was to borrow naturalism from the Italians as it was understood by the actor Salvini, who made a great sensation in London by the fierce realism of his performance as Othello. 'Staggering then to a seat,' says the Victorian critic, Joseph Knight, 'he commences, sitting and weeping, the final speech. Nearing the end he rises, and at the supreme moment cuts his throat with a short scimitar, hacking and hewing with savage energy, and imitating the noise that escaping blood and air may together make when the windpipe is severed. Nothing in art so terribly realistic as this death-scene has been attempted . . . Terror is, indeed, the aim of all tragic art. When for this is substituted horror, and even commonplace horror, the degradation of art has commenced.'

Zola does not discuss this point. Salvini's Othello left him uninterested. 'I am indifferent to it,' he says, 'because it is too remote from me . . . As for the performance, I am still more at a loss. I could call it sublime, but I remain cold. Perhaps it is my fault.'

The *coup de foudre* came for him when he saw the Salvini company in *La Mort civile*, a naturalistic play in which an escaped convict kills himself so as not to spoil the lives of his wife and daughter. Here Zola felt Salvini's full power. 'I have no need of readymade phrases . . . The actor seized and over-whelmed me. I felt in him a man, a living being with my own passions.' There was no rolling of the eyes here, nor waving of arms, nor beating of the breast; only the perfect imitation of real men's behaviour. The company was like its leading actor. 'Not once do they look at the audience. The auditorium does not seem to exist for them. When they listen they fix their eyes on whoever is speaking, and when they speak they really address the person listening. None of them comes to the prompter's box, like a tenor about to sing his big song . . .' The play, by Giacometti, did not strike him as particularly good. 'But it belongs to my time, it is in the air that I breathe, it touches me like something that happens to my neighbour. I prefer life to art, I have often said so. A masterpiece frozen by centuries is, after all, only a beautiful corpse.'

It is clear enough that what Zola was looking at in *La Mort civile* is less the play than the players. A convict who kills himself through compassion is not noticeably nearer to the daily life of ordinary people than a successful professional man who murders his wife through jealousy. What Zola was experiencing here was realistic acting in a melodramatic play. Not until Renard's *Le Plaisir de rompre* (1897) and *Le Pain de ménage* (1898) did the Paris theatre find a drama totally devoid of any melo-dramatic elements.

Jules Renard is the most memorable dramatist of the late nineteenth century, more memorable even than Maeterlinck. He was born in 1864 at Châlons-du-Maine, and died in 1910. His father was a railway engineer, François Renard, and his mother, Anna Rosa Colin. François Renard was a Freemason, twelve years older than his wife, who was a fervent Catholic. They had been married for several years before Jules Renard was born, and already they were beginning to find each other uncongenial. Exasperated by his wife's chatter, lies and continual complaints, François took refuge in an almost complete silence. Consequently it was not a happy household, and Jules Renard had a miserable childhood, for which he took what some critics have considered to be a brutal revenge in *Poil de carotte* and *La Bigote*. His mother frightened him 'with a sort of physical fear, an imaginative fear that he kept all his life'. Never knowing what she would say, whether it would be an endearment or a curse, it became second nature to him to be on the defensive. Throughout his forty-six years of life he did not know a moment's ease with her. 'Her terrifying eyes, her sharp, metallic voice,' says Léon Guichard, 'paralysed him to the end.'[7]

With other people his method was not so much defence as attack. Before he was thirty his savagery of speech had become notorious, so that many people, some of them famous, were afraid to meet him. But it is the unsuspected parts of his nature that are revealed (as nowhere else) in *Le Plaisir de rompre* and *Le Pain de ménage*. Renard as the world of his friends and acquaintances knew him is to be found in his *Journal*. Here he cut out from his writing anything ornamental or superfluous. He hated anything vague or symbolic. ('Mallarmé,' he said contemptuously, 'is untranslateable, even into French.') In his *Journal* his thoughts and daydreams (as well as some of his night dreams, which occasionally are horrifying) are set down in the fewest possible words, in bare statements just as they occurred to him. He makes no effort to mitigate or soften or expand them, or to provide them with any background or explanation. They are like unset diamonds; they glitter and cut.

On 18 February 1890 he notes: 'Her shift moved gently, as if animated by bugs.' There is no indication that the shift belonged to anyone in particular, or even that it existed outside his imagination. All we know is that this was the kind of fancy that gave him pleasure. Almost a year later he wrote, again without explanation, 'Sir, on a butcher's table I have seen brains like yours.' He contemplated writing a novel about the death of someone well known who was still alive, and he worked out the plot of a story in which an elderly neighbour, Mlle Blanche, should be murdered. The murderers should not be found out, and should feel no remorse. He resolved to make this

---

7.   GUICHARD, Léon: *Renard*, NRF Gallimard, Paris, 1961.

story 'coldly ferocious'. He had been annoyed by Mlle Blanche's pretensions in having each week a visitor's day, although she was very poor. He noted that no one came to it.

Like Bernard Shaw, his contemporary, though without Shaw's good nature and overflowing high spirits, Renard was in full revolt against what he considered to be the false romanticism of literature and the theatre; against the conventional idea that mothers are tender and kind, that children are pure and loveable, and that if a man and woman are left alone for five minutes they will instantly think of getting into bed together.

His bitterness, his morbidity, his capacity for making people miserable, for inducing a mood of taut nerves was hereditary. When her daughter-in-law said to Renard's mother, 'Yes, maman,' Maman replied, 'I am not your mother. I have no need of your compliments.'

Yet Renard's life was not devoid of affection. He was devoted to his wife, though by no means indifferent to other women. The sight of a dancer at the Folies Bergère would start roving fancies in his head, and when he first met Georgette Leblanc, Maeterlinck's mistress, he was so excited that he rushed out into the darkness to control himself. When he saw Marthe Brandès taking off her costume in *Le Pain de ménage* to put on a dressing gown, he felt himself on fire. He knew as well as Stevenson that to the end spring winds will sow disquietude, and passing faces leave a regret behind them, but in spite of this his private life never deviated from his prayer at the beginning of his *Journal* (1 August 1891), 'Lord help us, my wife and me, to eat our daily bread.'

She alone, with her cheerfulness and good humour, was able to banish his black tempers and resentments. It is strange that this bitter man, renowned for the cruelty of his ordinary speech, should have been so tender in marriage. Renard was one of those rare men who reserve their good humour for their wives, and their amiability for home.

Renard's parents brought him misery, his wife at least some comfort and peace; and both of them brought him plays. 'What do I owe to my family?' he asked; and answered his own question: 'Ungrateful fellow: plays ready-made.' This is unjust to Renard, who brought to his plays an incomparable naturalistic technique, and a unique emotion. But without the experiences of his childhood he would never have written *Poil de carotte* (1900) or *Monsieur Vernet* (1903) or *La Bigote* (1909); and had he not known his wife there would have been no *Pain de ménage* or *Plaisir de rompre*.

It was she, whom he called his Marinette, his Marinon, who, with her instinctive goodness of nature, enabled Renard to step outside himself, and to judge with a remorseful objectivity the defects of his own behaviour. One of the most illuminating passages in his *Journal* narrates with a contemptuous regret a grim tea-party in his early married life. Mlle Blanche had brought an Easter egg as a present. In her eagerness to be agreeable she quickly wearied Renard. She chattered about her dreams, and Renard found this insupportable. He either did not answer her questions, or did so surlily. She talked, he said, like a well-brought up teacher, and he despised her.

He plunged himself into his chair, his hands in his pockets, as chilling as a rich man who is being pestered by a beggar. He saw the two eyes of the old woman wander over his face, vaguely suppliant, and he knew that he was behaving badly, but in spite of this he could do nothing. 'Once more,' he wrote, 'I was convinced that we never forgive anyone except those whom it is our interest to forgive.' And he added, in ineffectual and bitter self-reproof, 'On the black pages of human baseness I marked one more victory for Satan.' It is this clear-sighted recognition of the evil in himself that constitutes the peculiar quality of *Le Pain de ménage* and *Le Plaisir de rompre*. What in fact makes Jules Renard's plays memorable, and unlike any others, is not their sharp wit, nor their skill in dialogue, remarkable as these are, but that in each of them Renard, like Judas, went out and hanged himself in contrition.

This is evident, though lightly, in *Le Pain de ménage* (1898). It is a simple dialogue, at holiday time, between a man, Pierre, and Marthe, his friend's wife. His friend is asleep, and his wife is looking after their sick child. The play begins with Marthe laughing incredulously at something Pierre has just said. 'What!' exclaims Marthe, 'since you were married, you have never had a mistress?' This, naturally enough, is the beginning of a flirtation, but a flirtation that does not follow the usual course of such things on the stage. Underlying the gaiety and provocativeness of the whole play is the feeling that Renard derived from his own marriage: that it is not worth sacrificing a quiet happiness for the excitement and passion of an amorous adventure. But such is the shame which had become a permanent part of his nature after incidents like that in which he had so unhandsomely figured with Mlle Blanche, that he could not ascribe to himself the credit for perceiving this. Such credit as there is goes to the woman.

Yet Marthe is not a prude. She is rather rattled when Pierre says that she is, and always will be, a good woman. 'You go too far,' she replies. 'I have been a good woman up to now. But I do not shout it upon the rooftops that I shall always be a good woman. How can I tell? I have no desire at all to deceive Alfred, and yet I should be desolated to be absolutely certain that I should never deceive him.'

But in spite of her spirited answer, and her opening remark, which is an excellently startling beginning to the play, it is she, not he, who is in no danger of behaving foolishly. 'It would be exciting,' she says, 'this little holiday, this rest from marriage, this truce to the daily affections of the home . . . But how long would it last?' It is significant that it is to the woman, and not to the man, that Renard looks for saving commonsense and faithfulness; it is due to the best part of his nature that this should be so.

Antoine, the founder of the Théâtre Libre, renowned as the exponent of naturalism, saw *Le Pain de ménage* again in 1927. By this time Antoine, who had done much to transform the French theatre into a living force in world drama, had sunk (or risen) to being, not an impresario, but a dramatic critic. He seems however to have had no bitterness, and he said of Renard's play that it was 'a masterpiece worthy of taking its place alongside the most celebrated pieces' in the repertoire of the Comédie Française. He had been associated with Renard in his youth, and was favourably disposed to him, but his opinion was not far wrong. It is an amusing and a touching play, and from its electrical beginning, comparable in its leap into the middle of things with the pistol opening of John Van Druten's *Behold, We Live*, it moves with grace and civilization to a gentle and satisfying ending.

Renard's generosity to women, except only his mother, is shown in *Le Plaisir de rompre* (1897) even more strikingly than in *Le Pain de ménage*. Perhaps there is significance in the fact that the heroine is called Blanche. That this should be so is in some measure a reparation for his behaviour to the elderly and irritating Mlle Blanche. But in the Blanche of the play there is also something of his wife, and again something of a mistress that he had himself discarded before his marriage. His contempt for himself burns throughout the play, which is in one act.

The situation in the play is the last visit of a young man, Maurice, to his mistress, Blanche, on the eve of his marriage to someone else, and all the sympathy is on the discarded mistress's side. Maurice behaves badly, without dignity, but not so badly that he cannot see that Blanche is behaving well. He suggests, with an astonishing callousness, that they should once more sleep together. In Blanche's refusal there is infinite tenderness and affection. Maurice himself recognises this, and his last words as he leaves her (the final words of the play) are 'Il vous reste le beau rôle.' They are as simple and banal as any phrase deliberately designed to be so by Maeterlinck, but in their context, as the climax and resolution of the play, they constitute one of the most resonantly memorable speeches in French drama.

Blanche was played at the first production in March, 1897, by Jeanne Granier, a singer who two years before had begun a second career as an actress. Renard was much moved by her performance. He wrote in his *Journal*, 'Granier, at the end, had silver tears in her voice,' and his mind turned with a vague regret and even remorse to Danielle Davyle, the young actress he had himself deserted some years before. *Le Pain de ménage* and *Le Plaisir de rompre* are Renard's best plays.

They are not generally considered so. Edmond Rostand thought they were no more than 'reportage malveillant', possibly because he suspected that *Le Pain de ménage* echoed an abortive flirtation between Renard and Mme Rostand. They show Renard's character in a more attractive light than usual, and they are less cruel than *Poil de carotte* and *La Bigote*. But this is not the reason for their superior position in the canon of Renard's work. That is due to the fact that they deal with a single complete action, progressing steadily and unceasingly towards the climax, with the characters continually developing.

Both Pierre and Maurice are wiser men at the end than at the beginning, and if Marthe and Blanche are not better women, they are at least confirmed in their goodness. But Renard's most famous play, *Poil de carotte*, is merely a series of episodes connected by the same characters, and time after time monotonously hitting the same target. The aim is accurate enough, but after the bull's eye has been hit once there is little point in repeating the shot.

In *Poil de carotte* Renard is concerned crudely to blacken his mother's character, to show that in her behaviour to himself as a child she had been uniformly unkind. There are some moving movements in the piece, and also in the stage directions, as when we are told: 'In hearing the door open Poil de Carotte is afraid. He is always afraid.' But the play is too neatly made, it has too many curtain-lines, and above all it is too obviously

7. *Le Poil de carotte* by Jules Renard with Suzanne Desprès (Théâtre des Varietés). Photograph by courtesy of Collection Viollet

determined to show Mme Lepic, Poil de Carotte's mother, as a monster.

So resolute is this determination that one ends by wondering whether there might not, after all, be something to be said on her side. Indeed there was, although it never occurred to Renard to say it. Renard greatly admired his father, but his father subjected his mother to intolerable torture by silence. He never spoke to her, and would not speak to anyone else whilst she was in the room. If she came into the room whilst he was talking to Renard he would stop speaking, and not begin again until after she had left, when he would resume his remarks where he had interrupted himself, and proceed in exactly the same tone of voice. This terrible domestic persecution aroused no pity in Renard. He transposed it to *Poil de carotte* with apparent approval. *Poil de carotte* was first produced by Antoine, who himself played M. Lepic, at the Théâtre Antoine, on 2 March 1900. It entered into the repertoire of the Comédie Française in 1912, and in the 1920s it furnished Berthe Bovy, the second wife of Pierre Fresnay, with her most successful part.

But in terms of immediate popular success *Poil de carotte* was eclipsed by a play written by Edmond Rostand, who in spite of the rumbling misunderstandings over *Le Pain de ménage*, was one of Renard's most intimate friends. All through 1897 Rostand (1868–1918) was in a mood of depression so intense that his charming young wife became afraid both for her own safety and his own. But on 27 December of that year, with the production at the Porte Saint-Martin of *Cyrano de Bergerac*, Rostand had an experience such as comes to few dramatists. Remy de Gourmont said that no poetic drama in any country at any time had had such a triumph. ' "Cyrano" . . . is a date in the history of our literature.' Émile Faguet, then one of the most influential of critics, compared *Cyrano* with *Le Cid*.

In spite, however, of his recognition of the play's wild success, Gourmont had reservations. 'It does not,' he said, 'mark the beginning of a new era; it marks the end of romanticism. This play is the last blinding flash of a fireworks gala.' Gourmont felt that for a moment Rostand had reversed a modern dramatic movement of which audiences were getting tired. 'For twenty years and more, when we have gone to the theatre, it has been to hear lawyers discussing the rights and wrongs of divorce, the rights of children, the rights of fathers, the rights of mothers, the rights of the State, the future of society, the city of the future . . . or else doctors talk to you about some wretched disease, some difficult surgical operation, the running of hospitals or prisons.'

Gourmont is speaking, not, as one might hastily suppose, of the social drama of the English Stage Company in the 1950s, but of fashionable Parisian entertainment sixty years earlier. 'Before the wit and bravura of *Cyrano* audiences felt themselves reborn . . . once again it was a question of love, heroism, and beauty.'

To a modern reader, although the Comédie Française has revived the play with considerable éclat, and Christopher Fry made a glittering translation for a Chichester Festival, this seems to be putting the merits of *Cyrano* too high. The verse has a splendid verve, and Rostand adapts it to the swift interchange of conversation as cleverly as he uses it in glittering outbursts of rhetoric.

Nevertheless, there is a romantic falsity in the play, as there is a dishonesty vitiating the whole of *A la recherche du temps perdu* in Proust's earnestly maintained pretence that he is heterosexual. When Cyrano browbeats the actor Montfleury in the opening scene and ruins the performance that a large audience has gathered to see, he is behaving no more attractively than the football hooligans who break up railway carriages, and Rostand's view of him as a romantic hero becomes, at its best, unacceptably naive. Rostand does not any longer convince us that this swashbuckling show-off is a figure worthy of admiration, and his dazzlingly cascading verse fails to wash away our objections. The play is one of the nineteenth century's brilliant mistakes.

Some of this disillusion with *Cyrano de Bergerac* entered into Patrick Garland's savagely condemned production of the play for the National Theatre in 1970. The condemnation with which this production was received was undoubtedly due to Garland's rejection of a romantic view of Rostand's seventeenth-century ruffian. But in 1897 the theatregoing public was quite unready to accept a view like Garland's; it was not in fact at that time in advance of the British public of seventy years later, for which perhaps it cannot be blamed. Anyway, Rostand's temperament, bathed in adulation, made a slight, but far from complete, recovery from its former gloom and despair. His near hope was confirmed three years later with Sarah Bernhardt's fantasy image as the tragic heir apparent in *L'Aiglon*.

8. Sarah Bernhardt in *L'Aiglon* (Théâtre des Nations 1900). Photograph by courtesy of Harlingue-Viollet

Another friend of Renard's, Tristan Bernard (1866–1947), was a total contrast to Rostand, not only in style, but also in disposition. Genial, kindly, and in private life extremely witty, Tristan Bernard is one of the most attractive figures in modern drama. His farces, which Renard seems to have considered superior to those of Georges Feydeau (1862–1921), were very successful, and several of them entered into the repertory of the Comédie Française in the 1920s. But they have not endured.

Feydeau did not secure full official recognition from the Théâtre National until after both men were dead, but his work has proved more lasting than Bernard's. Indeed, plays of his like *Le Dindon* and *Un fil à la patte* made the Comédie Française in the later 1950s the most popular theatre in Paris. The results of this were curious. When General de Gaulle came to power in 1958, his head filled with dreams he intended to realise to restore the greatness and the glory of France, he and his ministers resented the fact that France's national theatre, which they felt should be the symbol and banner-bearer of the country's international prestige, should have become, however splendidly, the home almost exclusively, not even of comedy, but of farce.

They did not realise that this eminence in farce, which had been brought about by the dynamic comic force of the leading spirit of the company, Jean Meyer, had rescued the Comédie from lethargy and atrophy. They demanded that the company should play the grand and stately Racine. Actually the Comédie had not the resources of tragic acting necessary to play this noble but difficult dramatist. Jean Meyer put on a production of 'Phèdre', but it was not a success. To the general astonishment, Meyer, who had been expected for the next quarter of a century to be the mainstay of the Comédie, was summarily dismissed.

After a brief period of confusion the Comédie partially recovered, such success as it achieved after Meyer's unfortunate departure being due to its following the path that Meyer himself had laid out. It had no success whatever with Racine, but its Feydeau farces continued to be very good. Meyer watched these developments with ironic amusement, and himself turned away from farce to the immense seriousness of Henry de Montherlant's *La Ville dont le prince est un enfant*. His extremely ascetic and Jansenist production of this play, as grave in temper as any of Racine's, ran for three or four years at the Théâtre

Michel. Why Meyer should have failed with exalted drama at the Comédie, and succeeded with it elsewhere, why the Comédie should have liquidated him, and then continued with his policy, are factors in the confusion which fell on the French theatre after its miraculous flowering at the end of the 1939–45 war.

None of this could have been foreseen in the easy days of Tristan Bernard. Even then the vital drama of France—the plays of Maeterlinck, Renard, and Jarry—was being created elsewhere, but this did not trouble the smooth surface of the House of Molière. In 1907 it took into its repertoire Bernard's *L'Anglais tel qu'on le parle*, which had been first produced in another theatre in 1899. It is one of Bernard's sprightliest pieces. A young Frenchman elopes with an English girl to Paris. They put up at a small hotel, whereupon the lover, with an excuse that dramatically is totally inadequate, leaves his fiancée to go to the post office.

Now Bernard's technique has been highly praised, but today it seems very clumsy. Julien's visit to the post office is not at all funny in itself. It is no more than a device, since the girl does not speak French, to introduce an interpreter into the play. This brings in the play's basic joke, for the interpreter speaks nothing else but French, and from this various misunderstandings arise. They are managed with nothing like the finesse and freshness of wit that Terence Rattigan later brought to a similar confusion of languages in *French without Tears*.

If Bernard has not Rattigan's sparkle, neither has he Feydeau's happiness of invention. In Feydeau not only are the misunderstandings amusing, but the devices that engineer them are amusing in themselves. Bernard's technical tricks, such as Julien's desertion of his fiancée, are without the wildly improbable wit that enlivens even the machinery of a farce like *Un fil à la patte* or *Occupe-toi d'Amélie*.

Renard was a regular theatregoer, and for some years a dramatic critic. In his professional career he did not discover, nor was he the first to hail, any new talent. He thus missed the chief pleasure of dramatic criticism, which is to perceive before anyone else the emergence of unexpected genius. Nevertheless his mind to a certain extent was open to new influences. Some years before his death he was elected to the Académie Goncourt, and it is evidence of the flexibility of his judgment that in 1909 he voted for a young and unknown writer, Jean Giraudoux, to receive the Prix Goncourt for his first work, *Provinciales*. Renard's was the only vote that Giraudoux received.

Renard's perceptivity is the more remarkable in that Giraudoux was not only passed over for the Prix Goncourt in 1909, but he received hardly any recognition till nearly twenty years later. It was not until 1928, when he was in his middle forties, that his first play, *Siegfried*, was produced. It is remarkable also that Tristan Bernard, who was a much more generous-hearted man than Renard, could, on the very eve of the 1939–45 war, see in Giraudoux none of the merit that Renard had clearly observed thirty years earlier.

Tristan Bernard did in fact watch the belated success of Giraudoux with an amused but uncomprehending irony. He thought that the vogue which the author of *La Guerre de Troie n'aura pas lieu* enjoyed in some circles would not last long. He would have been baffled to understand why Michael Redgrave made Christopher Fry's translation, under the title of *Tiger at the Gates*, a resounding success in the 1950s; or how Robert Shaw as an insolent, rasping sailor, imaginatively lecherous and socially aggressive, should have been able, in a single scene in this play, to rivet and tease the attention even of people who had never had an opportunity of seeing him before, and to whom he was a name then totally unknown.

Giraudoux reminded Bernard of Madame de Scudéry, who also, in the seventeenth century, had 'enthusiastic and pushing partisans'. A quarter of a century later her works aroused only indulgent smiles. This is a curious anticipation of some modern criticism of Giraudoux. Bernard told Louis Verneuil, a popular boulevard author of great personal charm who committed suicide in a fit of depression after the war, that admiration for "textes impénétrables" was merely a passing fashion.

The interesting thing is that Tristan Bernard, and not Renard, was right. Bernard saw in Giraudoux an author of great talent who spoiled the pleasure of his finest ideas by expressing them in a form intentionally complicated and sybilline. 'Clarity,' said Bernard, 'is the politeness of men of letters.' He added: 'I am the more astonished at the determined ambiguity of Giraudoux, because, as soon as he ceases to write, he is a man of perfect courtesy.'

He never changed his views about Giraudoux, even when Giraudoux became the most famous man of letters in the French theatre. He saw *Ondine*, a very celebrated work indeed, at the Athénéê in 1939. He told Verneuil that he listened carefully, and understood about half of what was said on the stage. 'Then I thought, this isn't a play to see. One must read it. I bought the text, and read it with the closest attention. This time I understood nothing at all.'

Verneuil believed that in fifty years' time the plays of Giraudoux would be forgotten, but that those of Tristan Bernard would still hold the boards. In recommending Giraudoux for the Prix Goncourt thirty years before the production of *Ondine* Renard clearly correctly anticipated the way that public theatrical taste would go. Bernard had merely the melancholy satisfaction of knowing which way it ought to go. But in respect of *Ubu Roi*, which, with its influence on Beckett and Ionesco, has become the most famous play of its period, he completely failed to see into the future. He saw no future, and indeed no present, for Jarry's *Ubu Roi*.

It is a common belief of dramatists that if they were judged by their fellow-playwrights they would get more enthusiastic treatment and deeper understanding than they are accustomed to receive from professional critics. We have seen that in the case of Jarry there is no foundation for this belief. Renard was his personal friend. He went to *Ubu Roi* in a state of private euphoria. He was not universally jealous, for he appreciated Giraudoux (admittedly this before Giraudoux became a dramatist, and therefore a rival). But the performance of the play filled him with a sense of shame and embarrassment for its author. For appreciation and comprehension Jarry had to turn to Catulle Mendès, that is, to a professional critic.

A greater writer than either Renard or Jarry, Maurice Maeterlinck, did not encounter the same critical perceptiveness. To a certain extent this cannot be ascribed wholly to the stupidity or conservatism of critics. The company that presented '*Pelléas et Mélisande*' in Paris in 1893 had a more than ordinary share of the superciliousness which often accompanies mediocrity, and sometimes—this is what makes judgment so difficult —genius. The great and to them outmoded Sarcey, with his frock coat, his tall silk hat, and his Edward Prince of Wales beard, responded to this superior attitude by making fun of it in a surprisingly gentle way. It was understood, he said, that only one performance of the play would be given, because in Paris, well known to be a city of idiots, there were not enough intelligent people to make more than a single audience.

He claimed that, as a plain, simple man, he did not understand even the very first scene, in which servants rush distractedly about, shouting for the door to be opened, and for water to be brought to wash the castle steps. 'You do not appear to comprehend what is happening', Sarcey alleges that a helpful neighbour of the female sex said to him: 'It is symbolism. These servants who call for water are preparing you for the extraordinary crimes that will follow, which all the water in the world will not wash away. There will be blood, and water will not cleanse it.'

'But so far there isn't any blood,' objected Sarcey.

'Of course there isn't any blood. It is a symbol. Either your intelligence is sufficient to understand symbols, or it isn't. Yours is not sufficient.'

After giving Sarcey time to digest this observation, his new-found friend remarked, 'You have a lot of prejudices to get rid of. You come to the theatre for entertainment. That is old-fashioned. Entertainment is not what the theatre is for.'

Some years later, when *Pelléas et Mélisande* was played in England, another critic, Max Beerbohm, took a different view. He found the play entertaining to a high degree. He took it for a play of action. He made it appear as though it were a piece as rich in incident as an ordinary melodrama. He talks of Mélisande being loved and wooed by Golaud, of the dawn of her love for Pelléas, of her dropping her ring in the well, of the fearful searching for it, of the waiting in the glade of poplars for the wrath of Golaud, as if they had the obvious dramatic impact of Sydney Carton mounting the scaffold to the angry roars of the crowd.

It may be significant of Beerbohm's attitude that, in this catalogue of mistaken and crude judgments, he misses the only scene that could legitimately have appeared there: the disturbing episode in which Golaud lifts up the boy Yniold so that he may spy upon the never revealed activities of Pelléas and Mélisande, which horrify the child as he sees them through the lighted and unscreened window.

Sarcey, a far less delicately civilised man than the exquisite Beerbohm, nevertheless was more perceptive than that. He said of this scene that it was very moving; that it was the work of a man of the theatre. At the same time he recognised its daring, its decadence, its possible corruption. 'All the same, I am not sure that if Sardou or Meilhac had risked anything like it, those who find it admirable in Maeterlinck would not have been shocked.' Sarcey was right. This scene, and there is another which is not dissimilar in *La Princesse Maleine*, is more suggestive to me of the impurely erotic, as distinct from that which is uncomplicatedly pleasurable, than anything I can remember in the uninhibited drama released by the abolition of censorship in 1969. Perhaps this is not surprising. Eroticism depends on the suggestion of the forbidden. So far as I am concerned where nothing is forbidden there can be no erotic pleasure.

Unlike the incomparable Max, Sarcey knew that the value, if it had any value, of *Pelléas et Mélisande* did not lie in its story, but in the way its story was told. In spite of his prejudices, of his devotion to well made melodramas, he did experience some aesthetic response to *Pelléas et Mélisande*. He thought it ridiculous, especially the fine, mysterious scene in which Yniold speaks to an unseen shepherd, tending his flock of sheep.

But he realised, as Beerbohm, so much more subtle in aesthetic appreciation than the rough, workaday Sarcey, appears not to have done, that what *Pelléas et Mélisande* was akin to, was not melodrama, but poetry.

> Rien de bruyant, rien d'agité
> Dans leur triste félicité;
> Ils se couronnent sans gaité
>
> De fleurs nouvelles;
>
> Ils se parlent, mais c'est tout bas;
> Ils marchent, mais c'est pas à pas;
> Ils volent, mais on n'entends pas
> Battre leurs ailes.[8]

Sarcey calls these verses of Casimir Delavigne delicious; and in scene after scene of *Pelléas et Mélisande* they were present in his mind. It was the right approach.

It is strange that, after showing his sensibilities to be so true, he should have gone completely wrong in his comments on the ending of the play. He knows, and shows that he knows, that

---

8. This musical little verse speaks of a quiet happiness that is akin to sadness. 'Without gaiety they are crowned with fresh flowers, and though they fly you cannot hear the beating of their wings.'

Maeterlinck is appealing to other, less logical, things than reason; and then is disturbed that the conclusion of the play is, in his eyes, unreasonable. Mélisande is wounded, but the wound is nothing. 'A bird would not have died of it,' says the doctor. 'But she cannot live . . . she was born without reason . . . to die; and she dies without reason.'

'Ah,' exclaims Sarcey. 'He is right, this doctor: and it is precisely of that that I complain: that she was born, lived, and died without reason. For it is only in learning of things that the theatre interests me.'

Finally Sarcey comments on the old king Arkel's words about Mélisande, that she was a 'sad little thing as mysterious as all the world.' 'Have you,' he says, 'noticed that word which seems so bizarre?' 'C'était un petit être mystérieux comme tout le monde. Very well, that is what is wrong with the play, that everybody is mysterious, that everything is affected with mystery.' Sarcey, with the self-confidence of the nineteenth century, of course knew better than Maeterlinck; to his dying day it seemed to him that he understood everything in life in the clear light of reason.

He thus rejected what is in fact the most valuable thing in Maeterlinck's art, the perception of strange forces controlling our destiny. But why should one blame him? Was Debussy any wiser, when he dismissed in his opera all the vague threats and impalpable horrors shadowed forth in the play's opening scene, which he omitted altogether? Sarcey at least responded to the *voyeur* scene with Yniold, for he perceived that it sent a shiver round the house. His emotions were, as they should be, complex; he was thrilled, but at the same time uncomfortable that a child should be compelled to watch the dishonour of his stepmother, and speculated that the small girl playing the part ought at that hour to be in bed.

The theatre to which Sarcey was accustomed was a theatre of sharp clear outlines, and plainly stated problems. For this Maeterlinck substituted a world, not of emotions, but of emotion, a dark brooding on the impalpable influence of death and doom. He agreed with Alfred Capus, who wrote, 'Quelle illusion de croire que les événéments de notre existence s'enchaînent et se commandent! Notre vie est une courte série d'anecdotes racontées sans lien: notre âme est changeante et variable comme elle; nos sentiments sont aussi imprévus que des rêves: et ce sont des lois éternellement ignorées qui nous donne avec indifference les joies et les peines, les matins lumineux, les heures lourdes et obscures.'[9]

Maeterlinck created this heavy, doom-laden world, not with the resounding Latinities of a Conrad, but with short speeches, simple words, and definite images. Jarry attacked and ridiculed the bourgeoisie, but Maeterlinck ignored it. His characters are kings and queens, princes and princesses. They are in themselves less important than the shadows in which they move, than the dark passions of incest they undergo in *La Princesse Maleine*, and than the criminal voyeurism of *Pelléas et Mélisande*. They live in gloomy northern castles where scores of servants rush about in panic; they wander through pathless woods in the company of an old nurse, meeting people who are poor or blind or lost, who regard them with malevolence and suspicion; they are lovers who encounter each other by the side of a fountain, under a moon obscured by flying clouds, in a wind that makes the willows weep.

When for a moment they are happy, as in the second act of *La Princesse Maleine*, the fountain turns to blood, and dries up. It is as if some cosmic drama were in progress dominating the human characters. This is the converse of the pathetic fallacy, in which nature is in harmony with humanity. In Maeterlinck humanity is dominated by the malevolence and misery of nature.

Allez une nuit dans le bois du parc, près du jet d'eau; et vous remarquerez que c'est à certains moments seulement, et lorsqu'on les regarde, que les choses se tiennent tranquilles comme des enfants sages et ne semblent pas étranges et bizarres; mais dès qu'on leur tourne le dos, elles vous font des grimaces et vous jouent de mauvais tours,'[10] (*La Princesse Maleine*, Act 3).

---

9. What a delusion to believe that there is order or logic in the events of our life! Our life is a short series of unconnected anecdotes; our soul shifts and changes; our feelings are as unforeseeable as our dreams; and it is laws which are eternally unknown that give us with indifference both joys and sorrows, the mornings that blaze, the hours that are heavy and dark.

10. Go one night amongst the trees in the estate, near to the fountain; and you will notice that it is only at certain moments, and when you are looking at them, that things stay still like well-behaved children; but as soon as you turn your back they will mock you and play you malicious tricks.

The second quality that Maeterlinck brought to the drama was a sense of the perverse. No dramatist has had a greater and more potent realisation of evil than Maeterlinck. In this he equals Henry James. In *La Princesse Maleine*, inside the castle the newly-married Queen Anne demands to be embraced in her husband's presence by her stepson, the young Hjalmar.

> N'y voyez-vous pas que je vous aime? Vous ne m'avez jamais embrassée jusqu' ici.'
> Vous embrasser, Madame?
> Oui, m'embrasser: n'embrassiez-vous pas votre mère? Je voudrai vous embrasser tous les jours.[11]

The echoes and repetitions of these simple words in these short sentences are characteristic of the way in which Maeterlinck creates, even in the cold, dark north, a hot-house feeling of obsessive and unhealthy passion. In the cool of the evening, walking in the village, Hjalmar says to his friend Angus: 'J'ai entrevu aujourd'hui les flammes de péchés auxquels je n'ose pas encore donner un nom.'[12] They look up and see the king and Queen Anne embracing at a lighted and uncurtained window. Angus wishes to turn away, but Hjalmar—he who had just been introduced to the presence of a nameless sin—is resolved to go on watching.

Rachilde's *Volupté* (May, 1896), studying the adolescence of two children given to curious pleasures, also brought perversity into the theatre. Mendès called the play atrocious, but found it delicate and almost chaste, filled with graceful phrases and happy images. If *Volupté*, he said, descends from de Sade it is from a de Sade who remembered Petrarch's Laura. There are no such pure remembrances behind the subtle and impalpable perversions of Maeterlinck. Not until *The Turn of the Screw*, or in the modern theatre, the namelessly corroded wedding scene in Howard Brenton's and David Hare's *Brassneck*, where the bride's uncle, making the wedding speech, dies as he rambles

---

11. 'Don't you see that I love you? You have never embraced me to this day.'
  'Embrace you, Madame?'
  'Yes, embrace me; don't you embrace your mother? I should like to embrace you every day.'

12. 'I have today caught a glimpse of the fires of sin that I dare not yet name.'

on about cannibalism in the Great War, and the bride herself rushes wildly about with white, uplifted skirts, all without reason, without explanation, do we encounter so all-pervasive a feeling of unanalysable evil as in the most important plays of Maeterlinck.

CHAPTER THREE

The Battle between Dramatists and Critics

The perversity which Maeterlinck so prodigiously and philo-
sophically put into his greatest plays rapidly became degraded
in other dramatists. This degradation is a chief reason why the
French drama declined in the early years of the twentieth century. This is not to say that there were no authors of talent or
even of sensibility except those who had already revealed themselves in the eighteen-nineties; nor that these never wrote for the
stage. Indeed, one of the ablest among them, Henry Bataille
(1872–1922), was a very prolific dramatist. He was born in
Provence, at Nîmes, and the sad beauty of his native countryside permeated his best work. He wrote a charming recollection
of his childhood, *L'Enfance éternelle*, and it is this, with his poetry,
that gives him his slight hold upon immortality. His poems are
fragile, as fragile as the sentimental lyrics of Noel Coward, but
they are also as haunting as the rays of the setting sun. The
critic Jean Lorrain found in them 'a kind of anguish and a
fleeting desire to cry.'

> Oui . . . Un soir d'août
> Quelque part, il me semble . . . un air de casino . . .
> Oui, c'est un air de la Bohème . . . Très piano
> Ecoute. Souviens-toi. C'est nous, la mer, les plages . . .
> valses de casino, grands soirs mélancoliques,
> aux terrasses, flots bleus . . . lumières, noirs ombragés.
> Ecoute . . . nous avons terminé notre conte.
> D'autres le referont avec les mêmes flots,
> les mêmes nuits très bleues sur les mêmes terrasses
> et le même air banal, nostalgique et tenace
> qui fait flotter sa traîne au bord des casinos.[1]

---

1. Like the once-fashionable song, 'These Foolish Things', Bataille here

Bernard Delvaille, writing in *Combat*, 25 May 1972, on the hundredth anniversary of Bataille's birth, remarked of the poems in *La Chambre blanche*, 'Toute la tristesse moderne y apparaît pour la première fois peut-être dans la poésie française:[2]

> Douleur, n'étais-tu pas dans le train qui s'en va? . . .
> Tu t'assiéras, le soir, aux vieilles tables d'hôte,
> Où se rencontrent toutes les douleurs en voyage . . .

'C'est ici,' says Delvaille, 'pour la première fois que passent aux vitres des grands express de nuit les lumières bleues des gares, que l'on découvre au soir des chambres d'hôtel inconnues où la solitude est toujours fidèle à elle-même, que l'on quitte à l'automne des villes d'eau qui ferme les volets. A cet abandon, il reste les larmes:[3]

> Les larmes sont en nous. C'est la sécurité.
> Des peines de savoir qu'il y a des larmes toujours prêtes.'[4]

Turner had painted a great express train of the west country cleaving its triumphant way through billowing clouds and mists; Cézanne had made trains an integral part of his landscape, but Bataille was the first to find in them a metaphor for the melancholy that descends on the spirit when it contemplates the brevity of existence and the evanescence of all joys. He did the same thing with telephones and electric lamps. Not until he began to write had such things entered the world of poetry.

Neither this modernism, nor this regret seen through the veil of trivial and prosaic things plays much part in his theatre. This is almost wholly concerned with the adultery of the rich. But the trouble with these plays is not their subject-matter. The trouble with Bataille is that, unlike Dumas *fils*, he did not care about this adultery. It was not an affront to him, but only a

---

recalls trifles whose memory still moves the heart: an evening in August, the seaside, a romantic air played very softly by a casino orchestra, all now ended.

2. Here, perhaps for the first time, appears in French poetry all our modern sadness.

3. It is here for the first time that the dim light of stations can be seen from the windows of the night expresses that pass through them, that in the evening one discovers unfamiliar hotel rooms that have their own peculiar atmosphere, that in the autumn one leaves holiday places that are closing down. In this mood only tears remain:

4. The same sadness, the same memories, with tears not far away.

means of devising a piquant story. In *Maman Colibri*, in *La Marche nuptiale*, which were immensely famous in their day, Bataille does not say, as he does in his poetry, what he really feels, but only what he thinks will startle his audiences to hear.

Nevertheless, despite this insincerity, Bataille's celebrity as a dramatist was very great. It is not merely that his premières were thronged with the rich and fashionable, glittering in furs and diamonds, attended to in their carriages by footmen and flunkeys, but that the finest players of the day—Berthe Bady, Réjane, Julia Bartet (an incomparable Bérénice), vied with each other for the honour of appearing in his daring melodramas. During the first decade of the century three or four of his plays were acted in Paris on the same evening, and he kept in touch with each of them by means of a *théâtrephone* installed in his apartment in the Avenue du Bois.

His international influence was not as great as it would have been had he written half a century later. The interchange of companies between France and Britain was already beginning; Bernhardt and Réjane were well-known on both sides of the Channel. But they appeared in pieces specially designed to show off their particular talents, not in the representative drama of modern France.

In the first years of the century there was nothing to compare in seriousness and scale with the World Theatre seasons of Peter Daubeny in the sixties and seventies. Shaw, Galsworthy, and Barrie made little impression in France before the Great War. In fact, more attention was paid to a pretty but trivial musical comedy like *The Quaker Girl* (London, 1910), which was brought to Paris in the summer of 1911. It had to compete with Nijinsky, Pavlova, Karsavina, Lopokhova; the flaming costumes of Bakst; and the other glories of the Russian ballet. It is not surprising that it seemed rather insipid.

Nevertheless, it was noticed, if not altogether favourably. It was remarked disapprovingly that the ladies of the chorus did not lift their skirts higher than their ankles. It is true that at this time Mistinguett was still wearing dresses that reached to the ground, but at the Alhambra Gaby Deslys was drawing full houses, and showing all she had in order 'to cement the Entente cordiale', and Cléo de Mérode was expected to crowd the Hippodrome in that hot summer of Halley's comet. Her dances, according to the French journals, did not matter much; her reputation in other matters was enough to guarantee success.

The boulevard theatres at this period were filled with audiences who revelled in high fashion. The stage itself was a leader in this respect. The great courturiers of the day—Paquin, Poiret—designed clothes for actresses to show off, and authors took care to write plays for which such clothes were suitable. A few voices—that of the critic, Léon Blum, in particular—were raised in protest, saying that the drama was being subordinated to a fashion parade. In the *loges* ladies wore wide-brimmed, feathered cavalier hats created by Gabrielle Chanel.

Occasionally the stage went too far. When Mlle Prévost appeared in a bloomer-suit in Henry Bernstein's *Après Moi* (1911) at the Comédie Française, the extra police that had been drafted into the theatre for the occasion failed to master the uproar she evoked. In vain it was pointed out that the clothes she wore were intended to indicate the loose character of the woman she was playing. Mlle Prévost, in spite of the sneers at the prudery of *The Quaker Girl* (which was said to come from 'the land of cant'), had to change into a more conventional costume for the second performance. Even so, the tumultuous protests of the audience continued, and the play was quickly withdrawn.

A wider licence was accorded to the ballet, where on one occasion the Russian Trouhanova danced without any clothes at all. She was accompanied by what is perhaps the most astounding cast that has ever been assembled on any stage at any time anywhere in the world. Even after the lapse of more than half a century the name of nearly every member of the company still remains famous. Amongst the ladies who appeared with the naked Trouhanova were Karsavina, Pavlova, and Lopokhova from the Russian ballet; Mistinguett and Loie Fuller, Polaire and her lover Colette from the music hall; Cléo de Mérode, Isadora Duncan, and la belle Otéro, for whom eight rich men are said to have committed suicide.

On the whole, it was an age of good feeling. Even critics and the people they criticised seem to have got on well together. In fact, to a degree quite unknown in either the French or the British theatres after the war of 1939–45, the most eminent people in all branches of the theatrical profession were close personal friends with each other. At the first performance of Rostand's *Chantecler* in 1910 Adolphe Brisson, the drama critic of *Le Temps*, was accompanied by Mounet-Sully, the leading actor of the Comédie Française. They shared the same box, and

9. Some of the resplendent and notorious cast from the famous matinée where the Russian Trouhanova appeared naked. Photographs from *Comoedia Illustré* 15 December 1910

no one seems to have thought it odd. It is as though, at the first night of a play by John Osborne or Harold Pinter, Irving Wardle, of *The Times*, should be accompanied by Laurence Olivier.

Mounet-Sully, far from concealing that he was with someone whose professional concern it was to criticise his own performances from time to time, appears to have done everything he could to draw attention to Brisson and himself. Adolphe Brisson's son, Pierre, then just in his teens, was with them, and says that Mounet-Sully's applause was so thunderous that it led that of the rest of the house. There was a great and jostling crowd on the pavement at the end of the performance, anxious to know how the play had gone. They stopped the people lucky enough to have seen it, and asked eagerly, 'What was it like? What was it like?' This, says Pierre Brisson, was the apotheosis of the theatre, the moment in time when the theatre was first amongst the arts, even with the man in the street; the age of Rostand, before it had become the age of Georges Carpentier.

Mounet-Sully was not the only great figure in the theatre who was an intimate friend of the critic Brisson. Every week Brisson and his wife held parties in their home. There was croquet on the lawn, billiards, quadrilles, and a valet in uniform darted in and out amongst the guests. Reynaldo Hahn, a glass of brandy in his hand, was dragged to the piano by the others, and played *La Boulangère*, and *La Tour Saint-Jacques*. Madame Paul Thomas danced a *Pas des patineurs*. Mounet-Sully hurled *Oceano Nox* to the stars. Amongst the other regular guests were Henri Lavedan, Hervieu, Maurice Donnay, Rostand, Porto-Riche, Maeterlinck.

More however is needed than friendship to make possible these joyous reunions of dramatists, musicians, and critics; money is as essential as mutual esteem. Few critics today have two houses, as Brisson had, one in the town, the other nearer the country; or a family capable of undergoing, or willing to undergo, the disruption caused by a party of fifteen or twenty guests every week; or, if it comes to that, the enthusiastic services of a valet in a striped waistcoat.

Out of this geniality grew a theatre intensely pleased with itself. In spite of the shocked outburst provoked by the *robe-pantalon* of Mlle Prévost, the French stage thought of itself as much more daring than the British. To this extent, though not without some moral misgivings, it considered itself more advanced. When Froyez, the French critic in London of 'Comoedia Illustré', made a survey of the English theatre, he came to the conclusion that its principal quality was wholesomeness. He noted that it was free of the French obsession with adultery and the problems of diseased psychology. It struck him as a place of family entertainment. Its sanity was evidenced by such plays as *The Arcadians* and *The Quaker Girl*.

He found, too, that its serious plays, of which he took Martin-Harvey's drama of the French Revolution, *The Only Way*, to be typical, were unobjectionable. Anything moderately daring was handled with perfect taste. He admits that an actress named Sahary Djeli, in *Salome*, went so far as to show her bosom. But she did it in half-darkness, a discretion still imitated by the nudes in *Hair* more than fifty years later. The bathing scene in *Kismet* (London, 1911) was done with such care that not even prudes could complain.

Froyez found this innocence endearing, but a bit childish. He does not really conceal his feeling that the febrile sexual excitement of a *Maman Colibri* or the emotional and philosophical brutality of an *Après Moi* is what gives true value to a theatre. The English, he says, are businessmen of incomparable sagacity, but at heart they are immature. Their theatre reflects this, being simple and sentimental. It is in fact years behind the French.

It is hard to agree with this. English drama in the early years of the century may have been less theatrically adroit than the French, less capable of evolving tightly knit and exciting situations, but it was more didactically expressive of the serious spirit of the times, for the very reason that it was, by Froyez's standards, more innocent. 'This period,' says Bernard Dorival, 'was in fact that of the anti-Bergsonian reaction of Julien Benda (*La Dialogue d'Eleuthère*, 1911), that of the revaluation of Thomist scholasticism by Maritain (*La Philosophie bergsonienne*), that in which Alain began the publication of his *Cent et un propos* (1908, 1909, 1914). Equally it is that in which appeared the most classical works of Gide, such as *La Porte étroite*[5] . . .

Psichari . . . wrote in 1913: 'Whatever we do, we always put intelligence above everything else.' Bernard Shaw and the writers of the Manchester school were considerably more inter-

---

5. *Histoire de l'art*, Volume 4: Sous la direction de Bernard Dorival, Encyclopédie de la Pleiade, Gallimard, Paris, 1969.

ested in intelligence than any of the leading French dramatists, precisely because they were less interested, and therefore more restrained, in portraying passion.

French art at this time was opening itself to new and in some cases exotic influences. The douanier Rousseau in his *naifs* painted what he knew rather than what he saw. Picasso's landscapes, Leger in *Nus dans le forêt*, Delaunay in his *Ville de Paris*, owe a great deal to him. But fashionable drama kept itself closed to this sincere simplicity, and preoccupation with technique continued to dominate the theatre in Paris. In 1905 Vlaminck discovered in a bistro in Argenteuil two negro sculptures. They were the first negro works of art he had ever seen, and he was astonished by a sense of 'profound humanity'. He bought them for two litres of wine, and showed them to Derain, who exclaimed, 'They are as beautiful as the Venus de Milo.'

About the same time Matisse saw in the rue de Rennes a statuette which he took to be from ancient Egypt. He was disappointed when the owner of the shop told him it was negro; nevertheless, he bought it. It was through him and Derain that the revelation of negro art broke on Picasso, and led to the geometricisation of Cubic art.

None of this intellectual and artistic disturbance and discovery appears to have had any effect on the reigning French theatre, which was then, in the opinion of the shrewd Pierre Brisson, either at, or approaching, its apotheosis. It remained closed to all influences outside itself. It was not until Samuel Beckett wrote *Waiting for Godot* in the middle of the century that the French drama showed any response to the structural geometricisation of negro and Cubist art, although Jacques Copeau (1878–1949) was influenced considerably earlier by the austerity and contempt for ornament of the new movements in painting. Copeau, however, at this time certainly, and probably for several years later, was not held to be part of the French theatre as the theatre was popularly understood.

The plays to which the public flocked were strong dramas like Bataille's *Maman Colibri* or François de Croisset's *Le Feu du voisin* (1910). Such plays were titillating and mildly shocking. They neatly packaged life in terms of powerful melodramatic situations, often contrived with considerable skill, and with telling curtain lines. One of the recurrent features of such plays was that they showed women of forty and men of fifty as sexually attractive to the young of the opposite sex. Middle aged audiences found this both flattering and reassuring.

François de Croisset handled this sort of theme with an engaging lightness of touch. In *Le Feu du voisin*, for example, Raymonde, a widow, had for ten years lived a quiet and happy but unexciting married life. She is about to enter on another marriage, similarly happy and uninteresting, with Fernand, who has long devotedly loved her. But even Fernand feels that she would be better if she were less serene. The problem is how to bring into her life an all-conquering affection, the Laingian ecstasy, without actually overdoing things, and making them worse than they were before.

Fortunately a young Englishman, with a title, too, Sir Harry Falway, is on hand to perform this delicate task. He awakens in Raymonde emotions that are delicious but disturbing. But he does not go too far nor too deep, and the ultimate beneficiary is the new husband. In dealing with this mildly perverse idea of making the tumult of the *chaise longue* the prelude to the rapture of the double bed, Croisset is both skilful and witty. But he is not possessed by it with that abandon that some critics believe to be an essential constituent of genius. He desires ecstasy (within reasonable limits) for Raymonde, but there is no ecstasy in himself.

The same remark can be made of *Papa*, by Robert de Flers and G. A. Caillavet, who for many years delighted fashionable Paris with their gay and ingenious plays. The upshot of *Papa* was to comfort men of middle age rather than women. Its central character is an ageing Vicomte who devotes his life to making conquests, and is shaken to his shallow depths when the girl to whom he is most recently attracted laughs in his face. Thus induced to think more seriously of life he recalls that he has an illegitimate son whom he has left neglected in the country for nearly thirty years. Stricken in conscience, he legitimises the young man, who, French law being full of mysteries, immediately becomes a Vicomte also. However the young man does not appreciate his rise in the world. Unlike Célimène, he prefers the country to the town, and returns to his rural solitudes, followed by his wondering father. This ageing roué warns his son against the woman he has chosen to be his wife, and then runs off with her himself. The scornful laughter had been premature, after all, and the male members of the audience were

10. Sacha Guitry and his wife confronting each other on stage just before
their divorce. Drawing by Paulett in *Comoedia Illustré* 20 December 1912

able to take their creaking bones out of the theatre, full of confidence, concupiscence, and hope.

   The same technical slickness, the same lack of any real conviction behind the writing, is seen in the young Sacha Guitry's
Le Veilleur de nuit, which was produced in 1913, the same year as
Papa. *Le Veilleur de nuit* may not be quite so geriatrically optimistic as the work of Flers and Caillavet, but it is by no means
discouraging. Its thesis is that if the elderly man about town
cannot eat his cake for forty years and still have all of it left,

nevertheless a few succulent crumbs remain. A famous but ancient Academician realises that his mistress is in love with a young painter. He cannot drive the painter away, but he has the bright notion that the two of them might happily share the girl. Guitry played the handsome and irresistible artist himself. His then wife, Charlotte Lysès, had hitherto played the heroine in Guitry's plays. On this occasion Guitry chose someone else for his heroine, his wife, hideously made up, taking the part of an ugly nurse. Soon afterwards they were divorced. *Le Veilleur de nuit* was written with Guitry's usual verve and vivacity, and contemporary critics wondered whether its author would fulfil all the promise that it showed. They could hardly be blamed for not seeing in which direction Guitry's talent would develop. It no doubt took Guitry himself by surprise.

In any case dramatists like Guitry and Croisset were the lightweights of the theatrical arena. There was about them an unpretentiousness and frivolity that gives them a certain charm even today, a charm that is lacking in the ponderously formidable works of Bataille and, to some people, of Bernstein. Yet Bataille's *Maman Colibri* was regarded for many years as the most significant drama of the decade. When it was revived by the Comédie Française ten years after the end of the Great War it was still thought of highly enough to draw the biggest receipts of the season. If Adolphe Brisson thought it immoral, as he did, he nevertheless admired it, and Brisson was a critic of great taste and perceptiveness. It has that interest in morbid psychology which Maurice Froyez took to be the sign of adult theatre; and if one is willing to accept theatre as theatrical, it is quite a remarkable work.

By their audacity and nonchalance its situations drained the blood from the faces of the audiences at the Vaudeville. The youthful Richard de Rysbergue suspects, but cannot be sure, that his mother, the Baroness Irène, is in love with his friend Georges, who is scarcely more than a schoolboy. In order to make certain he plays a trick that Brisson found rather shocking. Unobserved, he approaches the couch on which his mother is sitting, and when he gets close to her he hesitates. But only for a moment. Then he pulls himself together and places on her neck a kiss that is somewhat more than filial. The Baroness is completely deceived. She throws back her head and, thinking that she is delivering herself to her lover, she murmurs, 'Chéri . . . chéri.' The luckless, middle-aged lady is almost choked with emotion. Then she turns round and recognises the awful truth that when she thought she was giving herself, she was in fact giving herself away.

Brisson was present at the first performance, and he was completely bowled over. 'The eyes of the mother', he wrote, 'meet those of the son. The moment is overwhelming and terrible. They are both pale from the frightening realisation of their shame. Then Richard takes control of himself, and says tranquilly, "Bonsoir, maman." ' The amorous Baroness elopes with the juvenile Georges, and has a brief period of sexual gratification. But in the end Bataille elects for pathos, and the play finishes with the passionate Irène settling for the joys of being a grandmother. *Maman Colibri* is very clever, very well contrived, very dramatic. But it glitters with greasepaint instead of shining with the colours of life. Its eroticism is there for its own sake, not, as in *Pelléas et Mélisande*, as an integral part of a disgraced universe.

Yet some excellent judges thought otherwise. Henry Bordeaux, a stern moralist, and an incessant champion of the virtues of private life and marriage, found in Bataille's plays the very same quality which we today detect in his verse: a disillusioned poetry. But he found Bataille's characters lacking in nobility. This was especially the case with *La Femme nue*, the story of a rising young artist who after his first success marries his model. (If you are going to become a Marshal of France, says Bordeaux wisely, do not marry whilst you are only a sergeant.) The artist, in Bordeaux's opinion, is worthless as a man, and the girl has shown herself naked too variously and too often. But when the play was produced in 1908, Bordeaux, born in 1870, admired Bataille's compassionate attitude to her.

Bordeaux was greatly influenced by the work of Paul Bourget (1852–1935), who devoted himself to upholding the bourgeois virtues of religion and morality, and, like Bordeaux, became a member of the French Academy. Following logically the philosophic course that Bourget had marked out in his novels and essays, Bordeaux found in Henry Bernstein (1876–1953) none of the extenuating circumstances which he allowed for Bataille.

Bernstein created an immense sensation in Paris. During a career that lasted for more than half a century his plays shocked and delighted. Pieces like *Après moi* (1911) and *Israel* (Réjane; 1908) and *Le Voleur* were great scandalous triumphs. But there

was a solid body of middle class opinion which found no titilla-
tion in this scandal. In criticism it was represented by Bordeaux.
Bordeaux declared without equivocation that he did not share
the general admiration for Bernstein. Speaking with a concision
and directness rare in the criticism of the time he said that he
found in the work of Bernstein neither sombre power—'why,'
he exclaims, 'should I not speak out?'—nor character nor observation nor depth nor style. Bernstein, he maintained, excels
in putting his characters into situations in which, threshing
about in difficulties from which there is no escape, they make
terrible scenes and spit out their lungs at each other. Bernstein's
theatre is like those gymnastic schools in which athletes are seen
in every position but the normal.

Bordeaux had very little respect for the theatre of his day. He
preserved the tradition established by Janin and Sarcey, and
continued in our own time with immense verve by the brilliant
Jean-Jacques Gautier, whereby the most important Paris drama
critics are consistently hostile to whatever is new, challenging,
and radical in French drama. At the very beginning of his
career as a dramatic critic he visited with a German friend a
theatre in Mulhouse, which was presenting a French touring
play, *L'Age d'aimer*. Arnold Wesker in one of his plays says that
football is all right, but not football all the time. Bordeaux felt
the same about love as a subject for drama, and it disgusted him
that *L'Age d'aimer* should show no appreciation of the fact that
there are other things in life than sex. His friend said contemptuously, 'You (the French) are people of Venus,' and
Bordeaux writhed under the comment and its implications.

He seems to have dated the decline in seriousness of the
French drama from *Amoureuse* (1891), by Georges de Porto-Riche
(called by a recent French critic Georges de Porto-Pauvre).
In *Amoureuse* the hero, a man immersed in business, finds his
wife importunate. He cannot find the time nor the inclination
for all the sexual intercourse she wants, so he gravely solves the
problem by advising her to take a lover. *Amoureuse*, says Bordeaux, marks a date in the history of the French theatre, but it
also marks a date—and not one to be regarded with pride—in
French morals.

Bordeaux's constant complaint is that the theatre treats with
culpable levity the question of marriage. Hardly more than
once in a score of plays does he find anything of which to
approve. One of the rare dramas that please him is *Un Divorce*

(Vaudeville, 1908), by Paul Bourget and André Cury, adapted from a novel of Bourget's. This, he says, is a return to tragedy, to that 'tristesse majestueuse' of which Racine speaks in the preface to *Bérénice*. It sets in opposition religious marriage, civil marriage, and 'l'union libre'. There is in it a scene which Bordeaux found to belong to the 'beau théâtre, passioné et intelligent'; and his high opinion of it is due exclusively to the fact that it shows that civil marriage is morally no better than free love.

With patience, literary vigour, singleness of purpose, and quiet despair Bordeaux goes through, and deplores, the theatre of his time. In *Son Père*, by Albert Guinon and Bouchinet at the Odéon, a daughter reconciles her divorced parents, thus recognising an institution which fills Bordeaux with horror. *Monsieur de Courpière* (Athénée), by Abel Hermant, is about a professional libertine who settles into bourgeois virtue only when he no longer needs to make money out of his power over women. *L'Autre* (Comédie Française), by Paul and Victor Margueritte, is about the question of forgiving an erring spouse. Few things anger Bordeaux more than the forgiving of adultery by a generous-hearted husband or wife. Such an action seems to him atrocious weakness, and a betrayal of religion. It is the condoning of sin.

Romain Coolus's *Coeur-à-coeur* (Antoine) does in fact carry things rather far when its betrayed husband, in the charity of his heart, tries at revolver point to prevent his wife's lover from deserting her. It is not the melodrama of this that shocks Bordeaux, but what he considers its appalling immorality. He has no sympathy whatever for the husband; he calls him 'le Don Quichotte de cocuage'. Marriage, he says, is no longer a sacred institution to form a home and to establish a family. Children in modern drama are merely a disagreeable necessity, and people in plays now get married just to have pleasure, that is, sensual pleasure.

Bordeaux is important in the history of the early twentieth century French drama because he is the prime illustration of the vast gulf that separates the serious critics of his time from those of half a century later. These despise the pre-war French drama because it seems to be wholly concerned with individual relationships and apparently shows only the most tenuous recognition of the problems of society. Bordeaux despised it not because it was about personal relationships, but because in his opinion it expressed an immoral view of these relationships. Had he been able to reform the drama instead of merely criticising it he would have presented plays, not like those social dramas with which the English Stage Company achieved its reputation, but plays that examined private relationships in the light of Roman Catholic orthodoxy.

It is entirely because of his moral attitude that, of all the dramatists of his time, he most bitterly hated and despised Henry Bernstein. Bernstein was of a flamboyant personality, fond of gestures in life as extravagant as those in his plays, concerned only with sensationalism, and without that solid grounding in faith and honesty which Bordeaux judged to be the only things that really mattered.

Henry-Leon-Gustave-Charles Bernstein was born in Paris on 20 June 1876. His father was a Jewish financier, Marcel Bernstein, and he married a rich wife, Antoinette Martin, the niece of the proprietor of the big department store (which still exists) *Aux Trois Quartiers*. In 1904 Bernstein fled to Brussels after deserting from the army. He was already a dramatist; his first play had been presented four years earlier by Antoine at the Théâtre Libre, and another, *Le Bercail*, was to come on at the Gymnase in December; and he had no intention of being forgotten by the public. He wrote a celebrated letter to L'Aurore, then an anti-militarist paper, in which he declared, 'I am a deserter, and proud of it.' The affair was arranged, and Bernstein returned to Paris. But it was not forgotten by his enemies. There was an enormous scandal, and great disturbances broke out when the Camelots du Roi[6] resurrected and publicised this letter just before the production of *Après Moi*.

Most of the critics attributed the uproar at the first performance to Mlle Prévost's costume, but it is more likely to have been due to the noisy indignation of Bernstein's opponents. After all, even seven years before this, in February and March 1904, Mlle Cassive had, in a revival of *Nana* (adapted from Zola's novel by William Buznach) leaned in corsets and knickers against her dressing table, her clothes thrown over the back of a chair, as she received her male admirers in her loge. Mlle Cassive, though an actress much in vogue, created nothing like the furore that broke out over Mlle Prévost, and none of the critics ever mentioned the incident. But that may have been,

---

6.   A royalist right wing society.

given the circumstances of the time, and the prudery of their readers, that they could not think of phrases of sufficient delicacy.

Bernstein fought many duels as a young man, and René Prejelan, his squadron-leader at Salonika in the war of 1914–18, spoke very highly of his courage. After 1918 Bernstein moved to the right, and in 1923 wrote to Mussolini that the Duce was the 'great political thinker of the century'. He remained a Fascist until Mussolini adopted the same racial laws as Hitler, when he spectacularly returned all the decorations Mussolini had given him. After the débacle of 1940, Bernstein declared that after all he had written the Germans would gouge out his eyes. He prepared an ostentatious suicide, walking into the sea in a ski-ing costume, with a pistol in his hand. But when the water reached his waist, he turned round, got back to the beach, and fainted. When he recovered he asked for 300,000 francs, all he had left, to be sent to his wife and daughter. The next day he took a boat to London, whence he escaped to the United States. He was a convinced supporter of the war, but he thought the Germans would win. He spent much of his time in New York reproaching André Maurois for supporting Vichy. He was particularly annoyed that Maurois had abandoned his real name of Herzog.

Nowadays Bernstein, though generally little justice is done to him, nevertheless seems a much more considerable figure than Bataille. In fact he is beginning to emerge as a very significant dramatist, the foremost exponent of the ruthless ethics of high capitalism that the theatre has seen. Bataille shocked only in a way artfully designed to give pleasure, but the shocks that came from Bernstein were intended to hurt and affront. It is true that he is not the only dramatist of the Anglo–French theatre to write plays that attack other people's beliefs. Where he is honourably unique is that the people he attacked were the people on whom he relied to form his audience. However violent the Left wing writers of the 1950–60s Royal Court may have been, they wrote so that they had the bulk of their audiences with them. The people that they attacked were far away in the commercial theatre. But Bernstein wrote so that his *audiences* were against him. It was in the commercial theatre that he attacked the ethics of the people who supported the commercial theatre. For this he cannot be too greatly honoured.

If his enemies prefaced *Après Moi* with the letter that Bernstein had written to *L'Aurore*, Bernstein himself did his best to set the people for whom he was writing against him. He published a comment on the play in which he said, 'I am content to be a Jew. I do not say that I am proud of it; it always seems to me ridiculous to be proud of anything so involuntary as being born.'

This comment aroused enormous anger. Bernstein's audiences were rich, and they were snobbish. But they were not slow-witted. They saw that Bernstein's denial of pride in being a Jew was a slur on their own pride in being well-born. This was an insult that might not have meant much in Royalist England; but in republican France it carried far. There are at least 3,500 noble families in France, greatly in excess of the mere 900 that England can boast. Besides these 3,500 dukes, marquises, counts, viscounts, and barons, about 10,000 other families claim some sort of nobility through the use of the Portcaule *de*. These titles are based exclusively on birth, and they are taken very seriously. Several years after Bernstein's denial of merit to birth a respected employee of one of Paris's greatest and most famous hotels escaped dismissal only by an abject apology for failing to spring to attention when addressed by a duke.

All through his career Bernstein was derided by the eminent. André Gide declared that he trembled when he reflected that some future Taine might judge French society from the picture painted of it by Bernstein. Kléber Haedens, a critic of repute, called him one of Antoine's worst discoveries, 'an author of incredible nullity and vulgarity, whose success between the wars will be remembered with shame.'

But from 1904 onwards until his death the fashionable public which he insulted never deserted him. Though the critics of the day emphasise the enormous popularity of Bataille, statistically the advantage seems to have rested with Bernstein. In the early years of the century Paris did most of its theatregoing between January and April. Seven of the main theatres—the Comédie-Française, the Odéon, the Gymnase, the Renaissance, the Sarah Bernhardt, the Ambigu, and the Châtelet, all took more money in January during the typical year 1904 than in any other month. The best month of the year for the Vaudeville, however, was November. Bataille's *Maman Colibri* was produced there on 8 November. The receipts in October had been 103,691 francs, and Bataille's play raised them for November to 128,471 francs. This was a big jump, but it was not so great as that achieved by

Bernstein's·*Le Bercail* (1904) (yet another play dealing with marital forgiveness) at the Gymnase.

The Gymnase has always been a very successful theatre, and still continues so under the direction of Marie Bell. It was the first theatre anywhere in the world to stage Peter Brook's production of Jean Genet's *Le Balcon*. It had tremendous successes with Felicien Marceau's *La Bonne Soupe*, and William Douglas Home's *The Secretary Bird* and *Lloyd George Knew My Father*. But in November 1904, it had an unusually bad month, in which its receipts were only 76,001 francs. On 13 December Bernstein's *Le Bercail* was presented, and the receipts immediately shot up to 132,008 francs. This was a much larger increase than *Maman Colibri* had brought to the Vaudeville a few weeks earlier.

At the height of their respective popularity, therefore, Bataille's most famous play drew marginally less money to the box-office than did a comparatively minor piece of Bernstein's, in spite of the fact that the Gymnase seats only 1071 people against 1300 at the Vaudeville. Moreover in December the receipts for *Maman Colibri* dropped to 121,710 francs.

Both authors drew the same kind of audience. These were the days of the capitalist theatre. The rich and well-born had completely taken over the drama from the humble folk whose tastes dominated it before the *coup d'état* of 1851. Every night the stalls were filled with elegant ladies, whose rich robes were crowned by huge, elaborate hats. As they moved towards their seats, said a knowledgeable commentator, their silk underclothes rustled like autumn leaves disturbed by the breeze. The Gymnase, where the voice of Lucien Guitry, and his masterful male manner, sent a delicious thrill down their spines, was one of their favourite theatres. So was the tiny Capucines, where they were enchanted by Marguerite Deval in the operettes of Charles Cuvillier. The rich audiences of Bernstein and Bataille had a splendid, insolent confidence that the wealthy no longer have, even in France. When a celebrated financier died, leaving a million and a quarter pounds, the Baron de Rothschild remarked incredulously, 'Really, I had always thought he was well-off.'

They had the same nonchalance that the English aristocracy had had at the time of Dumas' *Antony*, though in less coarse circumstances. At a ball at that time a young girl inquired of her partner, 'Who is that sow of a woman . . . with her back to us?'

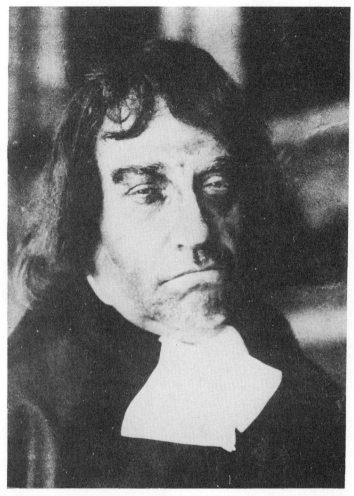

11. Lucien Guitry as Tartuffe. Photograph by courtesy of Harlingue-Viollet

'That sow of a woman,' replied her partner, 'is the Duchess of Bradford, and I have the honour to be one of her pigs.' The theatre, of which the French nobility were very fond, was, however, only the beginning of their evening's entertainment. After the performance, always accompanied by their father, husband, or brother, and never alone, its magnificent females would sup at the *Restaurant Durand*, in the boulevard de la Madeleine, at *Larue*, the favourite resort of Proust, or the *Café de Paris*. But

Mlle Cassive

Mlle Yvonne de Bray

Mme Jane Granier

Mme Bartet

12. Famous patrons of Maxim's: Madame Cassive, a favourite actress in Feydeau's plays, Yvonne de Bray, who appeared in Giraudoux's plays, Jeanne (Jane) Granier, who appeared in the plays of Renard, and Madame Bartet, who appeared in many of Racine's plays. Photograph from *Comoedia Illustré* 15 December 1910

never at *Maxim*'s, now in such high repute, which was reserved
for women of pleasure. No fashionable woman who was legally
married then ever went there.

Having dinner after the theatre doubled the cost of the evening. A stall at the Théâtre Antoine cost 5 francs. At the famous
Restaurant Marguery in the boulevard Bonne Nouvelle this would
have bought a salmon trout and a cup of coffee. For the price of
a stall at the Comédie Française (8 francs) one could have had
homard à la moùlaire, some asparagus, and coffee, and still have
had a little left over for a tip.

It is evident that in the huge inflation which has taken place
since 1900 the cost of theatre seats has fallen, rather than risen,
in relation to restaurants. It certainly would not be possible in
the 1970s to dine at Lasserre for the price of a stall at the
Comédie. In some of the best Paris restaurants today the guest
is given a menu on which no prices are marked. In 1900 at
places like the *Restaurant Durand*, for example, no prices were
given even on the host's menu. This gave scope for enterprise
and imagination. A grand duke, surprised at the price of a
peach when he was given his bill, remarked 'Peaches must be
very rare at Argenteuil this season?' The celebrated maître
d'hotel Nignon replied, 'No, monseigneur, it is grand dukes who
are rare in Paris.'

For the rich this was a time of serenity and happiness, which
they were convinced would last for ever. The splendour of
theatrical audiences was reflected in the ordinary way of life of
the exalted. Frenchmen of fashion, such as the Comte Greffulhe,
the Marquis de Lau, the Marquis de Breteuil, or the Marquis de
Jaucourt, were, like some less expected members of French
society, friends of Edward VII. They were to be seen in the
Royal Enclosure at Ascot: they were dressed by Poole of London, and they sent their sons to Oxford or Cambridge, whence
they returned to Paris with a slight English accent that was
regarded as a mark of the highest breeding.

One of the most carefully constructed and documented set
pieces in Zola is that in which he describes how Nana received
in her loge a foreign prince during a performance of an opera
bouffe which he calls *La Blonde Vénus*. This is the scene which, in
the stage version of the novel, was played with special zest by
Madame Cassive. With his young friend, the Comte de Muffat,
a man so virtuous that he has not even seen his wife put on her
garters, the Prince crosses during the interval from his box to

Nana's dressing room. The Prince's walk is meticulously described. He passes the scene shifters manoeuvring the scenery, brushes past small groups of *figurants* chattering in the wings, and, unlike Muffat, seems quite unmoved by the stifling atmosphere, the odour of soap, of dark, unsalubrious corners, of the chorus's doubtful underclothes. The flickering light of scores of gas jets continually threatens the theatre, the Variétés, with fire, and Muffat is taken by surprise when the stage shudders beneath his feet. He is taken by surprise also by the costume in which Nana receives the royal party. He is both religious and impressionable, and the sweat starts on his brow. 'Alors, tranquillement, pour aller à la toilette, elle passa en pantalon au milieu de ces messieurs.' And again: 'Nana, oubliant qu'elle était en pantalon, avec son bout de chemise, jouait la grande dame.'

The scene is authentic. The actress who thus received the prince in her loge was Hortense Schneider. She was playing 'La Grande Duchesse de Gerolstein', and, like Nana, mistook herself for a great lady. There was a ludicrous contrast between her drawers and the pretentious formality of her behaviour. She used the address 'Votre Altesse' almost every time she opened her mouth, and was secretly laughed at by everyone present in the loge except the Prince. Madame Schneider survived her royal admirer for many years, living until after the end of the 1914—18 war. Before she died she gave this advice to the young Gabriel-Louis Pringué, the commentator of Crapouillot 'Frivolity is the guarantee of wisdom and happiness. I was a frivolous woman, I lived at a frivolous time. Frivolous nations are happy nations. Try, monsieur, to be frivolous all your life. It is the best wish I can give you.'[8] There could be no better summing up than this of the spirit of the audiences who flocked to and acclaimed the plays of Henry Bernstein.

And the poor, did not one think of the poor, did no one realise that there was a world elsewhere than at Longchamps and Worth's and the loges of kept women? Yes, some people did, but not the leading dramatists or the audiences of the pre-war Paris theatre. There were men of clear eyes and compas-

---

7. Then, composedly, completing her make-up, she moved in front of these gentlemen in her knickers. Nana, forgetting she was in her underwear with her chemise hanging out, played the 'Grande dame'.

8. Crapouillot.

13. Orphans by Steinlen. Illustration from *Gil Blas* 17 June 1894

sionate hearts, men like Heidbrinck, Willette, and the incomparable, disconsolate Steinlen, to whom mean streets and starved faces were a reproach, and more real than diamonds and coaches and footmen. But they were artists, not men of the theatre; and the paradox is that their sombre, poetic accusations against the injustice and cruelty of an age which on the surface was brilliant and civilised appeared in the lightest, most libertine magazines of the 1890s and early 1900s: in *Le Chat noir*, *Le Gil Blas illustré*, *La Vie Parisienne*, *Le Rire*, *Le Courrier français*.

14. *Nos troupiers:* Cartoon by Poulbot from *Gil Blas* 19 July 1901

In *Le Gil Blas illustré* (19 July 1901) there is a drawing by the cartoonist Poulbot of a desolate scene outside the looming bulk of a huge barracks. It is a night of wind and rain, and the cobblestones gleam in the wet out of the gloom of an enveloping blackness. Struggling with an umbrella that threatens to blow itself inside out, a wretched *grue* offers to a hesitating *poilu* a last desperate inducement. 'In my home you can be certain not to meet any officers.' The restraint of this, the realism, the quiet bitterness, and the vista of poverty it reveals without emphasis or melodrama is far removed from the sentimental idealisation of *La Dame aux camélias* or the theatrical flourishes of *Nana*.

But the two great spokesmen of the poor and underprivileged were Steinlen and Willette: Steinlen with his wistful, starving children, his working girls, his modistes, his seamstresses, peered at by lubricious old men in dressmakers' changing rooms, or returning home to their lodgings up the steep streets of Montmartre under the pale light of forlorn lamps: Willette with his famished cats and gaunt chimney pots and broken Pierrots: the one even greater in realism than the other in fantasy and imagination. One in particular of Willette's cartoons, which occupies almost a full page in *Le Courrier français* of 25 April 1886, is unforgettable in its savage irony, its wealth of invention, its realisation of detail, and its bitterness against those in ascendency in this world, and against those who are expected to know about the next. The piquant-faced, upturned-nosed, fragile model Willette had in recent weeks been drawing (always in white lace bloomers, as she cascaded down the roof of the Moulin de la Galette, or waved an impudent fan at the crossing sweeper who with his broom represents Ash Wednesday), now lies stretched naked on a dishevelled bed, her despairing face buried in the pillows. The picture is called *Oeuf de Paques*; it is indeed Willette's comment on the great joyous feast of the Church, on the resurrection at Easter. In one corner a new-born baby, a pert little fellow, stands inquiringly in a broken eggshell. He looks across the disordered room, with its appalling poverty, its overturned, strawbottomed, broken chair, its pathetic sewing machine, its tumbled sheets: and he sees, for what comfort or reassurance it can bring him. nothing but a monstrous, vindictive Easter bell, ringing with menace, shaped into the face of an angry old man, its clanger sticking out like a lascivious tongue.

As the years went on Willette, who was prosecuted for the political implications in his drawings, seems to have lost something of his rage and attack. But sympathy for the poor remained in the lighter literature of the day. Set amongst erotic stories, constant insistence upon adultery and its pleasures, and pictures like that of a suggestively laughing girl holding up her skirts and inquiring of a passing man, 'Voulez-vous voir les dessous de ces dessous?'[9] there is social protest after social

---

9.   Would you like to see what's underneath these underclothes?

Le Numéro : 50 centimes.

14 Juillet 1895. 12ᵉ Année. Nᵒ 28.

LE COURRIER FRANÇAIS

ILLUSTRÉ PARAISSANT TOUS LES DIMANCHES

Littérature + Beaux-Arts + Théâtres + Médecine + Finance

ABONNEMENTS PARIS & DÉPARTEMENTS	BUREAUX & ADMINISTRATION	POUR LA PUBLICITÉ
SIX MOIS... 12ʳ50 — UN AN..... 25 Fr.	19, Rue des Bons-Enfants, Paris.	S'adresser aux Bureaux du COURRIER FRANÇAIS
SIX MOIS... 20 Fr. — UN AN..... 35 Fr.	**JULES ROQUES**	ou à l'Agence AUDBOURG & Cⁱᵉ, 10, Place de la Bourse.
Envoyer le montant en un Mandat ou Bon Postal.	Fondateur	ANNONCES............. 3 Fr. LA LIGNE.
On s'abonne aussi dans tous les Bureaux de Poste.		RÉCLAMES............. 6 Fr. —
Les abonnements partent du 1ᵉʳ janvier ou du 1ᵉʳ juillet de chaque année.	Les manuscrits non insérés ne sont pas rendus.	FAITS DIVERS......... 10 Fr. —

La Quarantaine

Dessin de A. WILLETTE.

— Ah! schoking, Monsieur, vous êtes nul comme..... un ver!

15. Cartoon by A. Willette from *Le Courrier* 14 July 1895

protest. It is as though the conscience of the 1970s resided in *Playboy* and *Penthouse*.

The first fine rage of the most admirable Willette passed imperceptibly into a quiet pity, and even tenderness, for the poor. After the turn of the century, whilst Bernstein was preaching the doctrine so detested by Bordeaux, that all things are justified so long as they lead to personal success, the belligerent note vanished from comment on the underprivileged. Paul Balluriau's drawing in *Le Gil Blas illustré* of shabby, middle-aged, working class woman holding the hand a a sad little boy with bare head and downcast, discouraged eyes is characteristic of the new mood of resigned acceptance. Willette's rebellion had now come to no more than that, to the sentiment of Achille Basile's little song called *Ballade des Pauvres Bougres*, to which a certain Gaston Perducet wrote the music.

> Oh! ces faces pâles collées
> Devant les vitraux éclatants
> Des cafés où sont écoulées
> Les liqueurs aux reflets tentants!
> Passant par bandes affolées
> Regardez ces magiques pouilleux
> Aux rouges paupières voilées . . .
>   Les pauvres bougres sont frileux.[10]

This kind of sentiment was far beyond the range of Bernstein, though here and there in the early twentieth century Paris theatre there were dramatists capable of generous feelings, even if they did not go out of their way to show it in their work. The most striking of these was Feydeau, who brought into his private life the tenderness he rigidly excluded from the clocklike intricacy and elaboration of his farces. The revue writer Max Aghion records that round about seven every evening Feydeau could be seen in the Café Napolitain, with a full glass of wine before him, which he rarely touched. In the first decade of the century the Napolitain was popular with journalists, men of letters, and dramatic critics. A regular visitor was Ernest Lajeunesse, the critic of *Comoedia Illustré*. His fingers were loaded with rings, and he dominated the noise of the café and the street outside with his high-pitched eunuch's voice. Jean de Bonnefon,

---

10.   The cold, starved poor peering through the windows of magnificent restaurants, where the wine flows glitteringly.

stout, solemn, Monsignorial, was invariably there, and Catulle Mendès, the only critic who had seen anything good in *Ubu Roi*: now ravaged and disfigured by every kind of excess.

Feydeau disliked Lajeunesse, and ignored Bonnefon, but Aghion noticed that he greeted Mendès with respect, though Mendès regularly pulled his plays to pieces. One evening Aghion asked him the reason for this. Feydeau told him that it was due to a memory of his youth, when his father had taken him to visit Théophile Gautier. In the poet's garden there suddenly appeared 'a magnificent couple aureoled by the sun. The woman was gentleness, charm, grace, and intelligence made flesh. The man, with his fine waist, his golden hair and beard, looked like Christ. He was Catulle Mendès, and the woman Judith Gautier. They had just become engaged. He murmured to her a poem of love, and she listened, radiant . . .' 'Exactly,' said Feydeau, 'the man you see over there, grey, fat, wrinkled, and not very clean, once could write without being ridiculous: Je porte avec orgueil la honte d'être beau.'[11]

Feydeau at this time was immensely popular, but he was not held in high regard by the critics of the day, who would have been amazed had they known that fifty years later he would be the most favoured dramatist in the repertoire of the Comédie Française. Madame Cassive had been the star of his *Un Fil à la patte* (1894) and of *La Dame de Chez Maxim's* (1899). When she played Nana in 1904 she doubtless thought that she was taking a step upwards in the dramatic hierarchy, for it was pointed out to her that she was now playing with 'a violence, a terror, a suffering, a genuine feeling for the horrifying and the tragic infinitely fascinating in an entrancing woman accustomed to triumphs in ephemeral comedies.'

But the public actually preferred these ephemeral comedies, and their taste has been ratified by posterity. In the first weeks of the two-month run of *Nana*, Zola's underworld and Madame Cassive's underwear in the fourth largest theatre in Paris brought in no more than 1946 francs a performance. Later this figure fell to 1514 francs. But when Madame Cassive left the serious social drama to return to Feydeau's 'ephemeral comedies' —comedies which have proved so much more lasting than the work of the critics who despised them—her triumphs returned.

---

11.   I carry proudly the shame of being handsome. AGHION, Max: *Hier à Paris*. Editions Marchot, Paris.

Her performances in *Occupe-toi d'Amélie* (1908) and in *Mais n'te promène donc pas toute nue!* (1912) were amongst her greatest successes, and have been repeated in the contemporary theatre by Madeleine Renaud with a provocative delicacy, a teasing *pudeur* without rival in the theatres of either France or Britain. When Vivien Leigh appeared in London in Noel Coward's *Look after Lulu*, which was adapted from *Occupe-toi d'Amélie*, she was very piquant and pretty. But it was obvious, to those who had seen Madame Renaud, that superlative beauty is not enough.

Feydeau did not concern himself with the poor any more than Bernstein did. But neither did he insist, as Bernstein did, on the rich's riches. Money, with sex, was the principal theme of the drama of his day. Paul Hervieu and Eugène Brieux showed in *L'Armature* how the most brilliant society is dominated by material necessities which push both love and pleasure into the background. Octave Mirbeau in *Les Affaires sont les affaires* and Emile Fabre in *Les Ventres dorés* each reveal the degradation that the love of money involves.

Bernstein's attitude to money is quite different. He sees it as the supreme symbol of power and success, the sweet fruition of earthly struggle. In *Le Retour* he reviles a respectable Protestant family which refuses to accept an old kept woman and her current lover. In *La Rafale* (1905), his first big success, he is contemptuous of an old man who declines to give 800,000 francs to his daughter to relieve her lover's gambling debts. In *Le Voleur* the heroine robs her friends so that she can buy clothes that will minister to the pride and sensuality of her husband. *Le Voleur* triumphed all through 1906; indeed, its vigour and elasticity are remarkable. The second act, in which husband and wife reveal all their conjugal secrets, was particularly popular. This was too much for Bordeaux. He recalls that after the Terror a little theatre in the Palais Royal offered the spectacle of the coupling of a savage with a prostitute, and every evening the place was crowded. Every evening, too, *Le Voleur* was crowded. Bordeaux saw a parallel between the two cases. Savages and prostitutes are really the characters in Bernstein, 'the painter of our civilised society.'

This exclusive interest in money cannot be found in classical French drama. It was the result of the decay of the territorial aristocracy, who, after the Revolution, ceased to fulfil the duties which were the sole justification of their power and influence.

When in *Israel* the Prince de Clar declares his intention of insulting the Jewish financier Gutlieb, his friend the Comte de Grégenoy tells him that the real enemy is not the Jews, but the Confédération du Travail. The young man expostulates that the workers do not march against the nobility, and that the nobility does not oppose their wage demands. 'What,' exclaimed the Count, 'Socialism doesn't frighten you? Wretched daydreams! There is the real enemy, and the only one.' 'To think that a nobleman should talk like this,' someone exclaims in disgust. In a memorable line, one of the few places in pre-war French drama that shows an accurate realisation of the movement of social power, the Count Grégenoy contemptuously replies, 'To my butler I am a nobleman! In the social battle I claim to be a member of a genuine class. I call myself a bourgeois!'

Bernstein and Bordeaux, despite their opposition to each other, or perhaps even because of it, remain the most considerable figures of their time in their respective professions. Bordeaux's criticism was of course essentially of a moral order. This narrows its scope, but gives it a precision and attack lacking in such an eminent rival critic as, for example, Adolphe Brisson. Whereas ancient tragedy did not question the moral order, the contemporary drama of France, in Bordeaux's opinion, envisaged the possibility of setting the individual above it. The dramatist Porto-Riche, commenting rather flippantly on the beauty of an actress who had recently played Phèdre, remarked that Hippolyte must have been a fool to throw away such a chance. This frivolous observation predictably shocked Bordeaux, who pointed out that for Hippolyte to go to bed with Phèdre would have been, in Hippolyte's eyes, a crime. It would have been a crime to Phèdre also, who never speaks of her incestuous passion except with horror. Neither Bérénice nor Titus seriously opposes love to the laws of Rome. Religious, moral, and political order are never called in question.

The climax of Bernstein's career came with the production in February 1911, of *Après moi*. It is in this play that Bernstein shows most clearly and brutally that for him the conventional moral order has no validity whatsoever. The principal character is a business tycoon who uses the money of his friends and family in speculations that bring him face to face with ruin and disgrace. The scene in which this man, with a savage directness and brevity, explains to the family he has made destitute exactly what he has done is a marvel of concision and force. In his love scenes Bernstein is usually strained and unconvincing, but in expressing the fierce scorn of powerful personalities for conventional restraints he was incomparable in his own day and has remained so to ours. Bernstein set aside the comparatively easy and sympathetic task of justifying adultery; he left that to men of lesser daring, and himself tackled the far less attractive and more difficult feat of uncompromisingly defending the right of the strong to swindle those less clever and astute than themselves.

Brisson was puzzled by *Après moi*. He felt that the hero, who was ready when unmasked to blow his brains out, did not meet his ruin with fortitude and nobility. In this, of course, he wholly misunderstood Bernstein, the central point of whose attitude to life was that fortitude and nobility were outmoded conceptions in which he took no interest. Brisson wished Bernstein to write in old-fashioned romantic terms of a man purified by failure. But Bernstein's merit and originality as a dramatist is that this is precisely what he had no intention of doing.

Nevertheless, a change was coming over the theatre, and the great problem was whether Bernstein, incomparably the finest craftsman and most strongly emotional dramatist in France, would bow to it, or ignore it and go his own way. The whole question of his future and his integrity as a dramatist were bound up in this problem. By the end of the first decade of the century he had become accustomed to overwhelming success. At *Le Bercail* (1904) the audience was in ecstasies. He was used to the services of the best actors and actresses, to actors like Lucien Guitry, and actresses who were perfectly suited to his farouche and brutal genius.

The most successful of these was Simone Le Bargy. In *Le Bercail* she gave a sensational performance as the dissatisfied wife who deserts her husband, and then, still ravaged by the inability of her temperament to come to terms with life, returns to him. She astounded Adolphe Brisson. He found her to be an actress thrilling with passion, certainly not pretty, perhaps even worse than that; walking badly and jerkily on the stage; without grace or feminine charm; but, infinitely more than making up for it, endowed with ferocious energy and strength of will; devoured by an interior fire that makes her voice hard, aggressive, wounding, scraping the words as she utters them. She seduces, he says, irritates, and wearies all at the same time; one wants to cry 'Stop it', and yet one never gets tired of applauding.

The resounding successes continued with *La Rafale* (Gymnase, 23 October 1905). Again Bernstein had Mme Le Bargy in his company. She was, as usual, tense, savage, with the terrible energy of a tightly coiled spring. In the big scene in the second act, when she attacks her father for his refusal to settle the debts of her gambling and criminal lover, she gave the feeling of a young lion following her prey with her eyes, and watching preparatory to leaping upon it. She has given up pleading, and threatens instead.

> You sold me through ambition and snobbery to a man that I hate. You will give me the money to save the man I adore.
> No.
> Then I shall join him. If he leaves the country, I shall go with him. If he is arrested, I shall kill myself. I shall shout my love from the housetops. You will never belong to the Circle in the rue Royale.

It is as though this young woman climaxed her speech with the words, 'You will never be accepted at Ascot.' In our own day it would not do at all. No living actress could now carry off such a speech. But in 1905 things were different, and the conquered Brisson reported that 'a triple salvo of cheers greeted this magnificent passage of arms.'

Three years later the tide has begun to recede from Bernstein. The atmosphere at the first performance of *Israel* was cold, the audience constrained and reserved. The young man who attacked the Jew in the club was thought to be ill-bred, and the Jew himself feeble-spirited. Everyone seems to have considered as a famous *coup de théâtre* the extremely improbable revelation that the Jew was actually his insulter's father. But even this did not reconcile *Israel* to the public. Perhaps it missed Mme Le Bargy, and found Réjane an inadequate substitute. Anyway, the reception of the play was sufficiently disappointing for Bernstein to be provoked to his tart words about the insignificance of birth.

But it was over *Après moi* that the storm actually broke. A cloud hung over it from the beginning. The resuscitation by the Camelots du Roi of Bernstein's celebrated letter on desertion of a few years before led to strong police reinforcements surrounding the theatre. But these were insufficient to prevent riots. The loud, sharp intake of breath reported throughout the whole house when Mlle Prévost appeared in her knicker-suit may have been complimentary, but when Guillaume Bourgade said of his approaching ruin 'Celui-là qui échoue dans une entreprise illicite est un misérable. Je n'avais pas le droit de ne pas réussir,'[12] the movement in the theatre was hostile. To suggest that swindling is wrong only when it fails was like adding warts to the unacceptable face of capitalism, and claiming that they increased its beauty. Après moi did not repeat the success of Bernstein's previous plays, and he became very bitter about it, as he showed in his fore-word to the published version. 'On se souvient de ce qui avait été machiné contre la représentation d'Après moi à la Comédie Française. Jamais une entreprise plus lâche ne fut plus basse-ment exécuté. Comme la plupart des vilaines choses, ce mauvais coup réussit.'[13]

But the relative failure of the play was not due wholly to political reasons, or to the plots of evilly-disposed enemies. Even Bernstein's admirers were beginning to revolt against his un-compromisingly vicious reading of human nature. In Après moi, Bourgade decides to shoot himself, but is prevented from doing so by the unexpected arrival on the scene of his wife. But his resolution was already faltering before she appeared. He later becomes pitiable in the extravagance of his humiliating pleas to her not to desert him. She accepts, and abandons her lover (one of the people Bourgade has ruined), not through any love or compassion for her husband, but because at 38, she feels too old, too weary, to leave him, and make a new life.

This deeply upset Brisson. He recognised Bernstein's mastery of furiously hostile dialogue, his capacity to create highly drama-tic scenes, and does not seem to have been distressed, as later audiences and critics would have been, by their artificiality. But he found nowhere in Bernstein's work any sense of nobility. This was not, of course, because he was short-sighted. There actually was no nobility there. Its absence is the hallmark of Bernstein's talent, and to ask for it is as foolish as to ask Beckett to fill his plays with optimism. Beckett finds no optimism in the world, and therefore it is absent from his plays. Bernstein found no

---

12. Anyone who fails in an illegal undertaking is a weakling. I had not the right not to succeed.

13. What was plotted against the production of Après-moi at the Comédie Française is easy to remember. No scandalous enterprise was ever more basely carried out. Like the majority of evil things, it succeeded.

nobility in the world, and therefore, being until this point in his careeer a writer of total aesthetic honesty, he did not in his plays pretend that he did.

It was now that Brisson, coming close to Henry Bordeaux, whom he did not otherwise resemble, made a memorable, and, as it turned out, effective, plea to Bernstein. 'Qu'une oeuvre idéaliste,' he cries, 'Qu'une oeuvre idéaliste, sans niaiserie, sans fadeur, qu'une oeuvre pathétique et vraiment belle soit représentée demain, elle obtiendra le triomphe de "Cyrano". Et un immense cri d'allégresse montera vers le ciel!'[14] Bordeaux also desired better and purer things. A few months later, reviewing a rather absurdly eloquent play about patriotism and spies by Henry Kistemaeckers, called La Flambée, Bordeaux said, speaking of 'la tendresse conjugale', that it was not convincingly portrayed by the author, and added, 'It is not to be found in the plays of M. Henry Bataille, nor in those of M. Henry Bernstein.'

The effect of this on Bernstein was disastrous. Hitherto he had been one of the century's most important dramatists. He was far and away the most vigorous incarnation of the philosophy of his time of whom we have any experience. He carried to extreme lengths the ethics of high capitalism; his plays are the limiting case, and their importance as social as well as theatrical documents cannot be exaggerated. He was the unqualified expression of individualism. But now he began to falter. He may have been unnerved by the attack of the Camelots and the hostility of the audience at the opening of Après moi; or he may have been affected by Brisson's eloquent sincerity.

His next play, L'Assaut (Gymnase, 1912), actually at one point compelled the admiration even of Henry Bordeaux. Mérital, a rising politician, is on the point of marrying Renée, a charming and innocent girl sincerely in love with him, who is much younger than he, when he is accused of having committed forgery in his youth. That such a devastating accusation should follow so instantly the happiness of his engagement is one of those melodramatic devices which neither the public nor the French critics were at this historical period ready to question. Anyway, the accusation was true, though there had been extenuating circumstances, which give Mérital the opportunity

14. If a work of idealism, without silliness or insipidity, were to be properly produced tomorrow it would obtain a success like 'Cyrano'. And there would rise to the heavens a great sigh of relief.

for a considerable oration later in the play. Mérital, as we should expect in Bernstein, is a man of strong nerve. Calling together all his resources, which we are not surprised to hear include blackmail, he makes certain that his accuser will be condemned. Overjoyed, he tells the trusting, simple Renée that he will be acquitted, and the man who has brought the charge against him will be imprisoned.

It is at this point that, for the first but not the last time in his career as a dramatist, Bernstein ceased to be true to himself, and to his real vision of life. Mérital is surprised that Renée shows so little emotion at the news that no harm will come to her powerful lover. 'I knew you were innocent all the time,' she says. This simplicity so moves Mérital that he tells her the truth. For the first time morality comes into a Bernstein play. Now in most plays morality is much to be desired, but not in Bernstein, whose social and dramatic importance was that there was no morality in him. Bordeaux naturally calls this a scene of 'unexpected grandeur'.

But worse was to come. When Bernstein wrote *Le Secret* (Bouffes-Parisiens, March 1913) Brisson greeted in it a new sensitivity to gentleness and goodness, a less complacent attitude towards duplicity and villainy, even a feeling for morality, and mistakenly thought that this was a move in the right direction. He praised Bernstein for ceasing to be Bernstein. Thereafter Bernstein's work steadily declined. The characters he wrote about after the war of 1914–18, in *La Galérie des glaces* (1924), *Félix*, or *Mélo*, are less sure of themselves than those in *La Rafale* or *Israel*. They are no longer bent on achieving their material ends at whatever cost to morality. They even begin to doubt themselves. Charles, in *La Galérie des glaces*, is a famous man, an artist, yet despite his celebrity he cannot believe that any woman can truly love him. In a scene written with considerably greater delicacy and less power than Bernstein would have employed fifteen years earlier, Charles in distress of spirit forces his former mistress, Madeleine, now herself happily married, to admit that though she had great affection for him, he had never been able to give her the sort of sexual excitement she gets from her husband.

The sentimental decline that set in after Bernstein had been intimidated by the reception of *Après moi* is to be seen also in *Félix*. The hero is a *coureur de jupes* who pities a girl in a brothel, and marries her. When she deceives him he nobly forgives her.

Bernstein's fall from what was really the thing which was in him to give the French theatre, and which he had given abundantly in plays like *Israel* and *Après moi*, came to its climax with the production of Jean Cocteau's *Les Parents Terribles* at the Ambassadeurs near the end of the thirties. The production was a triumph, but Bernstein, who then directed the Gymnase, intrigued with the municipality that ran the theatre to break its contract with the producer, Roger Capgras, an enlightened man of wealth who had presented plays by H. R. Lenormand, Cocteau, and Jean Anouilh. There is something ludicrous in Bernstein's claiming that Cocteau was an immoral writer, when he had himself, at his best period, profoundly shocked the *bien pensants* of the early part of ‚the century. Not many dramatists take advice from critics. What happened to Bernstein suggests that in this 'they may be right. Yet even today there are intelligent men of the theatre who prefer Bernstein's later period, and, like Pierre-Aimé Touchard, consider *Le Secret* to be his best play.

Bernstein was much criticised for the grossness of his language, even though this grossness was in some ways reluctantly admired. The critic Paul Léautaud did not much like Bernstein's *Samson* (1907), the story of an implacable Jewish industrialist of immense wealth who deliberately ruins himself so that he can at the same time ruin his wife's lover. But he admits that the scene in which these two men mutually expose each other, was 'un joli succès de grossièretés.'[15] He goes on to complain that Bernstein was excessively fond of using the most up-to-date slang, and alleges that the number of times he makes his characters employ the word 'chic' is incalculable. Bordeaux goes so far as to say that Bernstein does not write French at all.

The importance of Bernstein then is as much social as dramatic. It is that in his early period, the period when most drama critics were begging him to change his style, and become something other than he was, he revealed with unexampled energy, ferocity, and melodramatic power the ethics of capitalism raised to the extreme extent. He is the best authority we have in the theatre of the prevailing philosophy of his day unqualified by any considerations of morality or justice. He is the high priest of individualism. Man has a right to get what he can, no matter how he gets it. The only immorality is failure. It is not a

---

15.   A success of vulgarities.

pretty doctrine, but it makes Bernstein a primary authority for
the early twentieth century.

Hitherto the principal Parisian drama critics had been comparatively well-off members of the bourgeoisie, men with good
hopes of receiving the Legion of Honour and of being elected to
the Académie Française. But there now enters into the profession a man from an entirely different class. Paul Léautaud
(1872–1956) was the son of the prompter at the Comédie
Française. His mother deserted the Léautaud household when
Léautaud was very young, and he was brought up chiefly by
his father's mistresses. When he met his mother for what might
be considered the first time, he was grown up, and they both
conceived for each other a physical passion of extreme intensity.
Towards the end of his long life Léautaud spoke of his relations
with his mother in a series of remarkably frank radio talks, and
thus, when over seventy, became rich and famous.

But for the greater part of his life he was very poor. He had a
humble job at the *Mercure de France* when Vallette was editor;
and whilst there he suffered much from the intrigues of Vallette's
wife, the celebrated Rachilde. He was a man of bitter and acrid
temper, but showed a touching kindness to stray cats and dogs.
He cherished with unwearying affection 38 cats, 22 dogs, a goat,
and a goose, in his home. For these creatures he often deprived
himself of the necessities of life, and in his dramatic criticisms he
showed for them a compassion he rarely bestowed on either the
players or the authors of the works he was reviewing. He was of
mean appearance, dressed badly, and had a very ugly face.
Nevertheless he had considerable success with women.

Because of his father's connection with the Comédie Française, Léautaud knew the chief players of the National Theatre
intimately from the early days of his life. His principal admiration was for Marguerite Moreno. When Moreno played Aricie,
Léautaud wept silently; when she played in *Polyeucte* his efforts
to prevent himself from sobbing were so painful that they gave
him a headache. She was a woman of considerable wit, and
quite without vanity, though her legs were long and superb. In
Victorien Sardou's *La Sorcière* she made up as a wrinkled old
woman, and Léautaud was pained to see her looking so ugly.
'Sarah (Bernhardt: also an exponent of Sardou) wouldn't look
like that,' said a friend. 'Oh yes, she does,' replied Moreno. 'In
the morning.'

She was for some time the mistress of Catulle Mendès, and

later, when Léautaud was about thirty, she married Marcel
Schwob. Schwob was a Symbolist writer of great celebrity.
Brought up in circles of extreme, almost exaggerated, culture, he
gave many people the impression of having exhausted all litera-
tures and philosophies, and also, in the process, the impression
of having exhausted himself as well. At the time that Léautaud
frequented his house, though he was not much over thirty,
Schwob had become a valetudinarian, always moaning about
his health. Moreno did not allow this to depress her spirits. One
night when Schwob complained of a high temperature she took
Léautaud into her bedroom, and there, to his astonishment,
lifted up her skirts and danced the can-can. 'Have you seen the
fever dance?' she demanded merrily, looking as little like a
respected actress of the Comédie Française as it was possible
to be.

She was glad whenever she could to escape from the over-
heated atmosphere of continual ill-health in her home. There,
and at the Comédie, she had all the culture she could stomach.
She was at her best when playing Racine or Corneille. At other
times she yearned for Bohemian company, and the freedom that
it gave her. She was the intimate friend of Colette at a time
when Colette was a rather disreputable music hall actress,
appearing on the stage half dressed, and in a lesbian act with
the Marquise de Belboeuf which the Marquise, owing to the
protests of her family (the ducs de Morny), had to abandon
after the first performance. This friendship continued unabated
till Moreno died, long after Colette had become a famous
novelist, and one of the most revered figures in Paris and indeed
the world.

Moreno was quite without self-consciousness. Marthe
Brandès had excited Renard when she changed her costume
before him in her dressing room, and Moreno had an even more
troubling effect on Léautaud, for whilst stripping when he called
on her in her *loge* at the Comédie she without embarrassment
asked him very teasing questions. She talked eagerly of Schwob's
poor performances in bed. 'I don't want to wait till I'm sixty
before I make love,' she said. 'What shall I do, Léautaud? Tell
me what I should do.'

On no other occasion in his life did Léautaud show himself at
a loss in a similar situation. But he was awed by the consciousness that the lady who was talking thus was not a chorus girl
from the Folies-Bergère, but a great actress of the Comédie

Française, an actress moreover who at that very moment was in the middle of a performance of a grand and noble classical tragedy. The circumstances did not seem to him suitable to a gallant reply, but at intervals during the next fifty years he regretted his failure to inquire into what the words of Moreno really meant. Drama critics in the early years of the century had more delicate questions to resolve than merely evaluating the play they had been invited to review. So far as I know, the problems that contemporary critics face are more strictly professional.

For that matter it is unlikely that the solidly bourgeois and religious Henry Bordeaux often encountered experiences similar to Léautaud's. In fact the point of this story simply is to emphasise the great difference between the temperaments of the two men. Their social background was different; the circles in which they moved were different; their outlook on life was different. It is these differences that make it the more significant that in their views of the plays of Bernstein and of others of his kind they were identical.

People, said Léautaud, write only what they feel, and they put into their work just what is in themselves. The theatre of these dramatists is as sad as it is base. Never the least generous sentiment, or one of those touches that warm the heart, that give pleasure, and are affecting at the same time as giving pleasure. '. . . Let them,' he says, 'have their success—if that is what they call it. They are sad authors, and their theatre is a poor theatre.'

In all the hundreds of early twentieth century plays of whose production and performances long and detailed accounts exist, there seem to have been few that provided experiences which touch the imagination with pleasure, or which soften the feelings, or which suggest that it is good to be alive. Occasionally Léautaud had such an experience at a play by Sacha Guitry. That a man as misanthropic as Léautaud, as scornful of fashion and rich living, should find anything to praise in the light and pleasure-seeking Guitry is surprising at first sight. But he went further than this. He actually had an acute admiration for Guitry's work. Unlike the more serious critics of his time, he did not find Guitry's characters trivial and selfish.

On the contrary, he thought them frank, simple, and good-humoured, bringing gaiety to their peccadilloes. They do not search for pretty phrases with which to excuse themselves, and in the midst of their flirtations and unfaithfulness they still have qualities of generosity and emotion, and even a few scruples. In Guitry there is nothing that suggests the sham poet or bogus metaphysician. Throughout the period of Léautaud's active drama criticism, which lasted from 1907 till 1923, there is no writer who gets from him such consistently favourable notices as this provider of *jeux d'esprit* for after-dinner entertainment, whom most people wrote off with indulgent contempt as a frivolous and irresponsible dilettante. Léautaud placed Sacha Guitry infinitely above Bernstein, Bataille, and Paul Claudel. It is not a judgment that later generations, especially in the case of Claudel, have endorsed. But Léautaud was a man of sharp perceptions, as well as of cruel wit, and it is possible that, in respect to Guitry, it is not he, so much as his successors, who is wrong.

He was particularly affected by a piece of Guitry's called *Un Beau mariage* (1911). The heroine of this play was not *virgo intacta*, and for this Guitry was much criticised. Henry Bordeaux defended Guitry's choice of heroine on the equivocal ground that he would have been sorry to see any better girl married to the sort of man that Guitry had chosen for his hero. These gay and witty, but morally defective, people were played by Guitry and his first wife, Charlotte Lysès. Guitry was then in the flower of youth, not yet twenty-seven years old, and the sight of him touched Léautaud's sensibilities, particularly in the last scene of all, which lingered in his mind long after the curtain had fallen. It was a very simple scene, and would have been both beneath the notice and beyond the powers of any of Guitry's contemporaries. It represented a garden with real freshness, says Léautaud. 'M. Sacha Guitry in white, Mme. Charlotte Lysès in black, against the green background of trees' —it was nothing more than that; and yet, in the silence, and stillness, and colour, it was, said Léautaud, 'un Manet très réussi.'[16] He felt that these people would go on living in the freshness of spring, amidst the flowers of a garden after he had put on his hat and gone home in the cold and gloom of the November night. He was touched by the breath of immortality.

Out of the darkness this lone star shines. There was another moment that Léautaud remembered, another thing seen and heard in the theatre that enriched his being, and lightened the

16. A very successful Manet.

to him enormous and unrewarding weight of dramatic criticism. It is a tribute to the essential fairness of his sour nature that it occurred in a play written by two men whom he disliked, on an occasion that filled him with annoyance. This occasion was the production in 1907 by Lugné-Poe of *Le Baptême*, by Alfred Savoir and Fernand Nozière. Lugné-Poe had been responsible for the production in Paris of *Pelléas et Mélisande*. He was not of the school of Bataille and Bernstein, and Léautaud had therefore some reason to admire him. But to Léautaud's disgust he asked his friends at this performance to wear evening dress. Nothing could have been designed to upset Léautaud more than this. Some of France's greatest writers were there, he remarked sarcastically: M. Réné Maizeroy, M. Henry Bauer, M. Catulle Mendès, M. Jean de Bonnefon; and he added that one of the pleasantest things about such gatherings was that you saw people you thought had been dead for years.

Léautaud disliked Savoir and Nozière because they were Jews. He denies that he is an anti-Semite, but he never loses an opportunity to insist that Jews are not Frenchmen. In dealing with Savoir and Nozière he follows the literary system which is the foundation of his style. Not for him the thundering denunciation with which some critics announce their indignation at the very beginning of their review. His method is to open with a compliment that is apparently sincere, and then to develop it slowly in a series of simple statements that imperceptibly change its nature, and leave it at the end an unqualified insult. There is, he says, in *Le Baptême* an excellent moral directed at certain Jews. The authors express their shame at finding that there are Jews who change their real names for French names, instead of proudly telling the world that they are Jews, inspired by the courage and pride of their religion and their race. 'No words are too eloquent,' says Léautaud, 'to congratulate for these sentiments MM. Savoir and Nozière, whose real names are, the first, Poznansky, and the second, Weyl.'

Léautaud therefore had no predisposition to enjoy *Le Baptême*. But he found in it one of those scenes that stand out in the memory of critics, that remain as a permanent enrichment of life. That, for example, between the young boy Lucien and his father. The boy complains that he is unhappy at school. His comrades avoid him: he is a Jew. 'Look, father, if we are unhappy,' he says, 'I know why. It is because we are not at home. When you were a little boy in Frankfurt you at least were not unhappy. That's because you were at home. If you wished, we could return there, to our home.' Then the father lifts his head, and says gently, 'Alas, little one, there I was no happier than you, for that is not our home.' 'Then, father,' says the child, 'where are we at home?' And the old man says nothing, makes an evasive gesture of which he is hardly conscious, 'the gesture of the eternal wanderer.' Scenes of this kind, the strange, curious, and profoundly personal actor, Lugné-Poe, the only French actor of his time, says Léautaud, capable of acting in depth, played beautifully.

This is high praise, though not perhaps the praise that Lugné-Poe most earnestly desired. Lugné-Poe wished to be more than an actor. He was one of the two men who in the 1890s had tried to transform the French theatre into a thing of art and social service, and who had been overtaken by the abominable Bernstein and Bataille. The other was André Antoine.

CHAPTER FOUR

The Theatre of the People

In spite of its great popularity, there was much dissatisfacton with the boulevard theatre in Left wing political circles. Romain Rolland described the French theatre of the early years of the century as 'the brothel of Europe'. It does not seem to have occurred either to Rolland or to any of his friends that a writer like Bernstein, for example, was doing a great deal to discredit and weaken the capitalist system which they hated, and should therefore have been regarded as an ally in the enemies' camp. Nor did they harmoniously recognise allies even in their own ranks. Both Rolland and Antoine desired, if not the actual over-throw of the boulevard theatre, at least the erection of another kind of theatre which would be a viable alternative to it. But there was no agreement between them as to what sort of theatre this should be. Rolland spoke with the most violent contempt and hatred of the kind of play which Antoine produced as evidence of proletarian theatre. Antoine conceived of a People's Theatre as one which would deal with the problems of working class people: Rolland thought of it as a gigantic Fun Fair, designed to spread jollification and happiness, rather as Joan Littlewood did during the 1960s. There was no possibility of reconciling these two aims. Both men ignored the fact that during a large part of the nineteenth century the theatre had actually been a People's Theatre, and this was precisely what many drama critics held against it.

Rolland himself was well aware of his differences from Antoine. He declared that there are two schools amongst those who want a theatre of the people, and they are absolutely op-posed to each other. One wishes to bring the theatre, such as it is, to the people. The other wishes to make a new force, a new theatre, a new form of art, arise from the people. These believe in the People, whilst the others, in Rolland's view, believe only in the Theatre. Rolland, unlike Antoine, did not wish to make the theatre of the past accessible to the People, for he did not consider that there was anything in it of importance that had any meaning for them.

He grudgingly admitted that some of the more vulgar and knockabout comedy of Molière, such as *Scapin*, might have a certain amount of popular appeal, but he found nothing in Molière's masterpieces which had any significance for the people. *Le Misanthrope* is admirable drawing room psychology, but it bores a popular audience: and the long speeches in *Tartuffe*, and the peculiar devotional language of the play, are simply baffling. Nevertheless, Molière is the best of the past. Racine's plays are praiseworthy in some ways, but not interesting. Corneille is more robust than Racine, and has more action, but most of what he writes, apart from a few resounding speeches, is unintelligible. The abounding life of *Le Cid* arouses sympathy, but the chivalrous problem of its gentlemen duellists means nothing to the workers today. Except for the renown of Sophocles, and the imposing presence and voice of Mounet-Sully, the tenor of the Comédie Française, no one of any class would now distinguish *Oedipus Rex* from any other melodrama. Shakespeare is too remote, Ibsen is aristocratic, and plays like Tolstoy's *The Power of Darkness* are to be rejected with horror. We want to make the People healthy, not infect them with our diseases. These gloomy Russian dramas about misery and exploitation may rouse the conscience of the rich, but they give no pleasure to the poor. They appeal only to a few bourgeois, to 'a mere handful, the revolutionary élite'. Wagner is all right, especially *The Mastersingers*, which is vigorous, good-humoured, and sane. But unfortunately with Wagner you have to take the music as well as the play. Yes, all in all, the French theatre of 1890 to 1910 is 'the brothel of Europe'.

Antoine took a quite different view. It was he who, on 10 February 1888, at his Théâtre Libre, introduced *The Power of Darkness* to France. He had entered the artistic life of Paris only a few months before, in October 1887, when Edmond de Goncourt heard a rumour that Zola was spending every evening at the Théâtre Libre, where he was said to have taken out two season tickets. Zola was said every day to make Antoine extravagant compliments, and to kiss the actresses paternally. Goncourt felt that these actresses resented the fact that he himself had not yet started to join in the kissing.

Antoine himself did rather more than that. As the years went by Goncourt noticed that, in the most hallowed traditions of the commercial managers, Antoine slept with his actresses. This caused a great deal of trouble with his company, there was jealousy and recrimination, and it was felt with some justice that the best parts did not always go to the best players. Eugenie Nau, who toured as Poil de Carotte, and was a member of the Vieux Colombier company in its second visit to New York in 1918–19, created the part of Madame Coup-de-Sabre in Antoine's production of *La Fille Elisa*. She was greatly reputed for her beauty, which was said to be even more remarkable off the stage than on. Beauty or no beauty, Antoine took the part away from her, and gave it to Mlle Fleury, who became his mistress. Mlle Nau spoke angrily of Antoine's brutality to the women in his company, and said that the stage could be washed with their tears. It was not even as though his women players were in general good-looking. Jean Ajalbert, who adapted *La Fille Elisa* from Goncourt's novel, describes the departure of the troupe for Brussels one gloomy morning, and speaks of 'the wretchedness of the women's linen, faces, and toilette: it takes away any desire you may have to sleep with them.'

This does not appear to have deterred Antoine, who was a more romantic character than one might deduce from the rather drab fact that he was a not very important employee of the municipal gas compny. He had the faculty of charming people at the first glance. He dined at Alphonse Daudet's house on 6 April 1888, and immediately won the heart of Edmond de Goncourt, by no means an easy man to please, who was also present. He was slim, frail, and nervous, and his eyes, which were gentle and seductive, exercised an instant fascination. He was teeming with ideas, and, what is especially striking, to some of them he was faithful right to the end of his career. That night he declared that he looked forward to having a Government-subsidised theatre, an ambition he subsequently realised at the Odéon. He intended to run it with the help of actors discovered by himself, and reasonably paid. He was determined to give productions to everything written by the young that showed the slightest talent; and he was resolved constantly to change the bill. No matter what the success of a play, he would run it for no more than a fortnight. When he came to the Odéon he loyally stuck to this resolution; and it ruined him, and his whole theatrical enterprise.

Antoine is a melancholy proof that in the theatre keeping to your word, and following a consistent line of action, can lead as often to disaster as to success. But meanwhile all was hope and ambition. Goncourt felt that the intensity of his belief in his work could be seen in his brilliant, enchanted eyes, which he described as 'hallucinés'. Goncourt, indeed, who was uniformly jealous and suspicious, thinking that he was plagiarised by everybody, including Zola, Dostoevsky, and Tolstoy, and rating Maupassant as a writer of no talent, at once fell a victim to Antoine. The man was intelligent; he was forceful; he was prolific of ideas: and he was devoted to the theatre. It is a formidable combination of talents.

Very soon he used these talents on behalf of Goncourt and the theatre. It is really quite remarkable that these two men should ever have come together, and that, after coming together, they should have been united in an idea that for a certain length of time looked like revolutionising the French theatre. Goncourt was a comparatively rich man, and, as he was fond of reminding himself, an aristocrat. Antoine belonged to the lower middle class. But they were at one in recognising the theatrical and social importance, not of their own class, but of a third, the proletariat. As late as the time of Balzac the workers were entirely ignored in works of literature. Zola noted that in all Balzac's vast output, amounting to ninety-seven novels, there are no working class characters. The only reference to them occurs in four or five unimportant lines in the first chapter of one of his least known stories, *Pierrette*.

In 1879 Zola in *L'Assommoir* at the Ambigu had put working class characters on the stage, and, in Alphonse Daudet's opinion, had done so without enveloping them with the romantic trappings of the past. Zola regarded his work as revolutionary, and was so nervous of the effect that it would have on the public that he froze the actors with his miserable looks. He could not bear to watch the first performance, and passed all the evening turning the pages of a novel he had picked up by chance. To everybody's astonishment the play was well received, and this perhaps was its condemnation. *L'Assommoir* was not such a break with tradition as its author imagined. Only a few whistles pierced the applause at the end. Manet, wandering in the corridors, was distressed by the lack of opposition. Had the play been a success of the kind that was hoped for, there should, he felt, have been something more like a battle.

Sarcey was contemptuous. He dismissed it as merely an entertainment piece. He said that he had seen many plays like it, and expected to see many more. He poured scorn on the idea that the sight of real women on the stage plunging their hands into real warm water—one of Zola's big effects—was of any importance. Goncourt agreed with him. He denied that there was anything significant in *L'Assommoir*, which in his opinion told its story with the romantic artifice usual in melodrama. He may have been jealous. His own plays were not received with anything like the indulgence shown to Zola.

Six months after he had met Antoine, Goncourt had a memorable experience in the theatre. 19 December 1888 saw the first night of *Germinie Lacerteux*, which anticipated by more than sixty years the social drama of the English Stage Company and the Royal Court. Réjane was its principal actress, and the director was Désiré-Paul Parfouru, called Porel, who married Réjane five years later, and was divorced in 1905. He died in 1917, at the age of seventy-five.

Early in December it became apparent that journalists were determined to attack the play. *L'Echo de Paris* described the sufferings of its actresses, especially of Réjane, who endured the ignominy of having to utter the word 'putain'. (There was something in this. Putain is a word to tremble at. Even more than half a century later Jean-Paul Sartre could advertise one of his plays only as *La P——— respectueuse*.) Goncourt was disgusted at what he thought was the treachery of Zola, who chose this moment to write an article in which he said that journalism served the cause of literature well. The café proprietors of the Latin Quarter—the play was produced at the Odéon—were furious that Goncourt proposed to have only a single interval, reducing to one drink the several taken at a five-act play.

At a rehearsal the amiable Daudet actually wept in apprehension, and the painter Blanche forecast a stormy opening. Goncourt was well aware of the dangers he ran. In the preface to the novel from which he had adapted his play he had said that the public likes books which pretend to go into the great world: this book comes out of the street. The public likes dishonest novels: this novel is true. And it is austere and pure.

The week before the première was full of disasters. First of all, Réjane lost her voice. On 15 December she took an injection which sent her into hysterics. The same day Goncourt had a cold which twenty-four hours later turned to pleurisy. On the day of the actual performance even the weather joined in to make things more difficult. There was such a thick fog that Goncourt doubted whether cabs would be able to move through it. Despite this he reached the theatre. He hid himself at the back of his box. Daudet, ever his faithful friend, boldly leaned his elbow on the front ledge of the box. Porel said ambiguously, 'The Odéon has never seen a first-night audience like this.'

It was one of the most important evenings in the history of the theatre. It not only put the poor upon the stage, and showed that their lives and problems were as worthy of attention as those of their financial and social superiors: Zola's *L'Assommoir* had done that: but it also changed the technique of the theatre. *Germinie Lacerteux* was a plain narrative, without an artificially devised plot, and it dispensed with the *scène-à-faire* then, and for many years later, regarded as an essential feature of a wellmade play. There is nothing comparably explosive in the modern theatre.

The opening scene of the play passed without incident, and Goncourt's hopes ran high. But in the second scene there were whistles and protests. 'I can smell powder. I like that,' said Porel, in the tone of a man who did not like it at all. Daudet became restless, and to calm his nerves went out into the stalls, where his son Léon was sitting. When he returned, Daudet's face was so angry that Goncourt feared he might challenge someone to a duel.

The whistling and the counter-applause continued all through the scene of the dance, and that in which the unfortunate servant girl Germinie sets up the ignoble Jupillon in business with her meagre savings. It went on when, after Jupillon and his mother have discussed throwing her over, she announces that she is *enceinte*. Then comes the children's party given by the artistocratic old Mlle de Varendeuil, and served by Germinie despite her distress. Goncourt was convinced that the charm and vulnerability of the children would save the play. But the whole audience began to shout 'Au dodo les enfants' For a grievous moment Goncourt thought that the performance would have to be abandoned. But Réjane briefly managed to assert herself. Goncourt went out into the corridor behind his box, and found his child actors sobbing.

Thereafter the evening became a battle, and at the end, when the actor Du13 mény, who had played Jupillon, came forward, in accordance with custom, to announce the name of the author, the tumult was so great that for some moments he had to remain silent. Du13 mény did not flinch, but in a brief respite in the angry noise, threw out Goncourt's name as if he were issuing a challenge to a duel. Goncourt stood at the back of his box. He showed no emotion, but sadly reflected that he and his brother had not been born under a fortunate star.

Germinie Lacerteux was not produced by Antoine, but it was Antoine's kind of play, and it made a deep impression on him. Jules Lemaître jeered at Antoine for his eagerness in rushing ('se précipitant') to see the play, and Sarcey reviled it, but Goncourt received a letter from a young student at the École Normale which greatly encouraged him. This student with his friends had been to the third performance, and had been overcome with admiration and emotion. The letter said that it was a guarantee that what its young sponsors loved in the spirit of the play they would cause to triumph when they were older. 'Ce que nous aimons, nous le ferons triompher quand nous serons des hommes.'[1] The guarantee was never fulfilled, for the letter was written by Romain Rolland.

In spite of this communication, Goncourt constantly complained that not only were the established critics like Sarcey and Lemaître against him, but also the young authors of the day. He ascribed this to jealousy. But there may have been something instinctively unattractive in the spectacle of a rich man continually weeping over the miseries of the poor, and out of this no doubt quite sincere feeling making a good deal of money which he at least half seriously thought of spending on wines of great reputation and dishes of extreme fantasy. A young journalist in the *Décadent* called him 'a proud and jealous failure, who had not even poverty to excuse him for bringing the scandals of the Théâtre Libre to a bourgeois stage.'

Certainly Goncourt's temperament was less democratic than his themes, and this may have led to a certain falseness of tone which concealed from his critics his real merits and feelings. Speaking of the anger that the play's freedom of language provoked, Goncourt said that it was not merely the language of the working class Grande Adèle (shockingly played by Anna-Paula Dheurs) that upset the petit-bourgeois public, but that the effect

---

1. When we are men we shall make the things we love triumph.

of some of the things said by Mlle de Varendeuil was even worse on those who (unlike himself) were not born of a noble family, and consequently did not know how noble families talk; and much light is thrown on his private attitudes when the next evening he reflects that life has given him everything it has to offer except race horses and women of breeding. But two years later the long and sickeningly awaited triumph came.

It came with the production of Goncourt's *La Fille Elisa* on Christmas Eve, 1890. This piece was directed by Antoine himself, and was of that typically gloomy kind which Romain Rolland was to deplore a few years later. Its heroine is a pensionnaire of a brothel who kills her lover rather than allow him to have sex in a cemetery, and the second act largely consists of a twenty-five minute speech by Elisa's counsel. Antoine, says Goncourt, made the public swallow this speech, amidst frantic applause, without a moment's lassitude or boredom. In vain did Sarcey complain that the play had no action, no suspense, no development of character, no theatrical art. In the corridors people went up and down, saying 'It isn't theatre, but it's very interesting.' Goncourt commented with complacency: 'No, it isn't theatre as it used to be. It is the new theatre.'

This production firmly established the possibility of an important and prosperous theatre different from that of the boulevard, interested in more serious subjects, with a wider social range, and stressing the importance of *mise en scène*. The position won by Antoine with *La Fille Elisa* was consolidated by Lugné-Poe's production a little later of *Pelléas et Mélisande*, not at all the same kind of play as those that Antoine was interested in, but equally remote from the standards of the boulevard. And in its turn *Pelléas et Mélisande* was followed by Antoine's discovery of Renard, and, nearly ten years later, of Bernstein. Contempt for the conventional theatre and its defenders became an increasingly powerful force.

Despite his magnificent work Lugné-Poe never secured a position of any stability. He was an admirable actor; he made even Sarcey shiver in the scene in which, as Golaud, he questioned Yniold under Mélisande's lighted window. Twenty years after that his personality could still impress a critic as recalcitrant as Paul Léautaud. But he was perpetually in poverty in the most creative stage of his career. But for an English dramatist, Alfred Sutro, a man of wealth as well as talent, he and his wife would have starved. What should I have done, he exclaimed, without my good friend Sutro, who could be relied on to send him a cheque when he most needed it?

The story of his life after he had produced *Pelléas et Mélisande* was both sad and ludicrous. On one occasion when Maeterlinck came to Paris he stayed with the Lugné-Poes. Whilst they lay on a mattress in the passage, he slept in their bed, which broke, for he was a big man. For twelve months after that Lugné-Poe and his wife had to manage without a bed, for they were too poor to buy another. Often they had nothing to eat. They had the stomach of an ostrich, but nothing to put into it, not even a few dry peas. The summer was even worse than the winter. In winter they got a little money from their performances in Paris, but in the summer they had nowhere to go. To the end of his life Lugné-Poe remembered with bitterness how contemptuously Bloch, manager of the Casino at Dieppe, and Gandreyt of Aix, rejected his company.

Things went decidedly better with Antoine. Rachilde described the plays he produced as 'kitchen sink (la cuvette), confinements, and public miscarriages . . . le mot de Cambronne the highest expression of naturalist art.' But this did not prevent his being appointed director of the Odéon, France's second National Theatre, in 1906. For a brief brilliant time it seemed as though the avant-garde theatre in France was poised to achieve as much as the English Stage Company did in 1956 and after.

Antoine opened his administration of the Odéon on 24 October 1906, with the production of a small play by Lucien Descaves called *La Préférée*. It did not make much of a stir, but he followed it with a magnificent *mise en scène* for *Le Vrai Mystère de la Passion*, by Arnold Gréban. This was a triumph. The Odéon became a centre of furious energy, a veritable forcing ground for the advanced theatre. Léautaud was astounded at Antoine's activity; he thought it prodigious. Antoine would put on as many as three spectacles in fifteen days. People at the Odéon worked as they worked in no other theatre. Antoine, said Léautaud, is not only a remarkable director, an extraordinary man of the theatre. He is also a passionate lover of the theatre, who produces plays for his own delight, not caring whether people want to see them or not. He works his company like negroes. If it is true, as it is said in the army, that the years spent in campaigning count double, then years spent at the Odéon ought to count double, too. A good dozen members of the company appear in practically everything put on there, tragedy, comedy, plays in verse, or plays in prose, and always with verve, ingenuity. and diversity, knowing their parts perfectly.

This devoted attitude to the theatre reaped its reward, though undoubtedly Antoine made mistakes. After being struck by the talent of the young Bernstein he allowed him to go to other managers, and he did not whilst at the Odéon discover any further dramatist with either Bernstein's force or his popularity. But the splendid *mise en scène* of his productions won him a large public. The receipts at the Odéon began to mount almost as soon as he took over control. In 1908 the receipts rose to a record 725,000 francs; in 1910 they rose still higher, to 854,000 francs, and in 1911 to 904,000 francs.

But if his receipts increased, so did his expenses; so much so, indeed, that by 1913 he was on the verge of bankruptcy. Antoine was a spectacular example of the ruin that can be brought about by success, and by clinging tenaciously to one's principles. At the beginning of his career, when to come into the society of men like Alphonse Daudet and Edmond de Goncourt was still a great excitement, he had, as we have seen, resolved that he would maintain a constant succession of new productions, taking off even the most successful after a few performances in order to make way for something else.

This bold policy reached its ruinous culmination in 1913, when he put on *The School for Scandal* for a single performance; Goldoni's *La Locandière* for two performances; *Sylla* by the critic Alfred Mortier (whose wife was a literary lady so tiresomely pretentious that Maeterlinck, in one of his less spiritual moods, said that the only sensible thing to do was to lift up her skirt and smack her bottom), for another two performances; Racine's *Esther* for seven performances; Corneille's *Héraclius* for two performances; *Est-il bon, est-il méchant?* by Diderot for four performances; and Voltaire's *Zaire* for two performances.

Now this could easily have been a popular programme. Corneille, Racine, and Diderot all have their public. When Pierre Fresnay appeared in Diderot's *Le Neveu de Rameau* at the quite large Michodière in the 1960s the production ran for several hundred nights. But Antoine, like the fashionable ladies who that very year at Deauville launched the topless bathing dress, had a passion for taking everything off as quickly as possible. His financial resources exhausted, he had to give up the direction of the Odéon, and a notable period in the history of the French theatre came to an end. But despite his failure, the work of Antoine had a profound and lasting effect. It did not result in the discovery of many plays of permanent value, but it considerably changed the balance of power in the theatre. After Antoine the supremacy of the author was never fully restored.

Antoine was justly enough called 'the father of *mise en scène*'. He was the first to realise the close connexion between the acted character and his surroundings. This does not sound much, said Antoine; nevertheless, it is the secret of the feeling of originality that his productions gave. Even so fine a play as Renard's *Le Plaisir de rompre* seems to have been pushed casually onto the stage without anything that a later age would regard as production. There was no suggestion of a director. The morning the play was shown to the critics, Henry Mayer was still speaking slowly, trying each phrase over several times to see which way of speaking sounded best. Granier put in little words of her own here and there, whenever she thought they would improve the text. Renard resolved that later he would take them out, but there seems to have been no direction of either player by anyone.

Far from Antoine's close attention to the surroundings of the actor, décor for *Le Plaisir de rompre*—and in this it was no doubt typical of many other productions—was entirely haphazard. On the day the play was shown to the critics Granier brought with her statuettes, music, flowers, a lamp, and a lampshade she had herself made that morning. Renard saw nothing odd in the leading lady providing the stage accessories at the last moment. He thought her very pretty, and was moved by her for the first time.

Antoine set himself from the beginning of his career to reduce the authority of the star player. He wanted an ensemble theatre: a 'group of thirty actors of equal quality and average talent, uncomplicated in character, and always ready to submit to the law of the ensemble.' He wished to reform speech: he demanded a truer, calmer style than the exaggerated gestures of romanticism, and he judged all actors, even those as celebrated as Mounet-Sully and Julia Bartet, by their truth to life.

Improvements in lighting the stage made it possible for an actor to be heard when speaking quietly, and he increased the concentration of the audience by plunging it into darkness. He ridiculed the practice of painting furniture on the décor, and asked for solid scenery. What he did was to establish naturalism, though he resented the suggestion that he supported only one kind of drama. In this he resembled George Devine, who was always angry when it was maintained (quite truly) that the Royal Court Theatre in the 1950s and 1960s was a theatre of social protest.

He had a great contempt for actors. Léautaud believed that actors won a renown out of all proportion to their real achievements, but Antoine went further. 'Actors,' he said, 'never know anything about the pieces they play.' Though a man of advanced social ideas, and in principle opposed to feudalism and distinctions of class, he nevertheless regarded actors as slaves who fulfilled themselves in doing precisely what they were told. What actors have to do is 'honestly and as well as they can to interpret characters they do not understand.'

With Antoine a new spirit was coming into the theatre. The affairs of ordinary life were being brought into the drama. Lords and ladies gave way to seamstresses, prostitutes, and coal-miners. The breath of social reform refreshed the hot and dusty corridors of the old theatre. The aristocracy of dramatist and player was destroyed in order to establish a director's dictator-ship with benevolent social aims. The dramatic methods of Lugné-Poe, Antoine's contemporary, and of Copeau and Charles Dullin, the immediate inheritors of his work, were dif-ferent from his. But all believed in the supremacy of the director, and the relative humiliation of other workers in the theatre. Copeau declared that authors failed to co-operate with him, and said that he had found them to be either show-offs or children. Lugné-Poe maintained that 'the purely literary theatre is a heresy . . . Words are profoundly subordinate to the *mise en scène*.' Dullin said that authors, because of their technical in-competence, 'could be their own worst enemy'. All four, directly or indirectly, challenged the supremacy of author and actor, and saw as their ideal total theatre, a synthesis of words, spectacle, dance, and music instead of the word only.

The ultimate aim of these great renewers of the theatre was not understood at the time, but their actual work was enthusias-tically received by those whose appreciation of the theatre most closely resembles that of the generations which succeeded them. Léautaud[2] in particular was well fitted to receive their achieve-

---

2. LEAUTAUD, Paul: *Journal littéraire*, 19 Vols, Mercure de France.
    LEAUTAUD, Paul: *Le Théâtre de M. Boissard*, NRF Gallimard.

ments with rapture. With a wit and a virulence rarely equalled he overwhelmed the boulevard drama with contempt.

There were two actresses whom he admired. The first was Marthe Brandès, who played in Renard's *Le Pain de ménage*. There were nuances in her voice that roused in him an excitement that was as much sexual as aesthetic. The second was Marguerite Moreno. But for most other players he had nothing but scorn. He jeered at the young Pierre Fresnay, whose subsequent career outlasted Antoine's and Copeau's by decades. He showed his contempt for Julia Bartet, reputed the greatest Bérénice of modern times, and long an ornament of the Comédie Française, by asserting that her sister, Alice Regnault, was a former prostitute of the Second Empire. On the death in 1917 of Octave Mirbeau, who had been one of the few to recognise the genius of *Pelléas et Mélisande*, he recalled that Mirbeau had married Madame Bartet's sister, and that thereafter all the doors of high society had been closed against him. He recorded that when friends went to visit Mirbeau the actress's sister was always kept hidden. But he admitted that at the funeral she behaved with dignity.

With a rising star of the Comédie, Ventura, he went far beyond denigrating her family. When she appeared in Francis Porché's *Le Chevalier de Colombe* he wrote: 'The performance is enough to make one die of laughing. Whatever made Mlle Ventura think of becoming an actress? She is ugly, she is little, and she is badly built . . . She is better fitted to sell gewgaws in a shop than to appear on the stage of a theatre.' Nor was Léautaud's bitterness confined to actresses. Le Bargy, an actor of renown, whose wife had been enormously praised by Brisson in more than one play of Bernstein's, was also in *Le Chevalier de Colombe*. 'It is not true that ridicule kills,' remarked Léautaud. 'If it were, today M. Le Bargy would be dead and buried.'

During most of the time that he was drama critic of *Le Mercure de France*—from 1907 to 1923—Léautaud lived a rather shabby life. On at least one occasion he was reduced to wearing the cast-off clothes of a friend. He picked up mistresses in the street as he picked up stray cats and dogs. *Le Mercure de France* had a circulation of no more than 3,000 a month, so that in direct influence Léautaud could not compare with Brisson or Bordeaux. But he was more representative than either of them of the deeper movements that were transforming the theatre.

His contempt therefore for the plays and the players of his

time was significant. There was room in the theatre for someone other than author and actor, namely, the director. Antoine had prepared the way, and in the years that followed his brave but defeated efforts at the Odéon the directors came in large numbers and brilliantly: Jacques Copeau, Louis Jouvet, Georges and Ludmilla Pitoeff, Charles Dullin, Gaston Baty. For twenty years or so they triumphed, so that by 1936 Robert Brasillach was complaining that plays were now known, not by their author or their star, but by their director.

The new directors took over the position of importance achieved by Antoine, but used it to different purposes. Antoine had set himself a social aim, and tried to find new dramatists. The chief of the new influences, Jacques Copeau, when he established the Vieux Colombier in 1913, acknowledged the great importance of Antoine, but attributed his failure to his limiting his programme to revolutionary plays. The Théâtre du Vieux Colombier, he proclaimed, does not feel the need for revolution. Its eyes are fixed on the great permanent models that outlast changes in fashion and time. Copeau said that his theatre did not know what the drama of the future would be, but he promised that it would react against the drama of the present.

It was natural therefore for Copeau to look to the plays of the past. Unlike his contemporaries, he admired Porto-Riche's *Amoureuse*, which he said had more of the blood of life in it than any recent drama. But his real affection was for Shakespeare, and his productions of *A Winter's Tale* and *As You Like It* opened up a new conception of the theatre. He was the belligerent champion of simplicity, and attacked critics like Brisson who praised fine writing. It was typical of his attitude to the theatre that he ridiculed Brisson for admiring a play such as Paul Hervieu's *Le Réveil* (1906), which mixed up revolution with private matters like unfaithfulness. He was particularly scornful of a speech made by Prince Grégoire to his son that Brisson had singled out for praise.

Anything that was elaborate, high-faluting, or pretentious aroused Copeau's intense dislike. He believed with great conviction in the sovereign virtue of simplicity. To go into the Vieux Colombier at the height of its fame was like entering a cool, bare room after living in a baroque palace. To men like Léautaud, Copeau was a revelation, a saviour. The stage at the Vieux Colombier, said Léautaud admiringly, is always the same. At the back is a recess, on either side of which is a stair-case leading to an upper stage. The effects to be gained from this are marvellous. A few trees, or articles of furniture, or noth-ing at all, and you have anything you want, a garden or a field, a palace chamber, a bedroom, a shop, a dining room, or a public square or a street, whilst by an effect of lighting the recess can be transformed into an outlook on to whatever you wish; a street, garden, countryside, or even the sea. Copeau's influence upon the boulevard was of course limited; but he revolutionised the avant-garde. He gave it an austere and scrupulously dis-ciplined beauty. He was the Jansenist of the French theatre.

The great strength of the Vieux Colombier was its homo-geneity. Writing nearly thirty years later than the period of Copeau's triumphs, the American scholar Maurice Kurtz said that in this it had never had a rival since the days of Antoine. In this Copeau differed from his great contemporaries. Charles Dullin was the only real actor in the Dullin company. Louis Jouvet, in the Jouvet Company, even against his will outclassed his fellow-players. Gaston Baty had one or two good people in a troupe that was relatively weak. In Georges Pitoeff's com-pany, his wife Ludmilla outshone everyone else. But the Vieux-Colombier succeeded purely as an ensemble. Even after Dullin and Jouvet had left it, Copeau, though a good actor, never had to play, as Dullin often had, to raise the company's standards, which indeed were unequalled at that time in Paris. Moreover Copeau never, as Baty sometimes did, regarded the *mise en scène* as a thing in itself. He put it wholly at the service of the play. In this he resembled, in our own time, Peter Hall at his most devoted and understanding, *Blood Wedding*, best.

Copeau's most famous production was *La Nuit des rois* (*Twelfth Night*). He was known by it as John Osborne is known by *Look Back in Anger*. The main period of his activity lasted from 1913 to 1924, during which time *La Nuit des rois* had 187 per-formances. Despite his concentration on Shakespeare and other classics Copeau revealed seventeen modern dramatists (Antoine had found ninety-four). Still, it is a respectable total. In his first post-war season Copeau produced *Le Paquebot Tenacity* by Charles Vildrac; Georges Duhamel's *Oeuvres des athlètes*; Jules Romains's *Crommedeyre-le-Viel*; and Mazaud's *La Folle Journée*.

As a production *Le Paquebot Tenacity* did not rival *La Nuit des rois* in celebrity, but it exceeded it in popularity. This tender little story of two young sailors who wait in port a few days, and have their lives changed by a love which for one of them is fortunate, and for the other sad, has a gentle poetic spirit not unlike Tennyson's *Tears, idle tears, I know not what they mean*. It was received by most critics rather grumpily, but it pleased Copeau's audiences better than anything else he ever did. In its first season *Le Paquebot Tenacity* had 61 performances; in its second (1920–21) 54; in its third (1921–22) it fell to 23, but rose in the next season to 52. In the fifth and last it had another fifteen performances. Altogether it was played 205 times. It was the only one of Copeau's productions to reach 200 performances. Mérimée's *Le Carosse du Saint Sacrament* was played 179 times, but this was only because it generally appeared in a double bill with *Le Paquebot Tenacity*. Two other of Copeau's productions achieved more than a hundred (non-consecutive)performances: Renard's *Le Pain de ménage* (131), and Roger Martin du Gard's *Le Testament du Père Leleu*.

For once in theatrical history popularity coincided with merit. There can be no question that the finest original play which Copeau discovered was *Le Paquebot Tenacity*. The people who sat around the critic Alfred Mortier at its first performance said that it was 'a slice of life'. But in doing so they missed its resonances, its echoes of melancholy, its reverie and its poetry, as well as its tenderness. The scene at the end when the quiet Ségard comes down from his room in the modest little restaurant in Le Havre where he has been waiting for the boat to take him and his friend Bastien to a new life in Canada, and discovers that Bastien has left with the kindly and simple servant they were both in love with—left without even telling him he was going—is one of the most poignant in French drama. What is extraordinary about it is the simplicity, the reticence, of its means. There is none of the scandal of Bataille here, nor of the ferocity of Bernstein. Merely two friends leaving a third, all of them quite good, kind people, without the courage or the consideration to warn him of what they were doing; nothing more than that. Yet it is one of the unforgettable things in twentieth-century drama.

Copeau's activities at the Vieux Colombier were a reaction against and a condemnation of the commercial theatre of the days immediately preceding the war of 1914–18. They did not, however, disturb the complacency of this theatre. As yet virtually unthreatened by the cinema, the Parisian commercial theatre of 1913, and throughout the war, continually congratulated itself upon its present success and future prospects.

It was little moved by the strictures of such a critic as Léautaud; the fanatical denunciations which the ferociously self-righteous and devoutly believing Léon Bloy periodically issued against the work of his fellow-Catholic, Paul Bourget, did not move it at all. The wretched Bloy, the champion of Mélanie of La Salette against Bernadette of Lourdes, perpetually impoverished, driven from home to home, and from pawn shop to pawn shop, cursing the Pope Leo XIII for worldliness, bishops for not believing in Mélanie's vision of the Virgin Mary, and nearly all curés who did not accept his criticism of their conduct of the Mass, or who failed to lend him money, had not then acquired the fame that came to him after his death through the publication of his vitriolic and passionate *Journals* in the 1950s. In any case Bloy hated the progressive theatre as thoroughly as he did conventional writers. On 2 November 1907 he noted in his *Journal* that he was awakened at six o'clock by a scream so horrible that he said it could not have issued from any living throat. He saw considerable significance in the fact that next day he was invited to the funeral of Alfred Jarry, who had died about the time that Bloy's slumbers had been disturbed.[3]

The engaging and generous-hearted Louis Verneuil, who a few years later was to launch the red-headed Elvire Popesco, unrivalled in scatter-brained parts, upon her long and triumphant career, in his comedy, *Ma Cousine de Varsovie*, probably expressed the popular view when he said that the season immediately preceding the war of 1914–18 was a very good one, with an unusually high proportion of successes. Tristan Bernard's *Les Deux canards* filled the Palais Royal, and in her own theatre Sarah Bernhardt dazzled Paris in another play of Bernard's, *Jeanne Doré*. Sacha Guitry, then aged twenty-nine, had the third great success of his career with *La Pélerine écossaise* at the Bouffes-Parisiens. At the same theatre Max Dearly created what Verneuil calls the famous *Mon Bébé*, by Maurice Hennequin. Huge audiences applauded De Max at the Châtelet in *L'Insaissible Stanley Collins*, *Je ne trompe pas mon mari* crowded the Athénée, and at the Vaudeville *La Belle aventure* by Robert de Flers and G. A. de Caillavet, achieved a triumph. It gave its

---

3. BLOY, Léon: *Journal*, Mercure de France.

last performance three days before the declaration of war, as did Paul Gavault's joyous *Ma Tante d'Honfleur*, which was withdrawn from the Variétés on 1 August 1914. The celebrated actor Baron gave his last performance on the Parisian stage in this play at the age of seventy-seven. He ascribed his vitality to having a mistress of twenty-five. Joyous, famous, or merely triumphant, none of these plays, so confidently greeted by Verneuil, who was a highly intelligent as well as an agreeable man, has left any permanent memory.

About the entertainment provided on the last night of the war, 11 November 1918, Verneuil was even more enthusiastic. 'One might say that, when the Armistice was declared,' he wrote, 'all the theatres of Paris had determined beforehand to shine with the most brilliant splendour.' The Comédie Française gave Porto-Riche's *Amoureuse*, with Piérat, Georges Grand, and Henry Mayer in the cast. Sarah Bernhardt celebrated her five hundredth performance in *Les Nouveaux riches*, by Abadie and Cesse. At the Vaudeville Sacha Guitry appeared in his revue de Paris, with Yvonne Printemps. His father, Lucien Guitry, was in a revival of Bernstein's *Samson*, with Gabrielle Dorziat, who many years later was to play in a striking film with Edwige Feuillère. Réjane at the Théâtre Réjane played in Henry Bataille's *Notre Image*, and the Casino de Paris played to crowded houses with the revue *Paris qui rit*, which Verneuil said was one of the best in which Maurice Chevalier and Mistinguett ever appeared. Taking a somewhat different view the critic Edmond Sée remarked at the precise moment when Verneuil was filled with such exaltation that the French theatre was at its nadir.

These two opposing views are not really as irreconcilable as they seem. Edmond Sée and Louis Verneuil looked at the theatre from different standpoints. Sée judged the theatre by the contribution it made to the world of art; Verneuil saw it as a largely frivolous entertainment and a brilliant social occasion.

One afternoon about this time a young woman called Léonie Maria Julia Bathiat was strolling more or less aimlessly down the boulevards, not particularly averse perhaps to attracting attention. She later became celebrated under the name of Arletty in such films as *Le Jour se lève* (with Jean Gabin), *Hôtel du Nord* (with Jouvet), *Les Visiteurs du soir*, and above all in *Les Enfants du paradis*. Her walk was interrupted by a man of about thirty, who without more ado introduced himself as Paul

4ᵉ ANNÉE — N° 9   1ᵉʳ FÉVRIER 1912

Comoedia Illustré

REVUE·PARISIENNE·THEATRALE·ARTISTIQUE·LITERAIRE

Paraît le 1ᵉʳ et le 15
de chaque mois

52, Rue Louis-le-Grand
PARIS

DIRECTEUR :
M. DE BRUNOFF

Le Numéro : **1** fr. **50**   Abonnement : **12** fr. par an.

M. MAX DEARLY et Mlle MISTINGUETT, dansent la crapulette au troisième acte du " Bonheur sous la Main"
le nouveau succès des Variétés

Photo Bert

16. Max Dearly and Mistinguett dancing '*la crapulette*'. Photograph from
Comoedia Illustré February 1912

Guillaume. He said he was an amateur of art, and asked her to pose for certain painters. When she refused he proposed that she should go on the stage. Arletty burst out laughing, but he thrust into her hand cards of introduction to Armand Berthez, director of the Capucines, and to Gavault, who directed the Odéon. She left him with a casual 'A bientôt, Pygmalion.'

A few months later, in August 1919, Mlle Bathiat was again wandering along the boulevards. She noticed a sign which said Théâtre des Capucines, and went in. A very elegant man, who turned out to be Berthez himself, was directing a revue. The young woman asked to be included, and Berthez invited her to sing. She began 'It's a long way to Tipperary, It's a long way . . .' Here Berthez stopped her, and told her she could appear in the chorus and sing a song *On pince les parties naturelles, C'est nous les petites bourelles*.[4] She was to wear blood-red tights. One's career, said Arletty years later, depends on which pavement you walk down. Had she been passing the Odéon she would have turned to the classics. She adds: 'Phèdre, Bérénice, and Andromaque have had a lucky escape.'

But at the first performance Arletty, so baptised by Berthez, let her eyes rove round the audience.[5] From pictures and drawings she had seen, she recognised Colette with her husband Willy; Antoine; Cléo de Mérode; the dazzling social butterfly, Boni de Castellane; Anna de Noailles; Jeanne Granier, the days of *Le Plaisir de rompre* left far behind her; the dramatists Nozière, Alfred Savoir, and Robert de Flers; and Forain, a cartoonist even more famous than Steinlen, and a good deal less gentle: all these in a theatre holding hardly more than 200 people. This was the kind of evening, and this was the kind of theatre, even if entry into it were as casual and as dubious as Arletty's had been, which seemed brilliant to the amiable Verneuil, but was unlikely to yield much to an Edmond Sée.

---

4. We pinch where it's natural, we are the little balls of fluff.

5. ARLETTY: *La Défense*, Paris, La Table Ronde.

CHAPTER FIVE

The Separation of Boulevard and Avant-garde Defined

In the early 1920s the number *four* seems to have had a magic significance. In England Edgar Wallace wrote a very bad thriller called *The Four Just Men*. In Spain Vicento Blasco Ibanez wrote a rather better, or at any rate, a more ambitious one under the title of *The Four Horsemen of the Apocalypse*, which subsequently became the most grandiose of the films of Rudolph Valentino. In France it was to four men—Jacques Copeau, Louis Jouvet, Charles Dullin, and Gaston Baty, who later joined with Georges Pitoeff in what is known as the Cartel—that the Paris stage owed its resurrection from the graveyard of 1918.

In 1923 a young advertising agent from Le Havre, Armand Salacrou, wrote a few small pieces for the theatre. The poet and critic Max Jacob, the friend of Apollinaire, approved of them, but said that in his opinion the highest talent in the French theatre was Jean Cocteau. Salacrou has recorded his surprise at this, on the ground that at that time Cocteau had written nothing for the theatre except *Les Mariés de la tour Eiffel*. For Salacrou, and also for the dashing young Communist poet, Aragon, the French theatre in 1923 was synonymous still with Henry Bataille.

Unknown to Salacrou, but well within the knowledge of critics like Paul Léautaud and Lucien Dubech, Copeau, Jouvet, Dullin, and Baty had already undermined the traditional, romantic, contrived, sensational drama exemplified by Bataille, and begun to replace it with something saner and simpler. By 1923 Copeau had discovered Vildrac and Émile Mazaud. In that year Jouvet produced Jules Romains's *Monsieur Trouhadec saisi par la débauche* and *Knock ou la triomphe de la médecine*. Gaston Baty had directed H. R. Lenormand's *Le Simoun*, and Jean-

17. *Jean de la Lune* by Achard with Pierre Mondy and Dany Robin (Palais Royal 1967). Photograph by courtesy of Lipnitzki-Viollet

Jacques Bernard's exquisite *Martine*. Each of these dramatists, neglecting both artificial theatrical effects and attempts at shock and scandal, had introduced a new spirit into the French theatre. Its old fetid atmosphere had been blown away.

Amongst these famous men, only Dullin's discovery has later become the subject of misgiving and debate. In the 1922–23 and 1923–24 seasons Dullin produced two plays called *Celui qui vivait sa mort* and *Voulez-vous jouer avec môa*. These were by a very young, short-sighted, cheerful man called Marcel Achard. The reason for the misgiving over Achard is that during the next half-century he developed into being the most consistently dominating dramatist, not in the areas opened up by what was later the Cartel, but in that very boulevard theatre associated with Bataille and Bernstein.

Yet it was not only Dullin who produced the early work of Achard. Dullin's fondness for this young writer cannot be dismissed as a personal idiosyncrasy. Jouvet also produced his work. In 1924 he presented Achard's *Marlborough s'en va-t-en guerre*, a light-hearted charade which was the first play of the new French school of dramatists to be seen in England. During his famous management of the old Oxford Playhouse in the Woodstock Road, J. B. Fagan produced it soon after its Paris première, to the genial bewilderment of innumerable undergraduates. It was Jouvet who in 1929 (the season that Dullin produced Salacrou's first play, *Patchouli*) presented Achard's most celebrated and enduring work, *Jean de la lune*, a praise of inspired folly, trust, and simplicity that remains to this day moving and poetic. Nevertheless certain admirers of Jouvet, such as Clément Borgal, have been uneasy that the great man should not have been content to confine himself to the work of writers like Jean Giraudoux, Stève Passeur, Jean Genet, and Jean-Paul Sartre, but should have shown a decided affection for plays which were actually popular, and drew large audiences.

Both Copeau and Dullin despised popularity. Dullin, when he was very much in need of money, stopped the run of his famous production of *L'Avare* whilst it was still at the flood-tide of popularity, simply because he regarded the favour of the public with contempt. But Jouvet was quite different from this. He thought that if a play gave pleasure to large numbers of people, it must have some valuable quality in it. His attitude in this matter is particularly interesting, since it was he who first became associated with that notion of élitist drama known as the *avant-garde*.

It was not an association that he sought himself. It was thrust upon him by the commercial theatre which he was wrongly supposed to despise, but of whose virtues he was always

18. *Le Pain de ménage* by Jules Renard with Jacques Copeau and Germaine Rouet at the Comédie Française (1937). Photograph by courtesy of Lipnitzki-Viollet

aware. The sharp gulf which in the 1920s opened between the boulevard theatre and the avant-garde, a gulf which has continued to widen ever since, was first clearly perceived by the director of a Brussels theatre, Jean-François Fonson, of the Galéries-Saint-Hubert, as the unexpected result of a visit which Louis Verneuil had paid to London two years earlier. Its recognition and naming came about purely by chance, and would never have happened had it not rained heavily one night that Verneuil, who was of delicate health and much subject to chills, intended going to the theatre. Verneuil stayed at the Savoy Hotel, and the only theatre he could reach without getting wet was the Savoy itself.He had been enormously impressed by Lionel Monckton's *Tonight's the Night*, in which the whole audience hummed the refrain, 'And when I told them . . . How wonderful you are . . . They didn't believe me,' and by the simplicity, the absence of scenery, of Martin-Harvey's *Hamlet*, played only against curtains.

In contrast with his enthusiasm for Martin-Harvey and Lionel Monckton and an actor called Raymond Hitchcock, who was encored twice every night for singing 'All dressed up and nowhere to go' in the musical comedy *Mr Manhattan*, Verneuil had no interest at all in the piece at the Savoy. He saw it merely because it was important to him to escape the damp. The play was *The Barton Mystery*, by Walter Hackett. He was so bored by it that he wanted to leave after the end of the second act, but was persuaded to stay. In this third act there was a single scene that fired his imagination. He bought the rights of the piece, and, using only this one situation, wrote a new play called *Monsieur Beverley*.

Pretending to get advice from the Beyond, a detective brings together the family of a woman he suspects, and in a long monologue tells the story of the crime as he imagines it. He thus hopes to startle the criminal into a confession. At the moment he finishes he exclaims dramatically: 'The murderer is here. In this room.' At that moment a woman, whom no one had suspected, least of all the detective, thinks herself discovered, and cries, 'Yes, it is me. I killed Barton.' There is general astonishment, shared by the policeman who has thus discovered the criminal by mistake. But he recovers himself quickly, and says with conviction: 'Je le savais.'

The part was created by Firmin Gémier, who gave a magnificent performance, but who, Verneuil noted with some curiosity, could never get the laugh on this line which many lesser players, in revivals and on tour, obtained without difficulty. When Fonson decided to present *Monsieur Beverley* in Brussels in 1918 he asked Verneuil who should replace Gémier. This is where Jouvet comes, or rather does not come, into the story. 'Do you insist on a great name?' asked Verneuil. 'No,' said Fonson. 'Very well,' replied Verneuil, 'I have an idea. It is a question of an actor very few people have heard of, but whom I consider remarkable. His name is Louis Jouvey. Have you seen him?' (It was about this time that Jouvey changed his name to Jouvet.) Verneuil, who later recalled this incident in his autobiography, went on to say that Jouvet had been out-standing with Jacques Copeau at the Vieux-Colombier in the 1913–14 season. He had been irresistibly funny: as Sir Andrew Aguecheek in *La Nuit des rois*. But he was not only funny: he could be dramatic, too. He would in fact be an extraordinary Beverley.[1]

It was then that Fonson spoke the damning and divisive words that severed the two parts of the French theatre for the next half century. He would have nothing of Jouvet.

'Since you say it, I am sure he is excellent, but he is no good for us, because he is Copeau's right-hand man, that is, a man of the *avant-garde*, whilst you are a typical author of the boulevard, and between us and them is an unpass-able gulf. An *avant-garde* author is attracted by bizarre plays, unusual pieces, things on the margin of normal theatre, and between them and us is a difference, an antagonism as sharp and deep as there is in politics between Conservatives and Socialists. Lugné-Poe's Théâtre de l'Oeuvre, Jacques Rouche's Théâtre des Arts, and Copeau's Vieux-Colombier form an artistic group corre-sponding to the Socialist Party. In one and the other there is the same attitude of opposition, the same conviction that the salvation of the world lies in the collapse of the estab-lished order, and the triumph of the revolutionary theories they call new ideas. You are, and always will be, a man of the Right. Your masters are Dumas and Meilhac. There-fore never choose actors of the Left.'

Verneuil allowed himself to be persuaded by Fonson, and a decision was taken which had a profound effect upon the develop-ment of French theatre. Copeau, Dullin, Gaston Baty, and a few years later Georges and Ludmilla Pitoeff, who came from small halls in Geneva to present Chekhov memorably for the first time in Paris, had irremovable objections to the commercial theatre, and particularly to its doctrine of success. But Jouvet had not these objections. He liked popularity. He did not think that the taste of the public was necessarily bad. In other words he was seducible. Had he entered the commercial theatre with Verneuil he might never have left it, and the consequences would have been immeasurable. The paradox of the situation is

---

1. VERNEUIL, Louis: *Rideau à neuf heures*, Editions des Deux Rives.

19. M. Gémier in *César Birotteau* from *Comoedia Illustré* 15 October 1910

that Gémier was quite as highbrow as Jouvet. He had created the part of Ubu in *Ubu Roi*. He was associated with the Théâtre National Populaire. And in politics he was a good deal more Left-wing than Jouvet. Perhaps Fonson was aware of all this: aware too that Gémier had failed to get a laugh on a line which more commercial players found it easy to make hilarious.

The hostility of the commercial theatre to the *avant-garde* continued and increased. Verneuil was a generous man, and he recognised that in the 1920s and 1930s the *avant-garde* occupied a more important place in the theatre than it had done before. He admitted that Jouvet, Copeau, Pitoeff, Baty and Dullin gave to it an éclat it had not had in earlier days. He himself was surprised that this did not bring the boulevard and the *avant-garde* closer together. But it did not. They grew so far apart that Verneuil found it impossible to imagine a play by Giraudoux or Jules Romains (both of them Jouvet authors) being given at the boulevard Michodière. He thought that the popular actress Gaby Morlay, later very successful in André Roussin's *Lorsque l'enfant paraît*, would burst out laughing if it were suggested that she should appear in a play by Paul Claudel or Lenormand, whilst Dullin and Marguerite Jamois would consider themselves disgraced if they played Henry Bataille.

Jouvet's most popular discovery, after Jules Romains's *Knock*, a discovery that eventually obtained a far higher reputation than Romain's comic and extravagant masterpiece, was Jean Giraudoux, whose adaptation of his own novel, *Siegfried*, in 1928, had an unprecedented commercial and intellectual success at the Comédie des Champs Elysées. It was played by Valentine Tessier, Lucienne Bogaert, Pierre Renoir, Louis Jouvet, and Michel Simon. But Giraudoux was never accepted by the mainstays of the boulevard theatre. Verneuil, full of personal faith and loyalty, was moved to assert that Tristan Bernard's *Triplepatte*, because its character is eternal, true, strongly written, and magistrally observed, would still be played in 1990, by which time he was convinced that the very titles of Giraudoux's *Ondine* and *Intermezzo* would be forgotten.

Tristan Bernard's own low opinion of Giraudoux cannot be ascribed only to the jealousy of a rival and older dramatist, who in his own time had known tremendous réclame. It was shared by so judicious a critic as Léautaud. Léautaud had begun to hear the name of Giraudoux bandied about in artistic circles as early as 1922, six years before Jouvet produced *Siegfried*. He says that he would have to be paid very well indeed before he would read Giraudoux, to read whom is a sheer waste of time. His editor Vallette said that he had met no one who had been able to get through more than ten pages of Giraudoux's latest novel, which had just won a literary prize. Léautaud's opinion of Giraudoux was in fact worse than Bernard's. Bernard admitted that Giraudoux had interesting ideas, but obscured them by an over-decorated style. To Léautaud this elaborate style was merely a device for hiding the fact that Giraudoux had nothing whatever to say.

In these trenchant judgments there is a great deal of truth, and they expose cruelly Giraudoux's principal weakness, his constant straining after a filigree complexity and delicacy of poetic prose which does not illuminate the imagination, and wearies the mind. But it is not strictly true to suggest that he was incapable of writing directly, powerfully, and to the point. The last speech in *Pour Lucrèce* is proof of that. Moreover this capacity, which he used far too little for his permanent fame, lasted throughout his theatrical career. *Pour Lucrèce* was his last play, not produced until after his death. Years before that, in *La Guerre de Troie n'aura pas lieu* (1935), he wrote with equal power. One speech in it in fact has been much admired for that very directness for lack of which both Léautaud and Tristan Bernard more than plausibly condemned him.

It is not a speech which in the dread of war that followed the invention of the hydrogen bomb expresses what most people would like to think. One can even imagine that in certain climates of opinion it might be forbidden to be spoken. Nevertheless dramatically it is extremely forceful, and entirely free from the restless decoration that mars a great deal of Giraudoux's work, and to whose defects he seems to have been quite blind. The echoes and resonances which it roused in the minds of theatregoers in France during the Occupation, especially in the areas which the Germans left comparatively free, have been attested by Pierre Brisson, the son of the Adolphe Brisson who was on such excellent social terms with the leading artists of his time.

'Si toutes les mères coupent l'index de leurs fils, les armées de l'univers se feront la guerre sans index; et si elles lui coupent la jambe droite, les armées seront unijambistes; et si elles lui crèvent les yeux, les armées seront aveugles;

20. *La Guerre de Troie n'aura pas lieu* (Athénée 1937) with Louis Jouvet and Pierre Renoir. Photograph by courtesy of Lipnitzki-Viollet

mais il y aura des armées et, dans la mêlée, elles se cher-
cheront le défaut de l'aine ou la gorge à tâtons.'[2]

2. If every mother cut off her son's forefinger, then the world's armies
will make war without forefingers; and if she cut off the right leg,
there will be armies of cripples; and if she blinded him, armies of blind
men; but armies there will be, groping for the groin or the throat.

That is what the Giraudoux of the great days showed himself capable of imagining, feeling, and expressing, exclaimed Brisson in uncontrollable admiration. It is not a comfortable doctrine, but it is difficult to think of its being better preached. There is also in *La Guerre de Troie n'aura pas lieu* a scene which, when the play was produced in London in a translation by Christopher Fry, with Michael Redgrave giving a superbly noble performance as Hector trying to prevent, and ultimately by evil chance provoking the war, made an impression that in my memory at least has never been effaced.

It concerned an actor whom so far as I know, I had never seen before. Helen and Paris were being cross-examined on their behaviour during their passage from Greece to Troy. Helen claimed that Paris had treated her with the greatest possible respect. The furthest he had gone was when once, and once only, he had kissed her hand. Ulysses says to Paris, 'You had no desire for her, and yet when you carried her off she was naked?,' to which Paris makes the pious answer, 'A naked queen is clothed in her dignity.' There is a good deal of comedy in the scene, particularly when the Trojans are indignant at a suggestion that the Greek ships sail faster than theirs. Finally the Greeks are driven to the argument that Paris is impotent, and Ulysses suggests that in this he is like all Trojans, which provokes cries of 'Shame,' and 'Bring us your wife, and we'll show you,' and 'Your grandmother as well.'

Helen and Paris are thus confronted by a most embarrassing crisis. Paris can prove his innocence only by an argument which makes everyone laugh at him. But a champion arises, a Trojan sailor who had watched Paris and Helen on board ship when the rest of the crew had been ordered below deck. He had seen their naked bodies joined together in a fashion that effectively disproved the story of Paris's physical insufficiency. This is one of the best scenes that Giraudoux ever wrote, in the ambiguity of a defence which is actually an attack. Not that the sailor intends it as an attack. That is not the sort of question which is occupying his mind whilst he is telling the story that acquits Paris at the same time as it condemns him. He is far more concerned with his own lubricious enjoyment at seeing his betters nude when they think that they are unobserved, than he is with defending Paris.

At least that is the overwhelming impression which came over in the English production. The actor who played the sailor displayed in telling his story such an aggressive, insolent relish that I immediately looked at the programme to discover his name. It was Robert Shaw, who that night began the march that was to bring him to international fame.

In Jouvet's Paris production, Andromaque was played by Falconetti, who had been the star of Dreyer's celebrated film of *Joan of Arc*, in which the passion of Joan was depicted entirely in close-ups of Falconetti's sculptural face. The fragile, child-like Madeleine Ozeray was Helen, and the actress who played Cassandra was Copeau's daughter, Marie-Hélène Dasté, who after the war became well known to English audiences when she formed an important part of the company that Jean-Louis Barrault brought several times to England. Pierre Renoir, who Robert Brasillach thought had the finest voice on the French stage, played Ulysses, and Jouvet himself was the idealistic and fatal Hector. Alfred Adam was the sailor; I do not know what sort of effect he made, or whether he made an effect at all.

In reality during the early 1920s the boulevard theatre had no justification for its detestation of the *avant-garde*, for it was not the *avant-garde* that put it in danger. After films like Chaplin's *Shoulder Arms* and *A Dog's Life*, the comedies of Max Linder, and the vampire and *Judex* serials of Louis Feuillade, the cinema was beginning to make a bigger impression on serious audiences. It even took away from the stage some prominent players. Léautaud in 1922 expressed surprise to his friend Berthéllmy that he no longer saw the name of Jean Périer in the programmes of musical theatres. Berthéllmy explained that Périer was now in the cinema, where he earned as much money in two or three months as in the theatre in a year. He had been engaged for a film of *The Three Musketeers* at 1,500 francs a day, with a minimum of fifty days guaranteed. This meant at least 75,000 francs.

The cinema was thus becoming a threat, but not yet so much so as to damage the theatre's self-confidence, and reasonably make one section of it critical of another that it might consider its rival. There were still spectacular boulevard successes. In the 1921–22 season Sacha Guitry made nearly a million francs, which puts Périer's remuneration for *The Three Musketeers* into proper perspective. Nor was this success a secret between Guitry and his bank manager. At the *répétition générale* of Guitry's *Un Sujet de roman* in January, 1923, which several people found piquant because Sacha's father, Lucien, chose for the chief woman's part one Henriette Roggers, a mistress he had discarded many years before, Sacha's wife, Yvonne Printemps, wore round her neck a row of pearls worth several hundred thousand francs. In the previous year Sacha had given her jewels worth a million and a half francs. Immense as these sums were, they were apparently not enough. Within a comparatively short time Mlle Printemps had left Guitry to contract a marriage with Pierre Fresnay that lasted for half a century. These events sent Léautaud's mind into an oddly sentimental reverie.

What, he wondered, had become of Marthe Brandès? He thinks he recalls having heard somewhere that a few years ago she had had an affection of the chest, and had had to go and live in the Midi. No one, he says, ever speaks now of this actress who with Lucien Guitry had created the characters in Renard's *Le Pain de ménage*. He remembers that Marguerite Moreno had told him how Guitry had made Brandès suffer, so that she had almost died of love. He finds her warm, languorous, ardent voice, and her enticing mouth unforgettable. Now, at over fifty years of age, he thinks he had once been in love with her himself. He wishes he could see her again.

No other professional drama critic ever makes such personal confessions as Léautaud, or records so frankly the opinions that other people hold of him. This is why we know him more intimately than any other figure in the French (or British) theatre of the twentieth century. More mordantly bitter in his criticisms than any of his colleagues, readier with the wounding phrase and the judgment that kills, he was nevertheless in his private life extraordinarily fairminded. For example, in the early part of 1923 Lucien Dubech, who later became the respected critic of *Le Journal de Genève*, reviewed a play by Alexandre Arnoux called *Huon of Bordeaux*. This play is a transposition to the stage of an 800-year old *chanson de geste*. In very uninspired verse it tells the story of Huon, son of the duke Séguin, who comes to the court of Charlemagne, where, in legitimate self-defence, he kills Karlot, the Emperor's son. In expiation he is sent on a mission to Babylon. He is told to enter the palace of the Emir Gaudise, to strike the man seated on the emir's left, to embrace three times his daughter Esclarmonde on his right, and to bring back hair from the ruler's beard, and teeth from his mouth. Huon accepts, and accomplishes this fantastic mission.

In an enchanted forest he meets an exiled compatriot, Gériaume, who asks for bread and wine, of which he has been deprived for thirty years. When they are brought to him he bends down to drink, exclaiming:

Saint-Andoche, du vin de France!

Whereupon Huon asks:

Gériaume, que fais-tu?

and Gériaume replies:

Voyez,
Je mangeais, les genous ployés,
L'humble pain; mais ce vin de gloire,
Je me prosterne pour le boire.[3]

This preposterous dialogue caused Dubech, generally regarded as one of the most reliable of critics, to hail Arnoux as amongst the very best of living poets.

Dubech took as his motto the words: 'When have I failed to bark at thieves?' Léautaud remarks that in his review of *Huon of Bordeaux* in *L'Action Française* Dubech referred to a former observation of Léautaud's to the effect that the heroism of the characters of Corneille seemed to him the height of folly. Dubech is quoted by Léautaud as saying: 'Nothing could be more natural: a soul as absolutely vile as (Léautaud's) can regard Cornelian heroism only as a monstrosity, a personal offence, and a bloody reproach.' This amiable comment was brought to Léautaud's attention by his mistress, Madame Cayssac, whose prowess in bed Léautaud frequently praises, but a woman of uncertain temper. She had been given the review by her husband. Léautaud is puzzled when such things as Dubech's attack happen, but not angry or resentful.

The two or three million words of his *Journal littéraire* are of a rare frankness, and unlike such theatre volumes as James Agate's *Ego* diaries they conceal nothing. Léautaud's infatuation with Madame Cayssac even when she was approaching sixty, three years older than he was himself, coupled with a gimlet-eyed scorn for the pretentiousness of her *petit bourgeois* outlook; his steadfast refusal, sometimes at great cost to him-

---

3. Gériaume explains his strange conduct by saying that before humble bread he bows, but for glorious wine he prostrates himself.

self, not to say exactly what he thought of plays and books and people; his devotion to stray animals that no one else cared for; his poverty; his rueful feeling that he was not really as ugly as people made him out to be; his conviction that the only writing of any value was that which without artifice expressed precisely its author's meaning; these things make his *Journals* of extreme importance for the history of society and the theatre during the first fifty years of the century.

Léautaud lost his job as drama critic of *Le Mercure de France* through the malevolence of Rachilde, the defender of *Ubu Roi* and wife of the editor, Vallette, though he continued as an employé of the paper in other, and humbler capacities. He became critic of *La Nouvelle Revue française,* but his reign there was short. For a colleague, Jules Romains, wrote a play, *Monsieur Le Trouhadec saisi par la débauche,* which Louis Jouvet directed at the Comédie des Champs Elysées on 14 March 1923. Léautaud's review of this play was deeply ironical, and the paper refused to print it. Since he would not compromise he was dismissed, and his career as a drama critic came to an end.

What Léautaud was not allowed to say was said for him, surprisingly, by Lucien Dubech. In *Monsieur Le Trouhadec saisi par la débauche* Jouvet played the part of a venerable member of the Institute who falls in love with Mademoiselle Rolande, an actress in Monte Carlo. Le Trouhadec spends his meagre wealth on buying her jewels, and is mistaken by his dishonest landlord for a famous robber who has retired from business. He drops into the Casino and casually wins an immense sum of money, which he spends right and left in a temporary period of prosperity and popularity. His money gone, and having reserved a room for Mademoiselle Rolande and himself in the Hotel de Paris, he recoups himself by selling to a fraudulent acquaintance the right to publish under the illustrious name of Le Trouhadec a treatise on the art of making a fortune at roulette.

Romains saw himself as a philosopher revealing the disorder and folly that reign on the earth, and there was something about his personality that upset the equanimity of most people who came into contact with him. He was sublimely confident, too sublimely confident for popularity, of his ability to achieve anything and everything in the world of art. He was a living embodiment of the sense of intellectual superiority which pervades the Ecole Normale Supérieure, and this did not endear him either to other dramatists or to drama critics.

Simplicity was the note of Jouvet's *mise en scène* for the play. There was little more on the stage than a couple of palm trees, which looked dejected or revived according to the moods of Monsieur Le Trouhadec. This mood of simplicity annoyed Dubech. He thought that Romains had made his hero simple and innocent beyond belief. He said that he had himself known members of the Institute, and he had not found them to be absolute idiots. But he admitted that Romains was extremely intelligent, and that some of the scenes in the play are very well managed.

One of them is of fantastic ingenuity. Mlle Rolande and a friend carry on a conversation at one side of the stage whilst M. Le Trouhadec talks to another character at the other. Each set of speakers is inaudible to the other. Throughout the scene a remark made at one side of the stage is followed by a remark made at the other, and though neither speaker knows what the other has said, each remark is as relative to the remark preceding it, and in ignorance of which it is made, as it is to the remark to which it is intended to be a reply. Romains had some of the ferocious cleverness which Alan Ayckbourn brought to the English stage fifty years later. But according to Dubech he had one fatal defect. He had no comic force. He was not funny.

Funny or not, however, Romains's association with Jouvet was to become a primary fact of theatrical history in France. Almost everything that Jouvet later achieved was made possible by another play of Romains's. This was *Knock*. It was produced at the Comédie des Champs Elysées in the middle of December, 1923, and it is one of the two plays most famously associated with Jouvet, the other being Jean Giraudoux's *Siegfried*.

It is a remarkable play, and Jouvet was mortally afraid of it. He considered that some scenes in it were too brutal, and he worked himself up into such a passion of anxiety that on the night of the *générale*, when for the first time in his career he played without a wig, his body was covered with no fewer than forty-six boils. In the half century that followed *Knock's* first performance nothing about it staled. Its construction is of classic simplicity. In the first act Knock is swindled. In the second he lays the foundations of his wholly original counter-attack. In the third he conquers his enemy, wins an unparalleled success, and is left in the ambiguous and disturbing condition of a man who, beating his enemy, beats himself in the process without knowing it. Romains knows this. We know it. Knock does not. Such is the irony of the play, which is a comic but disorientating masterpiece, a landmark in the history of Jouvet and of the French theatre.

Dr. Knock, who has seen a good deal of the world but whose medical qualifications are doubtful, buys the practice of a certain Dr. Parpalaid in the small mountain village of Saint-Maurice. He finds that Dr. Parpalaid has sold him a practice which scarcely exists. There is not a single well-off invalid in the village who requires regular and remunerative medical visits. Knock learns this devastating truth as he travels to Saint-Maurice in Dr. Parpalaid's ancient motor car, whose intermittent progress is shown by the moving of the scenery behind it (Dubech thought this a very poor comic idea). Knock shows little emotion on realising that he has been robbed. Except at the very end of the play he never shows emotion. His strength is in arousing emotion in others.

In the second act he offers to genuine inhabitants of the village free consultations every Monday morning. This confining of free consultations to the actual villagers, and charging ordinary fees to everyone else, suggests to them that they are getting something valuable for nothing. They are blissfully unaware that Knock is working on a medical theory of the most alarming kind, namely that every healthy man is only a man suffering from a disease whose existence he does not suspect, but which it is Knock's duty to reveal to him. The greedy villagers, eager for something for nothing, and also wishing to make a fool of a man stupid enough to broadcast his knowledge without a fee, come in droves. One by one they enter his surgery, full of self-importance, utterly pleased with themselves; but after a few simple, but hair-raising questions, punctuated by a sinister silence or a long searching stare, they stagger out, each one thinking that he is seriously ill, when of course there is nothing wrong with him at all. In the third act practically the whole population is receiving paid visits from Dr. Knock twice a week. When the curtain falls, Dr. Parpalaid himself, trembling with fear, is about to become a patient.

During the play's long existence there has been an interminable debate as to what its nature really is. Dubech says that the play is not a satire on doctors, because Knock is not a doctor but a charlatan. Jouvet himself denied that Knock is a charlatan, and seemed to be impressed by the amount of knowledge that Knock must have picked up during his wanderings before he

21. *Dr Knock* (Athénée 1937) with Louis Jouvet and Odette Papazac. Photograph by courtesy of Lipnitzki-Viollet

arrived at Saint-Maurice. Romains never offered any opinion on the question. The only thing he ever told Jouvet about Knock was that he once met him whilst he was out motoring.

Romains was clumsily trying to get a speck of dust out of his eye. A magnificent car drew up, Knock got out, and instantly removed the speck. Whilst doing so he diagnosed from the white of Romains's eye that he was suffering from deficiency of the pancreas. On reaching home Romains took to his bed, and his illness went on without the slightest serious consequence. In fact he sometimes wondered whether without it life would have been worth living.

Dubech, whose criticism of *Knock* is worth pondering for the reason that it abundantly illustrates the blunders to which drama critics are prone, also complains that there is no movement in the play. This is quite untrue. Knock begins as a comparatively honest man. But when he is swindled he changes, and he goes on changing. The man who frightens the villagers in the second act is out for himself.

But the Knock of the third act transported by the vision of hundreds of his patients simultaneously taking their rectal temperatures at ten o'clock every night is a mystic more enthralled by his imagination than any of his victims. When he tells Dr. Parpalaid, in whom he has diagnosed awful things by merely giving him a casual glance during conversation, that he is so skilful at discovering illness by looking at a man that he is now himself afraid to see his own face in the mirror, Knock has travelled a very long way from the man in the broken-down motor car in the first act.

Knock, as few who saw the original production seem to have realised, is a brilliant satire on the credulity of humanity, and a reminder that those who enslave others may well enslave themselves. It is ferociously funny. Jouvet revived it many times, playing it for more than a thousand performances in the course of his career. It provided him with most of the money he needed for his other productions. For this reason he could not help being grateful to it.

Yet his attitude towards it remained ambiguous. He was generally identified with the character of Knock, and he resented this. He would declare irritably that unless an actor plays one particular part with conspicuous success people think he is no good. But as soon as he has done so they identify him with the part, and talk as if he never played anything else. Jouvet refused to be identified with Knock. He is not Knock, he said, and Knock is not he. For one thing he denied that he was as cruel as Knock. This may be so. Nevertheless, though in

his later life he became deeply Christian, he spoke publicly of
the actor (A. Heraut) who first played Dr. Parpalaid in very
wounding phrases.

Cruelty is no doubt a relative term, and Armand Salacrou
has some interesting comments to make on the cruelty of Jouvet.
Jouvet's mistress was Lisa Duncan, the adopted daughter of
Isadora Duncan. She left Jouvet for a young dancer named
Pomiès. Pomiès was a man of immense promise, and many
people expected him to transform the dance world of his time.
Lisa and Pomiès formed a programme whose striking originality
impressed all who saw it. They planned to tour the world with
it, but a few days before they were due to set out Pomiès suddenly died. Lisa was plunged into grief, and her career was
ruined.

A little later, one night when his performance was over,
Jouvet knocked on the door of Lisa's lodging. She rose from bed,
and let him in. He was full of sympathy and understanding.
He could imagine and enter into her great grief. He uttered no
word of reproach. Lying beside her on her bed, he spoke with
great tenderness. In such a position, at such a time, and in such
a mood of sympathy, old habits reassert themselves. Jouvet took
her gently in his arms, and they became lovers again. And then,
whilst they were still enlaced, whilst in fact he was still inside
her, he said in a hard and sneering voice, 'Well, Lisa, I fancy I
have now buried your Pomiès for you.' Salacrou remarks that
for a long time he found this vengeance repugnant, but later he
tried to find in it an explosion of jealousy of almost Shake-
spearian grandeur.

Nor was Jouvet lenient to his colleagues. On his return to
France from South America after the war of 1939–45 one of the
first questions he asked the newspaper reporters sent to meet
him as he got off the boat was, 'What! Steve Passeur? Isn't he
dead yet?' He immediately added, 'And Anouilh? Still as sordid
as ever?'

Jouvet seemed to be more jealous for the reputation of Knock
than for *Knock* itself; for the character than for the play. He
admitted that there were mysteries in Knock that he did not
understand, depths of character which he could never fathom.
But he refused to regard Knock as a charlatan. He did not find
his methods of diagnosis and the questions he asks any more
peculiar than those he himself had encountered when he had
consulted doctors. Jouvet's various periods in hospital had

helped him in his interpretation of Knock. In particular he borrowed from a surgeon under whose orders he once found himself that meticulous and endless washing of his hands whilst Knock developed his medical theories which he made such a frightening feature of his performance.

Jouvet's opinion that Knock's attitude was not very different from that of those doctors with whom he had actually come into contact is given credence by later students of modern French history. Theodore Zeldin[4] suggests that between the wars French medicine was in a condition favourable to the production of a whole army of Knocks. In Montpellier there was a doctor who diagnosed and offered prescriptions by post. The most celebrated French doctor of the nineteenth century, Philippe Ricord (1800–89), distinguished correctly between syphilis and gonorrhea, but thought that syphilis was not contagious through secondary lesions. There was a widespread return to medical theories of the past, and the study of 'humours' was revived. Medical astrology came into vogue under the name of cosmobiology.

For Jouvet the play was not about charlatanism or fraud. It was about what he calls the dominant aspect of the twentieth century, the domination of the spirit and minds of men by ideas and ideology. Knock has the gift of faith; he believes in medicine; and faith is sustained by great texts: this is why the Old Testament still influences us. At first he had been afraid of the long speech in the third act in which Knock is seized by a cold passion of medical enthusiasm, and exposes to Dr. Parpalaid his vision of a village in the thrall of illness. He takes him to a window, and then launches into his famous *tirade*:

> Regardez un peu ici, docteur Parpalaid. Vous connaissez la vue qu'on a de cette fenêtre. Entre deux parties de billard, jadis, vous n'avez pu manquer d'y prendre garde. Tout là-bas, le mont Aligre marque les bornes du canton. Les villages de Mesclat et de Trébures s'aperçoivent à gauche; et si, de ce coté, les maisons de Saint Maurice ne faisaient pas une espèce de renflement, c'est tous les hameaux de la vallée que nous aurions en enfilade. Mais vous n'avez dû saisir là que ces beautés naturelles, dont vous êtes friand.

4. ZELDIN, Theodore: *France 1848–1945*, Vol 1 Oxford University Press.

C'est un paysage rude, à peine humain, que vous contempliez. Aujourd'hui, je vous le donne tout imprégné de médecine, animé et parcouru par le feu souterrain de notre art. La première fois que je me suis planté ici, au lendemain de mon arrivée, je n'étais pas trop fier: je sentais que ma présence ne pesait pas lourd. Ce vaste terroir se passait insolement de moi et de mes pareils. Mais maintenant, j'ai autant d'aise à me trouver ici qu'à son clavier l'organiste des grandes orgues. Dans deux cent cinquante de ces maisons—il s'en faut que nous les voyions toutes à cause de l'éloignement et des feuillages—il y a deux cent cinquante chambres où quelqu'un confesse la médecine, deux cent cinquante lits où un corps étendu témoigne que la vie a un sens, et grâce à moi un sens médical. La nuit, c'est encore plus beau, car il y a des lumières. Et presque toutes les lumières sont à moi. Les non-malades dorment dans les ténèbres. Ils son supprimés. Mais les malades ont gardé leur veilleuse ou leur lampe. Tout ce qui reste en marge de la médecine la nuit m'en débarrasse, m'en dérobe l'agacement et le défi. Le canton fait place à une sorte de firmament dont je suis le créateur continuel. Et je ne vous parle pas des cloches. Songez que, pour tout ce monde, leur premier office est de rappeler mes prescriptions; qu'elles sont la voix de mes ordonnances. Songez que, dans quelques instants, il va sonner dix heures, que pour tous mes malades, dix heurres, c'est la deuxième prise de température rectale, et que, dans quelques instants, deux cent cinquante thermomètres vont pénétrer à la fois . . .[5]

---

5. Just take a look here, Dr. Parpalaid. You know the view from this window. Down there, mount Aligre marks the end of the district. The villages of Mesclat and Trébure can be seen on the left; and if the houses of Saint Maurice did not hide them we should have all the hamlets of the valley strung out before us. But you must not see only those natural beauties of which you are so fond. It's a rough countryside, hardly human, that you used to contemplate. But today I show it you inspired by medicine, life put into it by the hidden fires of our art. The first time I stood here, the day after I arrived, I wasn't at all proud; I felt that my presence didn't count for much. This great landscape took no notice of me and my sort of people. But now I am as much at ease to find myself here as an organist at the keyboard of a magnificent organ. In two hundred and fifty of these houses there are two hundred and fifty rooms where someone bears witness to medicine,

In considering *Knock*, Jouvet, despite his first misgivings, came to the conclusion that it was this climactic speech which assured its 'perennial authority'.

Yet he never really gave his heart to *Knock*. Romains provided him with a short curtain-raiser to *Knock*, called *Amédée*. It was about a shoe-polisher who one day looked up and saw that his client was a man who had seduced his wife. With great dignity Amédée rises and leaves the saloon, but he is forced into the humiliation of returning, and falling professionally on to his knees in order to finish the job. *Amédée* was a complete failure, and was soon taken out of the programme. But to the end of his life Jouvet maintained that it was a better play than *Knock*.

Yet whenever it was revived, *Knock* continued to reveal new depths and meaning. By 1938, when the critic Robert Kemp saw one of its many revivals, it had ceased to be a comment on men's capacity to be controlled by ideology, and become instead an example of another modern siren, that of growth. Knock exalted medicine, where Molière mocked at it. He saw it as a growth industry. He believes passionately in the expansion of trade, of *his* trade. His criterion is whether the number of his customers is increasing, decreasing, or standing still. He exists, not to cure disease, but to spread its bounds wider and wider. He is an early and explicit practitioner of a dominant twentieth century philosophy that man ought constantly to be increasing his productivity. He believes in the more and more, not in the better and better. He sets the example of absolute certitude. Kemp, in the year of Munich, looks across the eastern frontier, and calls him a little Führer.

---

two hundred and fifty beds where a horizontal body shows that life has some sense, and thanks to me a medical sense. At night it is still more beautiful, for there are lights. And almost all the lights are due to me. The non-diseased sleep in the dark. But those who are ill have kept their night-light or lamp. At night all those that remain outside the domain of medicine cease to bother and defy me. The whole area becomes a kind of firmament of which I am the continual creator. And I say nothing about the bells. Think, for all this world, their first purpose is to recall my prescriptions; they are my prescriptions giving tongue. Think, in a few minutes, it will be ten o'clock, and for all my patients ten o'clock is the second time they take their rectal temperature, and that in a few moments, two hundred and fifty thermometers will simultaneously penetrate . . .

ROMAINS, Jules: *Knock*, NRF Gallimard, Paris.

That *Knock* could go on, at least as long as Jouvet was alive, revealing new significances is the proof that it was one of the few outstanding plays of the 1920s that still rewards extended study. But it was important, not merely in itself, but in its material results. Creative, it was the cause of creativity in others, or at any rate it allowed their creativity to be seen. Its success made it Jouvet's cash box and banker, and rendered it possible for him to produce several other plays which, for financial reasons, he would never have been able, without it, to put on the stage.

Among these were Roger Martin du Gard's *Le Testament du Père Leleu* (October 1924) and Marcel Achard's *Marlborough s'en va-t-en guerre* (December 1924). Jouvet, as we have seen, has been much criticised for presenting the work of the young Achard, not because of any particular defects in the work itself, but because Achard had the luck, and indeed the merit, of becoming during the next fifty years the most characteristic and consistently successful boulevard dramatist of the century. Roussin and Barrillet and Grédy have had bigger individual popular successes than Achard; but none was so prolific, or maintained his position so long. Achard, even in the 1920s, was a vastly entertaining writer, and Jouvet always had the true highbrow's respect for entertainment. An improving boredom was never one of the aims of his theatre. Moreover, *Marlborough s'en va-t-en guerre*, with its elegant frivolity and toy theatre mannerisms, was a rather adventurous work. Jouvet also used the profits of *Knock* to present Charles Vildrac's next play, *Mme. Béliard* (which did not fulfil the promise of *Le Paquebot Tenacity*); Jean Sarment's *Léopold le Bien-Aimé*; and Stève Passeur's *Suzanne* (30 January 1929).

But in the previous year Jouvet had produced (3 May 1928) a play which by any standards must be regarded as of great importance, and which many people persist in reckoning to be the summit of his career. This was *Siegfried*, by Jean Giraudoux, the Giraudoux whose merits had been prophetically recognised a couple of decades before by Jules Renard, but whom Léautaud and his editor dismissed as unreadable.

Historically, *Siegfried* came at a very important moment. From the days of Racine onwards the French theatre had been the theatre of the word. 'Sieur le mot', Gaston Baty, one of the five great directors of the 1920s, called it. Baty was determined to overthrow the supremacy of language, and his work had great influence. He liked plays which did not do all the work themselves, but left the director plenty of scope for invention and creation. In actual fact, the theatre has in modern times gone the way that Baty directed. Antonin Artaud (1896–1948), who developed the theory of the Theatre of Cruelty in which gesture and movements, inarticulate cries and rhythms are more important than language, and who died shortly after spending nine years under restraint in a mental asylum, derived from him: Peter Brook and John Barton are more intelligently Baty's progeny.

Giraudoux, all unknowingly, blocked the way of these men. Like Jupiter, he came in a shower of gold: he was the extraordinarily supple and delicate master of the theatre of glitter. His prose exploded like fireworks: *Siegfried* is like a Brock's Benefit at the Crystal Palace of the 1920s and 1930s, so brilliantly do the phrases contrast the brooding forests, the gleaming ice, and the surging, irrational music of the German soul and soil with the cool reason of France, its peaceful chateaux on the hillside, its statues of Louis Blanc in the village square, which soar into the air and illumine the night with radiance.

There were people in France at this time who thought that the movement represented and led by that resolute Christian, Baty, would ruin the French theatre, just as many English people thought that the Stratford dominated by John Barton, with his disrespect for texts, would ruin Shakespeare. They wrote to Giraudoux to tell him this; and he turned out to be for a few years the saviour of the cause they held for lost. Daniel Halévy, the champion of the old French virtues of clarity of thought and grace of expression, exclaimed with suddenly renewed hope:

> Qui nous l'eût dit, que notre théâtre, perdu par nos hommes de théâtre, c'est vous peut-être qui nous le sauveriez? Nous attendons maintenant tous vos personnages, toutes vos héroïnes, Eglantine, Juliette au Pays des Hommes, celles qui sont nées, celles qui sont à naître.[6]

As long as he lived (and he did not die until 1944) Giraudoux did not fail those who appealed to him to preserve the old way

---

6. Who would have said to us that our theatre, lost to us by our men of the theatre, could perhaps be saved by you? Now we expect all your characters, your heroines, Eglantine, Juliette in the Land of Men, those, that are born, those that are yet to be born.

22. Louis Jouvet and Dominique Blanchar in *Ondine* (Athénée 1949).
Photograph by courtesy of Lipnitzki-Viollet

and the accepted verities: and his success with such plays as *Amphitryon 38, La Guerre de Troie n'aura pas lieu* (1935), *Intermezzo* (1933), and *Ondine* (1939), proved that those who urged Canute to turn back the tide were not such fools as they seemed.

It is an accepted truism that Giraudoux was the greatest discovery ever made by Jouvet: indeed Pierre de Boisdeffre remarks that he was the only one. During the two months of rehearsal given to *Siegfried* Jouvet, with his usual gloom, maintained that the play would not attract the public. But he declared at the same time that it would be the greatest honour of his life to have produced it. He was certainly wrong about the play's popularity. It ran for 283 performances, which in the conditions of the time was almost a record.

With *La Guerre de Troie n'aura pas lieu, Siegfried* is Giraudoux's most ambitious play. As the later play deals with the fear that trying to avoid war actually provokes it, *Siegfried* attempts the reconciliation of nations after war has broken out. There is in it no feat of construction so fine as that in *La Guerre de Troie* by which it is Hector himself, the passionate proponent of peace, who brings about the war between Greece and Troy: and it has no speech so savagely effective as that which concludes *Pour Lucrèce*.

There is quite a lot of humour in it, especially in the scene of the frontier post at the beginning of the fourth act, where the French *douanier*, at a time of the breaking of nations, thinks that the question preoccupying everyone must be speculation about who has got the latest promotion in the Customs. But there is no whimsicality in it so long and gracefully sustained as in that famous speech in *Intermezzo* which becomes a fantasia on the names of the cities of France on pretty much the same theme, investing with filigree poetry the drab material of bureaucratic transfers. Nevertheless it remains a striking and important play. Whereas England ten years after the war, in R. C. Sherriff's *Journey's End* looked back on that war with compassion, and sorrow, and admiration, Giraudoux was in his fantasticated way longing that war should never come again, for he loved both Germany and France.

Paradoxically *Siegfried* has extraordinary echoes, not of the past, but of the future. It is the story of a foreigner who, as Adolf Hitler would do a few years later, restored the power of Germany. But Giraudoux's foreigner resigns; and, unlike Hitler, returns to his native country. Siegfried is a French soldier who

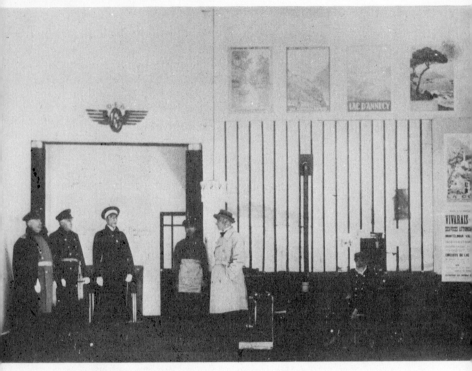

23. Louis Jouvet in *Siegfried* (1928). Photograph by courtesy of Lipnitzki-Viollet

has lost his memory, is taken to Germany, and by some process which Giraudoux does not attempt to explain, brings that defeated nation to the highest pitch of efficiency and power. But he wishes to solve the mystery of his past, and fruitlessly interviews many people who claim, falsely as it always turns out, to be his relations. But eventually a young sculptress, Geneviève, comes to his palace to give him lessons in French.

She is convinced, and she convinces the audience, that Siegfried is in fact her lost French fiancé Jacques. Giraudoux in his best literary style cannot refrain from reminding us that the situation is familiar; the hero is on the brink of learning what everybody else already knows. One of Giraudoux's characters, Count Zelten, says:

J'ai découvert ce que je soupçonnais depuis longtemps. J'ai découvert que celui qui juge avec son cerveau, qui parle avec son esprit, qui calcule avec sa raison, que celui-là n'est pas Allemand![7]

In a remarkable early example of Brechtian alienation, reminding us that what we are seeing is after all a play, an affair of prompters and scene-shifters, Zelten makes the comparison with Sophocles and Shakespeare:

> C'est même le moment où les machinistes font silence, où le souffleur souffle plus bas, et où les spectateurs qui ont naturellement deviné avant Oedipe, avant Othello, frémissent à l'idée d'apprendre ce qu'ils savent de toute éternité.[8]

But when the revelation is actually made that Siegfried knows that he is French, Giraudoux admirably throws aside literature and finesse for an excellent directness.

Geneviève says she would like him to give her lessons in German in exchange for her own lessons in French.

> J'ai l'intention de rester ici, d'étudier, avec un de vos sculpteurs, d'avoir une petite fille allemande pour modèle, de vous voir souvent, si je peux, de vous parler votre langue . . . Dans quelques mois, si je peux, de vous parler votre langue ...
> Un étranger apprend vite l'allemand?
> To which Siegfried replies simply:
> J'ai mis six mois.[9]

This is very clever, but perhaps a little too clever. What one misses in *Siegfried*, indeed in all Giraudoux's work, is any real feeling, either for his themes or his characters. His figures are

---

7. I've discovered what I suspected for a long time. I've discovered that the person who judges with his head, who speaks with his spirit, who thinks with his reason, that person is not German!
   GIRAUDOUX, Jean: *Siegfried*, Grasset, Paris.

8. This is the moment when the stagehands are silent, when the prompter lowers his voice, and when the spectators, who have naturally guessed before Oedipus, before Othello, thrill at the idea of learning what they have known from all eternity.

9. I intend to stay on here, and study with one of your sculptors, and have a little German girl as a model, and see you often, if you enjoy my visits . . . In a few months, if I can, learn your language . . . Does a foreigner learn German quickly?
   To which Siegfried replies simply: It took me six months.

merely figures of speech, dazzling, but without emotion or reality. There is hardly any greater depth in them than in the plays of Cocteau. The important critics of the first quarter of the century had been revolted by the heartlessness of the reigning drama of the day. They called for idealism and tenderness, and prophesied for them when they should come an immense success. Giraudoux was not the man to supply them. He would have been surprised had he been accused of the cruelty of Bernstein, but he was in fact just as heartless. For that reason, in spite of one's admiration for the skill of his legerdemain, one has not as much affection for him as for two writers, Emile Mazaud and Marcel Achard, one of whom failed to fulfil his high promise, and the other fulfilled the sort of promise which in his early days no one suspected that he was showing.

Mazaud's first play, in one act, was produced by Copeau at the Vieux Colombier in the early 1920s. It was called *La Folle Journée*, and critics went out of their way to heap extravagant comparisons upon it, mentioning Mazaud in the same breath with Becque, Maupassant, and Jules Renard. But Dubech says that these authors are too dry. If Mazaud recalls anything, it is the comedies of Georges Courteline, 'so free, so profound, and so sad'.

The story of *La Folle Journée* is simple enough, and, after the passing of more than half a century during which its author has been completely forgotten, it remains very touching. M. Mouton is an old waiter who has saved some money and retired into the country. He remembers his humble friend Truchard, who has not had Mouton's luck, and invites him on a visit. Truchard comes. He loses himself on the way. Then he eats and drinks too much. He has been ill, and the next day he is still in bed in the middle of the afternoon. Mouton is fed up with Truchard, bored by his clumsiness, and goes for his daily walk without him. Truchard is left behind with the maid of all work, and these innocent souls talk to each other.

Truchard explains his behaviour. He had so much wanted to come to see Mouton. Only, things had gone wrong with him. He had starved himself to get enough money for the train fare. He had worked till the last possible moment, and then run, not walked. When he arrived he was almost fainting. And, to do honour to Mouton, he had drunk too much, he who likes only milk. When he leaves (and Mouton does not try to keep him) he leaves behind a letter he had in his eagerness written before he set out, thanking Mouton for all the pleasures he was looking forward to: the poetry of the countryside, the fresh milk, the morning walk, all the things he had dreamt of in his life, and had not had.

'Make a note of this name, Emile Mazaud,' said Dubech: 'It is a long time since we saw anything so poignant and simple.' Almost the same words—'Make a note of his name'—were used of Harold Pinter in connection with his first play, *The Birthday Party*. But whereas Pinter became more and more famous, Mazaud has fallen into oblivion. Unjustly: for the best judges of his time saw in him notable quality and many virtues.

Jacques Copeau presented Mazaud's second play, *Dardamelle*, on 28 March 1923, a fortnight after Jouvet had begun his career as an independent producer with *Monsieur Le Trouhadec saisi par la débauche* at the Comédie des Champs Elysées. *Dardamelle* had all the qualities of tenderness and whimsicality of *La Folle Journée*, and it was in addition a full-length entertainment. Léautaud calls it 'a very pretty piece, curious and amusing.'

The hero is a man whose wife, in an unguarded moment, informs him that he is a cuckold. When the first minute of distress is past, he takes the news with gaiety, irony, sarcasm, and the wisest fantasy. Far from lamenting his situation, he boasts of it. Instead of concealing his misfortune from people, he draws their attention to it. There is something Shavian in the nonconformity of his attitude, something Barriesque in the pain underlying it. He intends that, whenever there is a visitor, the maid shall say, with all the amiability in the world, 'Please take a seat. The cuckold will be back in a moment.' He writes in huge capitals over his front door, 'Cuckold, first class'. His fame spreads, and people actually come to congratulate him. But he remains modest, and turning to his wife, points out quite reasonably that all the credit belongs to her.

Léautaud finds in this play a very agreeable playfulness, a profound and irresistible sense of comedy, and beneath its tone of farce a true humanity. But he has misgivings about the ending. The local notabilities ask Dardamelle to forgive his wife, and give up his jokes. 'That's all right,' he says. 'I forgive you. But don't do it again, please. For then it could well be that one of us two would die.' 'What!' exclaims his wife. 'You would kill me?' 'I said one of us two,' replies Dardamelle. 'I did not say it would be you.' Léautaud admits that this ending is touching, that in fact it spreads over the whole piece an emotion that through its three acts is hidden beneath its fantasy. But he thinks that it is perhaps rather too neat. With unusual modesty, however, he acknowledges that he may be wrong and the author right. Anyway, says Léautaud, the ending is even truer than the fantasy. He did not, during the sixteen years he spent as a drama critic, a drama critic with the most terrible pen in Paris, experience more than half a dozen moments which he felt so deeply that he described them in the detail he brings to *Dardamelle*. No other play seems to have moved him so much as this.

It is mildly surprising that it should have been Copeau who discovered an author as sentimental as Mazaud, for Copeau passed for being a hard man. He was implacable in his relations with others, whereas Jouvet, who could be horrified by the mockery of real grief and illness in *Knock*, was always ready to say the agreeable thing, but without necessarily intending to put his pleasant words and promises into practice. For a long period in the nineteen-twenties he teased Armand Salacrou, the young man who had come up from Le Havre with the resolution to become a great dramatist, with the prospect of producing his plays, but actually when Salacrou did get his work on the stage it was through Charles Dullin rather than Jouvet; and all the time that Jean Anouilh was his secretary Jouvet did not trouble to read seriously any of his manuscripts.

Nevertheless it was whilst Jouvet was a member of Copeau's company that *La Folle Journée* was produced, and his influence may have counted for something. But he had left to found his own company when Copeau presented *Dardamelle*, and the play, however much it pleased Léautaud and Dubech, did not attract the public. In any event it failed to prevent the failure that was rapidly enveloping Copeau's administration of the Vieux Colombier.

It was not until Marcel Achard's *Jean de la lune* was produced by Jouvet in 1929 that the success which had been confidently predicted for plays of tenderness and innocence nearly twenty years before, actually manifested itself. Valentine Tessier played Marceline, the mercurial, fascinating, selfish heroine, and Jouvet himself appeared as Jeff, called Jean de la lune, who meets all Marceline's betrayals with an absolute trust, an unshakeable faith in an integrity that is not there, but which the intensity of his own belief may actually create.

Jeff believes in Marceline beyond all reason. He is convinced, or he is convinced that he ought to be convinced, of her purity and love to a point at which absurdity has no meaning for him. The play has the same passionate certainty, the same total commitment that make the heroine of Terence Rattigan's *The Deep, Blue Sea* so overwhelmingly moving, and mark out the plays of Jean Anouilh above all others in French twentieth century theatre.

Like Rattigan, Achard in *Jean de la lune* eschews fine writing, and by putting the whole force of his play behind them gives to phrases of extreme simplicity a power often, indeed nearly always, denied to exalted rhetoric. Jeff's meeting the plainest evidence of Marceline's unfaithfulness with the simple statement, staggering in its sincerity, 'Tu es la droiture même:' and his 'Je crois en toi, je crois en toi, je crois en toi,'[10] in the third act are examples of the capacity of the most elementary words to express an unforgettable devotion. Achard has not Rattigan's mastery of construction. Even so Jeff's proposal of marriage, in the presence of the man with whom she has acknowledged herself to be in love, is an astonishing *tour de force*. Achard never wrote anything else on the level of *Jean de la lune*, which remains one of the best plays of the century.

Copeau, Jouvet, and Dullin were actors: Gaston Baty, who with them in 1936 was called on to form the 'Cartel' to save the Comédie Française, was the only one of the four who might be said to justify the cheap jibe that a director is a man who cannot act himself, and therefore orders about those who can. Copeau believed in a theatre of texts, Jouvet with Giraudoux restored the supremacy of literature on the stage, and Dullin was always alert to the task of finding new dramatists. Each of them gave fine personal performances, especially Dullin and Jouvet, but Baty never appeared on the stage himself.

He did not invariably recognise the merit of the work which these men who were both his rivals and his confrères accomplished. Armand Salacrou records that on the day of the first performance of Giraudoux's *Amphitryon 38* in 1929 he had a bitter quarrel with his wife Lucienne. Salacrou's nerves were still quivering when he took his seat in the audience, and he saw the performance through a mist of sorrow and exhaustion. Nevertheless he was enchanted by its delicate handling of the ancient improper legend, and by its verbal grace, which he

---

10. You are rectitude itself. I believe in you, I believe in you, I believe in you.

24. Jean Giraudoux and Louis Jouvet at a rehearsal of *Electre* (1940).
    Photograph by courtesy of Lipnitzki-Viollet

found all the more pleasant because it was completely inhuman.
Baty saw the play in presumably a state of greater emotional
stability, but Salacrou says that he hated it. Salacrou however
never liked Baty.

Baty was born at Pélusan in the department of the Loire on
26 May 1885, and died in 1952. He was formed at the University
of Lyon by an education unusually rigorous for a man who was
to make his subsequent career in the theatre. Of all the theatrical figures of twentieth century France, with the possible excep-
tion of Samuel Beckett, he had by far the severest intellectual
training. In fact he acquired in his early manhood a culture
which Clément Borgal describes as truly prodigious.

It was a culture firmly established in religion. He was a mili-
tant Catholic all his life, and wished to create a theatre 'according

to Saint Thomas', a spectacle which would reflect absolute beauty. His religious faith gave him a conviction of total certainty. This led him to refuse all discussion of his views, an attitude that some people admired less than others. He was the most mystical of the great directors. Only he would have seen, in the figure of the Marseilles prostitute who is the central character in Simon Gantillon's *Maya*, a symbol of something above this mortal world which obscurely draws her clients to her from all parts of the globe; or in Emma Bovary in his 1937 adaptation of Flaubert's novel a representation of passion to be celebrated at her death by long-robed ladies dressed, like the heroine of *Maya*, in scarlet.

'We wish,' he said, 'to found a theatre on faith, enthusiasm, and deliberate poverty . . . If today there is a state of decadence in the theatre, the cause must be found in the advance made by rationalism and intellectualism—in a word, by literature—which began with the Renaissance, and has been particularly aggravated since the eighteenth century. Conclusion: to save the theatre, recover the spirit of its great ages, and get rid of literature.'[11] He was utterly opposed to the Reformation, and Cartesianism, and to the spirit of Jansenism in the Roman Church represented by Pascal and Port Royal. It was only with reluctance that he recognised Racine, the supreme exponent of the power of the rigidly controlled word, of order and regularity, as a great dramatist. To him Racine was a step on the road to the nineteenth century middle class unimaginative realism of Augier and Dumas *fils* which he despised. His abiding conviction was that a text should be capable of expansion by the director. Giraudoux's plays did not meet this requirement, nor did Racine's. All that was necessary in either case was to speak the lines properly. They called for neither illuminating setting, nor expressive gesture.

This did not mean that the text need be bad, ill-written, or intellectually contemptible. It did not mean that Baty wished to devote himself to poor plays: only to plays, good or bad, that admitted of directorial creativity. For instance, two days before the beginning of the First World War a young man of twenty-five had come into Paul Léautaud's office at the *Mercure de France* with a collection of stories about children. Léautaud refused them impatiently. There were too many stories about

---

11. BATY, Gaston: *Le rideau baissé*, Bordas, Paris, 1949.

children: everybody was writing them. The young man then said: 'Very well, what is one to write about?' This irritated Léautaud extremely. 'I told him straight,' he wrote in his *Journal* that night after he got home. 'Good God, sir, you write what is in you, not what happens to be fashionable.' 'That,' he went on, 'is what all young people are like nowadays: they write about topical things, or imitate a success. As for having something in themselves that simply has to get out, well said or badly said, that is not their style.' This young man's name was Simon Gantillon. 'We shall see,' said Léautaud not very hopefully, 'if anything comes of him.'

As a matter of fact, something did come of him. Nearly ten years later he became the author of *Maya*. This semi-mystical treatment of a prostitute, without as Gantillon himself stipulated, any 'dessous graveleux', as a symbol of men's desire for escape from the world of material reality, was written in several brief impressionistic scenes, showing the heroine in her sordid Marseilles home amongst other prostitutes meeting men brought to the Vieux Port by ships from all parts of the world.

These scenes are artificial, ill-written, and unconvincing: *Maya* is a very bad play. But it gave Baty great scope for saying things to the eye that the ear might have missed. At the beginning he dressed the heroine in deep red; as a religious man aware of the reality of sin, he appears to have been very susceptible to the implications of this particular colour, and to what its gradations might mean. So the redness of the heroine's costume diminished as the play proceeded. *Maya* is an example of the type of bad play which nevertheless lent itself to Baty's theory of theatre.

But there were good plays also. One of the most important of these, and amongst the least pretentious, was Jean-Jacques Bernard's *Martine*. Bernard was the direct antithesis of Giraudoux. With Giraudoux the words told everything: with Bernard they told practically nothing. Everything was in his silences, his pauses, and his gestures. Martine is a country girl who is dazzled by a young man who comes to her village for his vacation. Without any ill intention he bewitches her with the incomprehensible fascination of his city manners and his breeding. Gauche, silent, and understanding nothing of what he is saying, she listens adoring and entranced. It is in this mute and futureless affection that the heart-rending charm of *Martine* lies. Baty was well qualified to give it great power on the stage. It is quite wrong to think of him as a man who overwhelmed the theatre with scenery and spectacle.

Nevertheless he brought off many remarkable stage effects. Robert Brasillach, who found much to criticise in Baty's theory of the theatre, says that with the work of Simon Gantillon he did incomparable, incredible things. Never on the stage had Brasillach seen the wonder of the sunrise expressed with such magnificence, with such a joy of colours. He recalled in Gantillon's *Départs* a quay by the side of which slumbered a ship: I would not, he said, have believed such an evocation possible. The very scent of the sea, and the wind, filled the theatre. Amongst many marvels he remembered with particular emotion *Maya* and its shadows; the twisting staircase of Baty's own adaptation of *Crime and Punishment*; the heavy magic desert of H. R. Lenormand's *Le Simoun*; the leprous attics of *Le Beau Danube rouge*; the high, mounting streets in *Prosper*, bursting with sunshine, through which between the yellow houses there appeared in a rough jersey the marvellous, enrapturing, melancholy Marguerite Jamois. Baty was unrivalled in effects like these, but they were not essential to his work.

Baty would not have approved of the wave of irreligion that has engulfed the modern world. It is ironical to reflect that the dominance of the appeal to the eye in action and movement, the insistence that the voice is only one factor amongst several, which are evident in the modern theatre, should have derived through Gaston Baty from religious ritual. Describing the medieval Good Friday services he says that as the Gospel proceeded, the candles were one by one put out, until as Jesus uttered his despairing cry the last was extinguished, and the church was covered in darkness as the service ended.

This was Baty's idea of a perfect *mise en scène*: the reinforcement and illumination of the text by visual means. The rock on which he founded himself, or at least wished to found himself, was this: 'Every sacrament is composed of a formula which embodies its essence, and of an external rite that expresses this essence in another language, and gives it weight and emphasis.'

When in *Godspell*, in a supremely moving moment, the actors, who are dressed as clowns, rub off their make-up and throw aside their hats, suddenly awed and grave, as they begin the scene of the Last Supper, the modern theatre perfectly exemplifies the theory bequeathed to it by Gaston Baty. It is a scene that would have deeply moved him. There is in his famous essay on the theatre's historical development, *Le Masque et l'Encensoir*, a passage of considerable eloquence, in which he says that in the preceding generation the theatre touched the bottom of the abyss, and had now begun to ascend the other side.

> But it would be vain for us to hope to reach the summits. In the night of ages the moments of perfect beauty shine at immense distances from each other, like the stars which were nevertheless sufficient to show the pilgrim the road to St. James (of Compostella), and to ensure him that he had not lost his way . . . Let us give our life to work that is imperfect and necessary, in the hope of that perfect work which we shall never see, but that others, should it please God, will realise after us, thanks to us, and of which we are content that they should have all the glory.[12]

The same humility is not apparent in the foreword he wrote to this book, in which he claims that two million people had in the course of the years come to his theatre in Montparnasse. But this fact affords him no pleasure. The great men of the first half of the century, the men who rejuvenated the French theatre, and at one time seemed likely to save even the Comédie Française, finished their lives in disillusion and sadness. In 1949 Baty wrote that 'a life devoted to the theatre can be nothing but a great love disappointed,' and turned from a theatre of actors and actresses to a theatre of marionettes. Jouvet, despite the huge success of his production in 1945 of Giraudoux's posthumous *La Folle de Chaillot* (in which the now aged Marguerite Moreno, who forty years earlier had provoked teasing doubts in the nervous young Paul Léautaud, achieved a legendary triumph), finished his career in gloom and misgiving. He was tired by his years of wandering during the German Occupation of France: depressed by the deaths of Giraudoux and his magical designer, Christian Bérard: and suffered a bitter sentimental disappointment over a young actress he had fallen in love with: he ended his life aloof, secretive, and silent.

So did Charles Dullin, but for a very different reason. He desired what Jouvet abundantly got: the approval of the Paris critics. The adhesion of the public was for him no substitute for a kind word from Lucien Dubech, or Robert Kemp, or indeed Robert Brasillach. Dullin's swansong was *King Lear* at the Sarah

---

12.   BATY, Gaston: Op. cit.

Bernhardt during the 1944-45 season. It is thus that Jean-Jacques Bernard remembered him most poignantly: Dullin grown old. His Lear was derided by the critics, though in this character, wounded and already angered by life, he surpassed himself. He was incurably sad, thinking of the critics. 'They haven't understood me. They never will.' The public, says Bernard, was overwhelmed, and applauded endlessly. But Dullin was inconsolable.

If Giraudoux is generally accounted the most important dramatist revealed by the great directors of the 1920s, the second place should probably be accorded to Armand Salacrou. Jouvet discovered Giraudoux, and he had the opportunity of discovering Salacrou, as he had the opportunity of discovering Anouilh. But as the most successful both with critics and public of the leading directors, he had less incentive than the others to find new authors, and, though he was interested in Salacrou's work from the beginning, he let this ambitious and forceful young writer slip through his fingers. If Jouvet noticed Salacrou's work, it was Charles Dullin who took the risk, with *Patchouli* in 1930, of putting it on the stage.

As a poor boy in Le Havre Salacrou decided that one day he would own the biggest house in the town. This ambition he achieved in 1974, when after living for thirty-five years in a palatial apartment in the Avenue Foch, he and his wife left Paris to return to his birthplace. He was also determined to be as great a dramatist as Shakespeare. Perhaps he has been less successful in this ambition than in the other.

Salacrou came up to Paris in the 1920s, when he lived a life of turbulence and passion in striking, indeed in irreconcilable, contrast with the good-humoured, tolerant, and cool temper in which, in the notes to his published plays, he discusses their often stormy reception. It is in these notes that he shows himself at his most engaging: zealous for his reputation, but generous and friendly in his estimate of those who passed unfavourable judgment upon him.

The hero of *Patchouli* is a young student preoccupied with the great love which had led an archduke at the end of the last century to shoot himself because his passion was not returned. Patchouli meets the girl the duke had been in love with, and is horrified and desolated by the frivolity with which she treats the memory of so great an affection.

Patchouli is very interesting technically. It does not tell a story, but is a study of love disillusioned, shown first in the meeting with the girl, now a very old but remarkably unfeeling and sprightly lady: then in a low café, and finally in a third-rate cinema studio. Its originality, its contempt for narrative form, its neglect of a tightly constructed plot, would, despite the grace and charm of its style, have condemned it anyway with an audience accustomed to well-made plays. But whatever chances it may have had, slender as they may have been, were destroyed by the mishaps of the opening performance. The c 'rtain at the end of the second act stuck, and was ironically applauded by the audience; in the third act, when the attractive actress, Tania Balachova, sat down, saying something disastrous was bound to happen, her chair broke, she crashed to the ground, and her legs flew up in the air. Its run lasted for only thirty performances, and in the last fifteen of them Dullin himself did not appear.

It is easy now to see that *Patchouli* was a major work in the development of the modern drama. Its bad reception was due solely to the fact that its audience, and most of the Parisian critics, were unable to make the adjustment from what the theatre had been before Salacrou to what he was to assist in making it become. The influential, and by no means ill-disposed, critic, Edmond Sée, had appreciated the first act of Achard's *Jean de la lune* on its production a few months before *Patchouli*, because its tenderness was shown through a plain, straightforward story of a man proposing marriage to a flighty girl who thought herself in love with someone else. This story followed a logical, reasonable, realistic course. But he objected to the third act, which shows Marceline suddenly and immediately transformed in character by the strength of the hero's confidence in her. This was not realistic: according to Sée, the transformation should have taken time, and developed slowly.

Sée criticised *Patchouli* from the same point of view. He admitted that there were some good scenes in it, particularly one in the first act in which Patchouli meets and is turned to desperation by the insensitive conversation of the aged beauty of the Second Empire. That is because up to this point *Patchouli* is following the rules of ordinary realism. But when in the second act Patchouli's grieved mother pursues him to his wretched *bistro*, and the door opens and his middle-aged father with a troupe of prostitutes bursts in on them from the street, the coincidence is altogether too much for Sée's powers of credulity.

It was also too much for the audience, who ended the act in disorder, with Dullin tearing at his hair in his distress: Salacrou watched the drops of sweat pouring down his cheeks as if they were tears. That night, Salacrou said later, the audience refused all cooperation with the play. They looked at it as they would have looked at a drunkard in the gutter. Giraudoux said that he listened to the piece with emotion, but the majority of critics *en titre* agreed with the public, and before long even Dullin lost faith in it, and abandoned his part of Patchouli's father, which Jouvet said was the finest of his career, to an understudy. 'M. Armand Salacrou's new play,' said Pierre Brisson in *Le Temps*, 'certainly rings false.' 'I will not tell you the story of *Patchouli*, you would think I was making a fool of you,' said another admired critic, Paul Reboux, in *Paris-Soir*. 'M. Salacrou's play seems to me detestable,' wrote Louis Leloy in *L'Ere nouvelle*. 'Better not talk of it any more,' said Edmond Sée in *L'Oeuvre*.

Patchouli, like the last act of *Jean de la lune*, was condemned on the ground that it was not realistic. One of the most important plays of the century, it was met, on the part of the public and the official critics, with the same unadventurous incomprehension that twenty or thirty years later greeted *Waiting for Godot* and *The Birthday Party*. It was not realistic, and therefore, because realism was the order of the day, it was wrong.

It does not seem to have occurred to anybody that it was intended to be, not realistic, but lyrical. It was not the story of a young man who deserted historical and biographical studies in order to go to the bad: it was a cry of distress that love should be corrupted: perhaps not even corrupted, but corrupt. It is strange that this theme of the destruction, or perhaps the non-existence, of innocence, should also be the mainspring of the work of Jean Anouilh, a man with whom Salacrou has always appeared to me to have little in common.

Salacrou wrote *Patchouli* at a time of extreme emotional disturbance. On the one hand he was showing great commercial, as well as artistic, acumen by buying Braques and Picassos at derisory prices. He was also devising advertising slogans for the Marie-Rose liquid for killing lice which had been invented by his father. It was thus that his feet were set, as happens often to people of extreme Left wing views, on the road to immense wealth. But emotionally all was far from well. He had married young a girl from Le Havre, Lucienne. She was of better family than he, but she seems to have adapted herself competently and good-humouredly enough to his then difficult circumstances. There were many cheap but more or less happy evenings spent entertaining, or being entertained by, Marcel and Juliette Achard: Lucienne and he were also much in the company of Steve Passeur and his wife. Passeur was shortly, with a play called *L'Acheteuse*, to have a success surpassing in financial terms anything that Achard or Salacrou was to achieve for many years.

But beneath this apparently calm and conventional surface, Salacrou was fermenting with passion and discontent, which sometimes broke out in a decidedly alarming way. Lucienne and he had agreed that they would have no children. One excited night, when she became *enceinte*, he knocked her down in the street because she was wearing high-heeled shoes. He became infatuated with another girl, and forced his wife into the humiliation of inviting her to dinner. He spent the entire night that Lindbergh landed at Le Bourget roaming the streets searching for this girl, shouting her name as if he had gone out of his mind. He did not find her, and has never seen her since. It is not surprising that Lucienne tried to commit suicide by drinking a bottle of iodine. Salacrou saved her life by making her drink so many litres of milk that she vomited. It is out of states of mind like these that drama makes its great advances.

The tumult in Salacrou's life and in his mind was continued throughout the 1930s, producing theatrical consequences of outstanding importance. He wrote during these years plays which, like *Un Homme comme les autres* (1936: Théâtre de l'Oeuvre, with Jacques Dumesnil in the chief role, and the young Jean-Louis Barrault in a minor but important part) and *Histoire de rire* (1939: Théâtre de la Madeleine: Alice Cocéa, André Luguet, Fernand Gravey, and Pierre Renoir), were as concerned with private relationships as *Patchouli* had been. But he began to show an uneasiness of conscience, a desire for self-justification seen in the very title of *Un Homme comme les autres*, and a questioning of the moral bases of existence which emphasise the originality of *Patchouli* with a new significance and importance. In this play Salacrou shows a man who is loved by his wife, but who wishes to be loved by her knowing exactly what sort of man, reckless and unfaithful, he is. This leads to a confession scene of probing power, ending in the wife's disillusioned words to her husband, 'Don't you understand that to forgive only means to accept going on suffering?'

Lucien Dubech, who greatly admired Salacrou, whilst critics like Robert Kemp and Gérard Bauer continued to underrate him, declared that there is a resonance in Salacrou's writing which echoes in us more profoundly than does the work of any other writer. 'No one is his equal in finding the unexpected word that overwhelms and illumines.' There is a great deal of truth in this, though it must be remembered that the most important plays of Jean Anouilh had not yet been written.

There is in Anouilh a greater intensity than in Salacrou: a wilder grief, a deeper pain, a more bitter rebellion. Where Salacrou finds his greatest importance is in his philosophic questioning. 'He is haunted,' said Dubech, 'by a single thought: the density of a humanity which does not believe in God.' In *Un Homme comme les autres* an old woman is reproached with drinking rum. 'You have taken God away from me,' she says: 'what will remain if you take away rum as well?' This is one of the high points of Salacrou's art; and Dubech was right in saying that if Salacrou could more often make his characters reveal themselves by their actions and the poignancy of their instinctive expressions of disarray and sorrow instead of by lucid and theatrically inventive analysis, he would rank with the very greatest dramatic authors.

This poignancy he attains in an almost unexampled degree in his autobiography, *Dans la salle des pas perdus—c'était écrit*, which will take its place amongst the saddest, greatest, frankest, and most moving revelations of what the human heart can suffer, and what suffering it can inflict on others. The summer of 1939, so terrible in its public anxieties, which Salacrou fully shared, was also for him personally and for his wife a time of desperate anguish. On the evening of Wednesday, 9 August, his fortieth birthday, Lucienne wrote to him a letter of extreme pathos. 'Dear Armand,' it began,

> my very dear Armand, I have wanted to write to you a long time, . . . without really knowing whether I shall be able to disentangle all my thoughts, to see clearly, and to make you see clearly . . . I have lost all confidence in myself, and when I am with you I wonder whether you would not be happier with someone else. You destroy all that, for a few moments, there is to be proud of in my life . . . The sole justification of my life is to have met you, and to have loved you. I shall have created nothing, but it seems to me that I may have

helped you to create. This thought gives me comfort, as you say, and when you reproach me it is as if you flung me back into that void, that uselessness, of which I am afraid.

You will think that I am talking very much about myself. But, my dear, to talk to you about myself is to talk of you. I cannot think of life without you; you are my only friend. During the days of distress through which I have just passed, remember that it was my only friend who made me suffer, that I had none, no one, and that I was alone in the world, and that, to add to all this, I thought: 'How he must be suffering, that he should torture me like this.'[13]

That same evening Salacrou himself wrote in his diary the following words:

I am in utter misery. I am married to an admirable woman; and after being close to her for seventeen years I no longer find that emotion of love the exaltation of which I caught a glimpse of in the last few months by the side of another for whom I have no respect . . . I lunched today with Raymond Bernard, Anouilh and his charming wife, and the Tristan Bernards. It was a painful luncheon; Tristan and his wife are both deaf, and talk without stopping, simultaneously, of different things.

A few days later the war broke out, and Salacrou wrote:

I met Steve Passeur. He is liable to military service. So am I. Salacrou: 'And Achard?'
Steve: 'Achard? No. He has fourteen dioptrics and is hump-backed. He will stay behind and write plays brimming with heroism.' (What is astonishing is that Steve's jealousy of Achard gives him such a precise memory of Achard's infirmities.)

It was out of this period of hopeless distress, both public and private, that Salacrou wrote one of the most remarkable of his plays. With the shame and agony of unfaithfulness tearing at him he completed *Histoire de rire* in the summer of 1939. In form *Histoire de rire*, with its ironic title, for there is nothing to laugh at or to deride in the theme of the play, is merely a boulevard

---

13.   SALACROU, Armand: *Dans la salle des pas perdus,—c'était écrit*, NRF Gallimard, Paris.

sex comedy in the then fashionable three acts. But in content it is deadly serious. It was into the least creditable of theatrical bottles that Salacrou poured the bitter wine of his self-disgust and the desolation of his want of faith.

When war actually broke out, Salacrou debated with himself whether to allow the play to be performed at the Comédie Française, where he feared the reception it might receive from the first night audience. Eventually it was presented on the boulevard at the Théâtre de la Madeleine on 22 December 1939. In the first act infidelity is treated entirely frivolously. Gérard Barbier, aged thirty-one (Salacrou is meticulous about ages), played by André Luguet, formerly of the Comédie Française himself, is delighted to hear that his great friend Jean-Louis Deshayes (two years younger) played by Fernand Gravey —their friendship, given the development of modern suspicions, is insisted on with rather embarrassing innocence—is about to run off with a married woman, Hélène Donaldo, aged twenty-six. Salacrou shows him somewhat authoritarian and dictatorial. He adopts an attitude of light-hearted raillery to the situation; it fills him with a prurient enjoyment. He argues that it is preposterous to expect a woman to remain with a husband with whom she is no longer in love. But his cynicism and strength collapse into gloom and a sense of outrage as soon as he learns that his own wife Adéliade, aged twenty-four, (Alice Cocéa) is determined to leave him for a young lover Achille Bellorson, aged twenty-three (Jean Mercanton).

In the second act the mood of the play changes from the vaudeville gaiety of the first, which is very witty, to bitterness and disillusion. Salacrou had spent three days of a rainy July in Deauville, more or less with a woman called Jysette in order to forget another called Line. Perhaps he had not enjoyed himself very much. At any rate Hélène and Jean-Louis quickly tend to get on each other's nerves. Their infidelity, which had begun so joyously, soon turns to bickering and boredom.

They have taken Gérard away to the seaside to cheer him up, and he proves, as they might have forseen, a companion little caculated to add to the happiness of nations. He refuses to be comforted. He is wholly self-centred, and sees his own misfortunes as the only things that matter in the world, either to himself or anyone else. He ludicrously exaggerates his misery, but what he exaggerates is perfectly real. 'I am not sad. I have merely discovered, as millions and millions of men have discovered before me, that we are much more miserable in our misery than we are happy in our happiness. On earth, hell is far more efficient than Paradise. On earth, Paradise seems to be run by well-meaning old women, and hell by young people, people full of activity and enthusiasm, and who are not without subtlety.' This is a very unusual speech to be encountered in an apparently boulevard, drawing room, French-windowed light comedy, played in a boulevard theatre by a boulevard cast.

But a more remarkable speech still was to come a little later. Salacrou introduces into the seaside hotel Jules Donaldo, aged forty-six, Hélène's supposedly unfortunate husband. This Jules Donaldo is a most formidable character: in fact he is probably the coolest, the most intellectually distinguished character in Salacrou's whole work. He is as little disconcerted by his ridiculous situation as Mazaud's Dardamelle had been. But instead of treating it with a controlled buffoonery, and gaining the upper hand by the inner joy of his high spirits, he establishes mastery by the imperturbability of his presence, his seriousness, his philosophy. It astonishes Gérard, who has been howling like a lost dog, that Jules should take his wife's infidelity so calmly. He breaks out into incredulous questioning in a passage which is one of the key scenes in contemporary theatre.

> GERARD. If I understand what you are saying, you are not revolted by your wife's behaviour? You regard her conduct as almost normal?
> JULES. Normal? I am twenty years older than my wife: do you call that normal? Now if of course I were a romantic poet, or perhaps a great explorer, or something else like that: glamorous, idealistic, starlike, well, but I am only a contractor!
> GERARD. And because you are only a contractor, you accept lies and betrayals?
> JULES. You are using old-fashioned words to describe a new situation. It is by doing just that sort of thing in the Board Room that great companies are brought into bankruptcy. You talk about betrayal. You can't betray what doesn't any longer exist. It's only in days long gone by that men married in order to found a family, that they married their wives for eternity! Today, my dear fellow, our wives are not religious any more. And whose fault is it? Do we ourselves go to mass? Of course we don't. Well? The single

scrap of morality that remains is love. And love is the most uncertain word, the most ineffectively defined, the vaguest in the human vocabulary. On one occasion or another, and sometimes on the very same day, it expresses feelings that are different, and even flatly contradictory to each other. Have you tried to explain to your wife in the name of what morality it is her duty to love you for always, and nothing but you? and nobody else? and for what reason?

GERARD. But . . .

JULES. For the simple reason that that happens to be agreeable to us?

This speech asserts what it appears to deny. Saying that Christianity no longer exists, it declares it to be necessary to happiness and decent behaviour. It is in this respect that its importance in the history of the modern French drama lies. But the main religious French dramatist of the century is Paul Claudel (1868–1955), and the famous religious dramas, which burn with the devouring fire of an inexorable Catholicism in sharp and to many people distasteful contrast to the tolerant cynicism of Salacrou's Jules Donaldo, are *L'Otage* and *Partage de midi*. *L'Otage* had been presented many years before *Histoire de rire*. In translation it was seen at the Scala Theatre in London in 1919, when Sybil Thorndike is said to have given a remarkable performance as Synge du Coûfontaine. *Partage de midi* did not reach the stage until the late 1940s, when it was produced with profound understanding by Jean-Louis Barrault. Barrault is the only director who has ever been able to control the difficult rhythm of Claudel's poetry. He brought *Partage de midi* to the St. James's Theatre in 1951, in a season arranged by Laurence Olivier that was the precursor of the brilliant World Theatre seasons of Peter Daubeny.

A play by Salacrou about the 1939-45 war—*Les Nuits de la colère*—was included in the Olivier season, which marked another cardinal point in the history of post-war drama. It cannot be too strongly stressed that Olivier is the man who opened the eyes of the English-speaking world to the great outburst of French theatrical genius that followed the end of the war. This season was in fact a stupendous achievement in the career of a man whose life has been full of stupendous achievements. It

---

14. SALACROU, Armand: *Historie de rire*, NRF Gallimard, Paris.

introduced to us the entrancing personality, the illimitable creative enthusiasm of Jean-Louis Barrault, and the subtle, capti-
vating art of his wife, Madeleine Renaud. It would also have
introduced to us Jean Vilar, in André Gide's *Oedipus*, had not
Vilar been called back to Paris in the course of the season to
give new life to the Théâtre National Populaire. But what made
it so supremely memorable was that it brought to England for
the first time the greatest of all actresses that I have seen—
Edwige Feuillère's sensuous smile, the caressing music of her
incomparable voice, her pealing laughter, and the supple grace
of her body as she lay languorously back in a chair on the deck
of a yacht blazing in the white light of a tropical midday sun
made on me an impression that has never been either effaced or
equalled. It was like seeing a goddess for the first time; it was
like first opening Chapman's Homer.

Partage de midi, in its more thunderous, threatening way, is
like *Histoire de rire* in that it is a denunciation of adultery, and an
oblique assertion of Christianity. It goes further than *Histoire de
rire*, because in an apocalyptic last scene, after the damnation of
Madame Feuillère's adulterous and tempting Ysé has been
accomplished, and Barrault's Mesa has committed the crime
that David committed in putting Uriah the Hittite in the mur-
derous front of the battle, it makes a positive statement of
Christianity: as Mesa dies on a stage dark but for the glittering
fires of the stars, his priggish heart is burst open with the
realisation of the immensity of the love of Christ. This scene, a
very long and difficult monologue, was delivered by Barrault
with an intensity that cut like a sword. This was a season of
great acting. Of the three greatest actresses I have seen, two
appeared in it: Feuillère and Madeleine Renaud. The third,
Peggy Ashcroft, has never attempted the part of Ysé.

Although *Partage de midi* was not actually produced until
several years after *Histoire de rire*, Claudel had written it in the
first decade of the century. Jules's speech becomes therefore the
last straightforward assertion of the Christian faith in modern
French drama. I say 'straightforward', because there is the
extraordinary phenomenon of François Billetdoux, whose
methods of establishing Christianity in *Tchin-Tchin* are so ruthlessly unexpected that most audiences take them to be blas-
phemous.

It does not seem however that religion has brought to Salacrou the sardonic serenity that it brought to Jules Donaldo.

25. *Histoire de Rire* by Armand Salacrou with Pierre Dux, Jacques Clancy, Marie Dälmas, Yves Robert (Théâtre St.-Georges 1955). Photograph by courtesy of Lipnitzki-Viollet

Donaldo had made his terms with the conditions of life. When I knew Salacrou in the fifties, gaily opening a bottle of champagne in the sumptuous Socialism of his apartment in the sixteenth arrondissement, or excitedly trying to recall some youthful years he had spent in England during the First World War by eating steak and kidney pie at the Caprice restaurant in London, or exclaiming with rapture '*Sensationnel*' as he waved a favourable review of his latest play in the air, still determined to be as great a dramatist as Shakespeare, Salacrou seemed to have done so too. To anyone who visited Henry de Montherlant, the dramatist of grandeur and royal splendour, in his bleak room on the Left Bank, furnished only with the cold glares of the busts of Roman emperors set on chilling pedestals, it came as little surprise when in the end he severed with his own hand his connection with this world. But Salacrou in the fifties was immune from care, revelling confidently in a certainty of enduring fame.

Twenty years later all that happiness had gone. In 1974 he could endure Paris no longer. As with Baty and Jouvet the theatre turned to bitterness in his mouth. In his great house in Le Havre, watching the ships in the estuary, he now sits gloomily brooding. He wonders whether after all in the twenties he did not make a mistake when, seeing the Chaplins and the Max Linders and the Buster Keatons, he thought them only a diversion. Are they not, he despondently reflects, the real art of the century, whilst the theatre, which he so exuberantly preferred, is merely a sham? Now not even an attractive sham. He could no longer endure to sit through a *générale*; half way through, utterly bored, he would wander off to some bistro and dispiritedly swallow a Calvados until it was all over.

A book has been published in England which is a conspectus of recent French drama. Salacrou notes that only two very early pieces of his are included in it: nothing from *Atlas Hotel* or from *La Terre est ronde*, his mature work. This dispirits him still further. He asks himself in misery whether he has not failed in his work. After writing some of the most memorable passages to be found in French drama in one of its greatest periods Salacrou was overcome from the beginning of the seventies by that darkness and gloom which has enveloped in the end so many outstanding figures in the modern Paris theatre. Yet one would have thought that his reasons for confidence and satisfaction were very considerable. For his work will certainly live in the history of modern French drama.

Salacrou's *Histoire de rire* was produced in a boulevard theatre, and played by boulevard actors, though one of them, André Luguet, had been a sociétaire of the Comédie Française in the days before it had been reformed by the administration of Edouard Bourdet, and the renovation of its *mise en scène* by the Cartel. It was also preoccupied, like the vast majority of boulevard plays, with sex. What distinguished it from these plays was not its subject, nor its wit, but the *gravitas* that underlay them. In a way it was concerned, like any typical boulevard entertainment, with who gets into bed with whom. But unlike them it treats this as a serious, not as a frivolous, matter. The distinction between the boulevard and the avant garde theatre is not one of subject so much as of treatment. It is not the thing looked at that matters, but the manner of its being looked at. This remains true all through the 1930s.

Whilst Jouvet, Baty, Dullin, and Copeau brought the avant garde theatre into the forefront of the modern consciousness, the glittering, fashionable boulevard theatre, designed only to titillate and amuse, produced hundreds of light comedies for the diversion of *le tout Paris* and of its midinettes. These comedies reached a high degree of technical competence, but, threatened on the one hand by the overwhelming competition of talking films, and on the other by the intelligence and brilliance of the productions of the men who in 1936 joined together to form the Cartel, they no longer dominated the theatre as they had done in the halcyon days of Bataille, Bernstein, and Sacha Guitry. Bataille had died, but his plays, such as *La Vierge folle*, with Yvonne de Bray in the part formerly played by Réjane, were revived from time to time. Bernstein and Guitry continued to write, but Guitry especially, according to Pierre Brisson (not a particularly reliable judge), had lost much of his youthful skill.

The plays that occupied the commercial stage between the wars were frivolous, sexy, witty, salacious, amiable, daring, but in the end afraid. Salacrou's attitude to infidelity remains unchanged throughout *Histoire de rire*, but the boulevard drama invariably changed its moral stance a few minutes before the fall of the curtain. They then embraced and endorsed the conventional principles they had been engaged in deriding all through the evening. However far they ventured into the territory of the forbidden at ten o'clock, they were always back in the safe land of middle class morality by eleven forty-five.

A typical example of this last-moment forsaking of provocative

gesture for a quick scurry back into respectability is *Avril*
(Variétés; 1922) by Louis Verneuil and Georges Berr. Philippe
Memeray, charming, still seductive at what the authors apparently regarded as the advanced age of thirty-nine, becomes, for
purely financial reasons, the husband of his own illegitimate
daughter. But he is resolved to respect her virginity, and at a
suitable moment, to seek divorce, and let her make her life
anew. Things of course do not work out like that. Philippe falls
into incest, and awakens overcome with horror, thinking that,
like a tragic hero, he ought to behave as one pursued by remorse: while his innocent little wife is thrown into transports of
joy by the revelation, and is ready to continue happily with
married life.

Faced with a situation like this a dramatist such as Salacrou
or Anouilh would inquire into the emotional condition that
finds excitement and gratification in incest. But naturally Verneuil and Berr do nothing of the kind. Before the play ends it is
discovered that Philippe is not the father after all, and the two
lovers are free to continue their felicity without sin. What makes
the boulevard play is not its daring, but its ability to create
situations in which at the final moment it shows that it has no
daring at all. If *Avril* were the work of an avant garde author
the wife would lose all her love for the husband, once the thrill
of incest was removed.

A great change was coming over the theatre in the 1930s.
Even though these years saw Salacrou establish his reputation
and Jean Anouilh emerge from the shadows, authors were
beginning less and less to dominate the stage; the drama was
giving place to theatre. The critics of the first quarter of the
century gave nearly all their attention to the written work.
Their principal preoccupation was to detail its plot, and then to
subject it to moral scrutiny. But in the thirties younger men,
like Robert Brasillach, found that their imagination was stirred,
not by words in a script, an argument, or a story, but by the
fugitive intonation of an actor's voice, by the passing illumination of a shaft of light on a fragile set. Louis Jouvet addressing
the dead in *La Guerre de Troie n'aura pas lieu*: Georges Pitoëff in
Le Canard sauvage: the wonder of the light on the stairs of Algiers
in Baty's production of Lucienne Favre's *Prosper* (1934): the in-
describable and unimaginable thing that Valentine Tessier was
in the last act of *Siegfried*, and Pierre Renoir's phantom voice in
the same scene: the collapsing face of Ludmilla Pitoëff, shining

with tears and stammering, or her drunken dance of despair, in
La Maison de poupée, or the same actress, light, aerian, fluttering
across the stage 'like a bird whose grace astonishes us': Marguerite Jamois's extraordinary performance in Baty's production of H. R. Lenormand's *Les Ratés*, overcome by life, passion,
and unhappiness but carrying through all a sort of instinctive
nobility, a royal allure, in her long supple body and her pure
voice: bringing all her charm, all her melancholy to Emma
Bovary in Baty's adaptation of Flaubert's novel; these are the
things that impressed Brasillach in the French theatre in the
decade before the war. The new plays of the period seem to
have left him unmoved, even, in fact, uninterested.

It is not that Brasillach was indifferent to the written word,
at any rate when that word had been written in the past. There
was Corneille's pretty conceit about the sun's arrangements for
getting up being upset one morning because the Dawn could
not be found to help him:

> Le soleil fut un jour sans pouvoir de se lever,
> Et ce visible dieu que tant de monde adore,
> Pour marcher devant lui ne trouvait point d'Aurore:
> On la cherchait partout, au lit de vieux Tithon,
> Dans les bois de Céphale, au palais de Memnon,
> Et faute de trouver cette belle fourrière,
> Le jour jusqu'à midi se passa sans lumière.[15]

Brasillach was entranced by these verses in Jouvet's production
of *L'Illusion comique*, even when spoken by the artists of the
Comédie Française, whom he called 'the worst actors in Paris',[16]
especially naming two whom he thought to be quite particularly incompetent, the comparative veteran Dorival, and a
newcomer, Clariond, who seemed to Brasillach to be a carica-
ture of all the faults of the past.

Salacrou himself had noted, years before Brasillach, and
regretted, that actors were beginning to be more important to
the public than the plays they appeared in, even if these plays
were amongst the world's supreme masterpieces. As a young
student he saw Sarah Bernhardt, in her great theatre near the
Châtelet, now the Théâtre de la Ville, play Racine's *Athalie* for

---

15. Dawn was searched for everywhere, but could not be found, so there
     was darkness till midday.

16. BRASILLACH, Robert: *Animateurs de théâtre*, La Table Ronde, 1954.

the last time. She was then old, and one of her legs had been amputated. When she came to the princess Athalie's narration of her famous dream about her mother Jezebel, the same Jezebel who was torn to pieces by dogs, she turned to the audience, and declaimed

> Même elle avait encor cet éclat emprunté
> Dont elle eut soin de peindre et d'orner son visage
> Pour réparer des ans l'irréparable outrage.[17]

There was a thunder of applause. The public had excuses, Salacrou admits: but they were watching the personal tragedy of a great actress at the end of her life. They were not sharing in the tragedy of *Athalie.*

Brasillach criticises the Comédie Française even after the appointment of the Cartel in 1936, when Edouard Bourdet was made Administrator, with Jouvet, Copeau, Baty, and Dullin as *metteurs en scène.* But before that date its condition had been deplorable. Yet it was not without some very fine players. Madeleine Renaud, Marie Bell, and Mary Marquet were elected sociétaires in 1928. (It was Mary Marquet, following Yvonne de Bray, who delivered the concluding speech in *Pour Lucrèce,* entering the play at the last moment like a whirlwind.) But there was great disunion in the company. Béatrice Bretty, who had been a pensionnaire since half way through the 1914–18 war, did not become a sociétaire until 1929. The year before she had been put back in favour of Marie Bell and Madeleine Renaud, which she admitted was fair. But she resented the election of Mary Marquet, who was a more recent member of the company than herself, and in Bretty's opinion no better an actress. But every one knew, said Madame Bretty, that Marquet had a friend at court.

This discontent and jealousy amongst the players resulted in a great deal of irregular behaviour. Players made all kinds of excuses when they wanted to take a day off on which they had been billed to appear. On 17 February 1927, Mlle Fontenay announced that she was too ill to play Madame Lepic in *Poil de carotte.* On 8 January 1929 André Luguet, due to appear as the Marquis de Presles in *Le Gendre de M. Poirier,* did not turn up

---

17   In this powerful and angry verse Athalie says that her mother, Jezebel, was still powdered and rouged, as she had to repair the irreparable outrage of the passing years.

for the performance. Two days later Berthe Cerny did not play
because her mother had died. In the same month Brunot was
ill. On 1 February, Dessonnes was taken suddenly ill during a
performance of *Sapho*. On the fourteenth Denis d'Inès was ill.
On the twenty-eighth he was ill again. On 18 March Montreaux
had to be replaced by Marchat. Donneaud was ill on 8 May,
and Renaud on 13 June.

But the biggest rows concerned Mary Marquet. On 10
February 1931 Mary Marquet told the theatre as late as
six o'clock that she would not be able to appear that evening.
As the curtain rose it was announced that 'Mlle M. Marquet,
our comrade, being unwell, Mlle Ventura has agreed to read
the part in ordinary clothes.' The actor making the announce-
ment could not proceed, because of the uproar that broke out.
The house was angry that Marquet had no understudy. There
were cries of scandal, and much whistling. The curtain was
brought down, and when it went up again the tumult continued
until one of the actors offered another performance free.

Mary Marquet was little troubled by such demonstrations,
for she was of an extraordinarily imperious disposition. She
would ring up complete strangers in the middle of the night,
and tell them to take a message immediately to one of her
colleagues who lived in the same building, but was not on the
telephone. The remarkable thing is that, even at two o'clock in
the morning, they would actually do what she told them. But
others were disturbed by the internal quarrels of the company,
and their own disagreements. Sylvain and Maurice de Féraudy,
who disputed the title of doyen, had once been friends, but at
this time were not on speaking terms. An acquaintance of both
of them remarked that formerly they had been very close. 'As
close as arse and shirt,' said Féraudy, adding bitterly, 'and I
was the shirt.'

Moreover the very constitution of the Comédie Française
breeds suspicion and jealousy. Its sociétaires constantly expect
to be stabbed in the back by their colleagues. Every year there
is a committee meeting of sociétaires. Each sociétaire leaves the
room in turn, from the doyen to the one who has been most
recently elected. Whilst he or she is out of the room, the rest
vote on whether the absent player is to be put into retirement,
or to remain for another year. In such circumstances a high
degree of nervous tension is inevitable. Nor were matters
improved by the fact that in real terms the remuneration of a

sociétaire in the thirties was less than it had been in 1900, and
went on diminishing until it became only a sixth part of what
it had been fifty years earlier. Madeleine Renaud, Marie Bell,
Berthe Bovy, Marie Ventura, André Brunot, René Alexandre,
Denis d'Inès, and of course Mary Marquet, received the top
salary of 72,000 francs annually. But Pierre Bertin had only
48,000 francs, and Pierre Dux 39,000. The belligerent Béatrice
Bretty, whose famous pealing laugh in petit bourgeois parts
belied the fierceness of her ambition and the determination of
her character, received 54,000 francs.

The most talented players in the company were deeply dis-
contented with their rates of pay, especially as the invention of
the talkies opened up vast visions of wealth. The Comédie's
feelings of uncertainty and temptation were encapsulated in an
incident connected with the Gala performance of a fantasy
ballet, *Cavalerie*, on 19 November 1932. The choreography of
this ballet was by Serge Lifar, and it was danced by Madeleine
Renaud, Berthe Bovy, Marie Bell, Mary Morgan, and a newcomer to the company, a young pensionnaire named Edwige
Feuillère. A rehearsal left one member of the Comédie's official
staff with an excited memory of Edwige Feuillère, wearing, as
he said twenty years later, little either above or below, sending
a troubled sexual thrill along the row of stalls in which he was
sitting. He mentioned his *ravissement* to Charles Granval, one of
the most respected actors in the company, who directed many
plays with talent, and was Madeleine Renaud's first husband.
Granval replied: 'That is someone who will not long ripen here.'
He prophesied truly. Soon afterwards Granval himself, weary
of playing too rarely, left the company. But not before Feuillère,
who went, said her manager, to earn on the films in three
days as much as she would get in ten years at the Comédie
Française.

The thundering success of Marie Bell in the film *La Nuit est à
nous* was an ominous blow to the Comédie Française, which the
public began to desert in ever-increasing numbers. Nevertheless the National Theatre continued to have occasional successes, Charles Vildrac's *La Brouille* being prominent amongst
them. Béatrice Bretty was enthusiastic about this quiet domestic
play about a disturbed family friendship, and wrote: 'I created
a ravishing part in *La Brouille*, a play of rare quality, like everything done by Charles Vildrac. The success of the *générale* was
magnificent, unqualified, and the criticisms such that, not only

was my sociétariat justified, but from that day my career passed to a different level.'[18]

Here Madame Bretty exaggerates. *La Brouille* has not the simple tenderness and innocence of *Le Paquebot Tenacity*. It is a rather confused play, and its naturalistic technique, compared with Salacrou's *Patchouli*, or with the symbolic threat and daring of Roger Vitrac's *Victor, ou Les Enfants au pouvoir* (directed by Antonin Artaud, Comédie des Champs Elysées, Christmas Eve, 1928) gives it an old-fashioned air. Nor did Bretty's career take the leap forward that she here suggests. She remained to the very end of her career at the Comédie Française a soubrette, with a jolly, buxom appearance, and an incomparable and justly celebrated cascading laugh which are hard to reconcile with that capacity for inveterate hatred she showed in her relationships with Jean Meyer in the 1950s, a hatred which led to her being put into retirement after an honourable career of forty years.

In the early 1930s the Comédie passed through one of the worst periods of its history. Its decline had begun soon after the end of the First World War. Players, once they had secured hold of a leading part, hung on to it desperately. Talking of Duflos's Alceste, Dubech says that he has not the age of his part: and adds, or rather, like all the chief players of the Comédie Française, he has twice the age of his part. Some of the Comédie's principal actors were exhibitionists. In *Britannicus* Edouard de Max as Narcissus mutters and screams. As a matter of fact de Max appears to have been in advance of rather than behind his times. He brought into his performance suggestions of sexual perversion which would have been perfectly acceptable fifty years later, at Stratford upon Avon if not in the rue Richelieu. He fondled the Emperor's knees, and licked his hands. This was altogether too much for the sensibilities of the time. Dubech no doubt expressed a widely held opinion when he said that, whatever he did, de Max looked like an old lady with a pain in her stomach. His Narcissus, he said, is nothing but 'une vieille cocotte.'

De Max in *Britannicus* clearly was trying to give a memorable performance. He had little interest in the play as a whole. This was characteristic of the Comédie. It had no sense of ensemble. Each player aimed, not at the success of the production, but at

18. BRETTY, Béatrice: *La Comédie Française a l'envers*, Fayard, Paris, 1957.

his own personal triumph. The more famous of them expected to be received with a round of applause when they entered the stage; to be recalled individually at the end of each act; and to be cheered after the delivery of any celebrated speech.

This was true chiefly of the older members of the company. There were younger players of very high quality, such as Madeleine Renaud and Marie Bell, who had a more modern idea of the theatre. But critics, even comparatively young critics, though friendly, gave them little real support. They did not perceive their immense potentialities. No critic appears to have recognised, for example, that in these very young ladies there were two of the greatest actresses of the twentieth century. They wrote of Madeleine Renaud merely as if she were a piece of Dresden china, or a piquant figure in a cartoon by Fragonard. When she appeared in Edmond Sée's *La Brebis* on 3 January 1927, André Billy commended her 'silhouette cocasse' and her 'jambes rondelettes'. These terms would have been adequate to describe some new queen at the Folies Bergère. They were no doubt true also of Madeleine Renaud. But they were not the whole truth, nor the most important truth, about her.

There was some excuse for the older players of the Comédie. The Comédie was a society of actors, not of directors. Bretty said approvingly that when she joined the Company players just came on to the stage and acted for all they were worth. They never bothered about the producer. But times were, apparently unperceived by the Comédie, changing. Acting was still enormously important, as we have seen from Robert Brasillach. But it was being subordinated by Jouvet, Copeau, Baty and Dullin to the whole composition of a production. This insensibly affected the attitude of critics and of the general public. Madame Bretty herself has to admit that the Comédie no longer attracted full houses, and people like Paul Léautaud treated it with contempt.

In August, 1936 a change was made that proved, for the space of ten years, revolutionary. The Popular Front Government deposed the Administrateur, Emile Fabre, and put in his place Edouard Bourdet, a skilful dramatist who had written an excellent play (*La Prisonnière*) about lesbianism. A striking and paradoxical change immediately took place. Whereas under Fabre the sparse audiences had been shabbily dressed, under Bourdet, the nominee of a left-wing Government, they became a practical exhibition of *la haute couture*. In the years before the war it was the done thing to go to the Comédie Française; unless one was an habitué of the National Theatre one could not be counted a member of *le tout Paris*.

The success achieved by Bourdet in bringing back audiences to the Comédie could not be disputed. But it was alleged by the friends of Fabre, and above all by those who, like Edouard Champion, the historian of the Comédie, and his colleague Paul Vinson, preferred actors to *metteurs en scène*, that he was given immense advantages. The chief of these was that the Government relieved the Comédie of financial anxiety. The Comédie's subsidy was increased from 2,276,000 francs in 1936 to 5,476,000 in 1937, and to 6,976,000 in 1938. This was truly a stupendous rise. Bourdet used it vigorously. He put up the salaries not only of sociétaires, but of pensionnaires as well, and he gave additional payments for each performance. He promoted some players, and demoted others, and for this he was much criticised. But he was a man of strong will, and would not allow himself to be deflected from anything he wanted to do. He greatly reduced the number of performances given by Mary Marquet.

He brought order into the Comédie. He almost succeeded in completely stopping last minute changes in programmes. He stabilised the beginning of performances at 21 hours, and both lessened the number and shortened the duration of the intervals in performances. Leading players were no longer allowed to disrupt the continuity of the Comédie by going on personal tours, and there were no more winter holidays, when of course the Comédie was at its busiest in the rue Richelieu. If Bourdet made the players better off, he saw to it that they obeyed a sharp discipline. The result was a steep increase in audiences and receipts.

There was no denying that under Bourdet (who remained *Administrateur* until he was knocked down in the blackout in 1940, whilst riding a bicycle), the Comédie became a stronger and more efficient organisation than it had been before. The defenders of what the Comédie had been in the past, when all the attention was concentrated on the players, and the *metteur en scène* was hardly noticed to exist disputed hotly that the improvement had anything to do with the directors Bourdet brought with him—Baty, Jouvet, Dullin, and Copeau—who became known as the Cartel. Vinson bitterly pointed out that when *L'Illusion comique* was presented Jouvet's name was printed in red to distinguish it from the ordinary black of the players. This was done with all the directors of the Cartel, and it marked a revolution in the relative status of directors and actors.

What the French public delightedly discovered, after Bourdet and the Cartel had taken over the Comédie Française, was that the things which Corneille and Racine had written were coherent plays, united wholes, not a collection of isolated pieces of bravura rhetoric. This change was marked particularly by Copeau's production of *Bajazet*. Instead of having each couplet of Racine resoundingly declaimed, especially those that concluded a speech, Copeau flung himself heart and soul into the story of the play, and the Comédie Française immediately began to excel the commercial theatre in importance.

But this was accompanied by some disadvantages. New plays diminished in stature. Robert Brasillach noted that the productions of the second half of 1936 which were most eagerly discussed were not original works, but revivals of the classics, such as Baty's *Le Chandelier*, Dullin's *Jules César*, and, of course, Jouvet's *L'Illusion comique*. The defenders of the pre-Cartel Comédie, a Comédie which after all had produced actresses like Madeleine Renaud, Marie Bell, and Edwige Feuillère (even if she did not stay with it long), felt it was not to be despised. Vinson even brought mathematics to assail the Cartel. After the first performance of *L'Illusion comique* the players were recalled five times. (Mounet-Sully had once been recalled 22 times after a matinee of *Oedipus Rex*.) But *L'Illusion* received only 31 performances, which Vinson calculates were a mere 31/472nds of the Comédie's total activity in 1937.

Better judges than Vinson were also severe on individual members of the Cartel. In the late 1930s Brasillach pursued Baty with increasing animosity. In Baty's *Le chapeau de paille de l'Italie* (1938) he accuses him of slowing down the action in order to show off his 'precious little lights'. He exclaims irritably at the idea that one can reform the Comédie Française with a director, infatuated with the theatre, it is true, but full of false ideas, clinging desperately to his unchallengeable title of the enemy of real dramatic art. He calls Baty's production of Marcel Achard's translation of *La Célestine* monstrous. Baty habitually abuses the lighting and spectacle. Never let it be forgotten, says Brasillach, that he is the man who, in the opening dialogue of *Faust*, replaced the voice of God by the light of a projector.

The Cartel clearly did not have an easy passage. Nevertheless, their triumph was complete. By 1939 the work they had done at the Comédie Française had revived it so spectacularly, and so much of the credit for this had been ascribed to them, that those who looked with optimism to the theatrical future put their trust, not in dramatists nor in players, but in directors. The man chosen by the far-sighted as the natural successor to the Cartel was a young actor, Jean-Louis Barrault, then under thirty years of age, who in the previous season had been a 'truly unforgettable' Alceste. 'No one,' wrote Brasillach, 'has so much invention, authority, and youth as he.' Yet Brasillach had doubts even about Barrault. He feared that he was too much preoccupied with *mise en scène*, that, like Baty, he paid too little attention to real drama.

Thus for the first time there walks upon the stage, young, enthusiastic, alert, progressive, courageous and attractive, the man who was to dominate the French theatre for many decades, the man who has made it famous throughout the world, and has inspired its greatest writers and players: the man devoid of jealousy or emulation, desiring only the best and the most just, who was betrayed by both his friends and his enemies, and who rose triumphant over both.

CHAPTER SIX

The Occupation

In June, 1940, when the Armistice between France and Germany was declared, French intellectuals and artists, in common with the rest of the population, were faced with a problem that their British counterparts were happily spared. How the British would have behaved in similar circumstances no one can tell. Their nerves remained steady under the threat of invasion, but had the invasion actually occurred what the attitude of the British people would have been is now only a matter for speculation. Probably, as in France, there would have been several attitudes.

Two of the people already mentioned in this book took a resolute decision immediately. They acted at once and without wavering or misgiving. Robert Brasillach put himself on the side of the Germans. He unhesitatingly upheld their cause in the periodical *Je suis partout*, and he regarded the Allied landings in Normandy as a grave danger to the welfare of France. What to the orthodox view was the Liberation of France was to him its enslavement. He continued to review plays with undiminished zest as the Allied armies drew near to Paris, but there was despair in his soul.

Béatrice Bretty acted with equal swiftness and certainty in exactly the opposite way. She refused to stay in a France occupied by the Germans. With her friend, the Resistant, Georges Mandel, one of the few members of the French Government who was of strong mind, she went to North Africa, where for some years she lived in conditions of discomfort and poverty. She was dismissed from the Comédie Française, and was bitterly scornful when on a celebrated occasion the French National Theatre received with formal honours its 'camarades allemands' from the Schiller Theatre in Berlin. Towards the end of the war

26. Actors rehearsing (1935). Béatrice Bretty on the right. Photograph by
courtesy of Lipnitzki-Viollet

Mandel was assassinated, but he left with Bretty the firm conviction that England would never surrender. She was reinstated
in the Comédie Française after the war, and when she came to
England for one of Peter Daubeny's World Theatre seasons,
and was presented to the Queen at a reception at the French
Embassy, she was so moved at the thought that she was in the
presence of the Head of State of a country in whose resolution
Mandel's faith had never been shaken, that when she made her
curtsey she almost fell.

Not many French players, however, shared Béatrice Bretty's
keen sense of public events. They were content to carry on their
own lives unharmed in the shadow of national disaster. One of
the chief members of the company with which Bretty came to

England was the late Jacques Charon, who afterwards directed John Mortimer's highly successful adaptation of Feydeau's *A Flea in her Ear* for the English National Theatre. Charon, then about twenty, was demobilised in 1941, and returned to the Conservatoire, where he had been a student. He says that if he is honest the first words that spring to his lips when he recalls 'la France humiliée' are 'Oh les beaux jours!'

When he became a pensionnaire of the Comédie on 1 January 1942, and was given the smallest dressing room on the topmost floor, he felt that he was living in an earthly Paradise. The theatre, he said years later, was then passing through an age of gold. For Charon the German Occupation was a time of joyous, carefree friendship in sharp contrast to the cold, businesslike atmosphere that he found at the Old Vic, when no one invited him out to drink champagne after a performance, and the only solace he found was the sumptuous lifestyle of Albert Finney, who he was charmed to discover had a real butler.

The people who enchanted Charon most at the Comédie during the war were Madeleine Renaud and Marie Bell. Renaud received the young Charon with gentleness and wisdom, and when, calm and decided, she left the Comédie, as he phrased it, on the arm of a young man who passed through it at the gallop, all the world looked on in astonishment; and Marie Bell was all flowers and passion and intensity. Charon was also impressed by the tremendous Mary Marquet, a veritable *monstre sacré*, with a superb and colossal voice that was capable of every incantation. One morning during the Occupation she brought her huge four-poster bed into her dressing-room, and stayed in the theatre all through the war.

However, there were some other artists besides Bretty who removed themselves from Paris. André Gide withdrew to the Unoccupied Zone and spent the early years of the Occupation near the Côte d'Azur. He noted sadly that the working people of this area showed no sign of appreciating the disaster that had befallen their country. So long as they could carry on their daily lives unmolested they were not interested in what was happening in the north of France, or at all concerned that the Germans were victorious.

Their lack of interest was shared by some more famous people; Gide was disturbed to hear that Henry de Montherlant, the most grandiose of living French dramatists, the undisputed master of the heroic style, had declared that 'the war did not bother him.' Gide was also disheartened by what he considered the diabolical cleverness of Hitler's policy towards the French people, by his seductive talk of 'ni vainquers, ni vaincus', and his meretricious appeal for 'collaboration loyale'. But in the autumn of 1940 Gide's spirits appeared to rise, without apparent reason. He seems to have heard of the beginnings of resistance, but not of the failure of the German attempt to invade England.

What principally maintained the spiritual morale of the French people during the Occupation was the theatre. For Gide, hidden away near Grasse, with occasional visits in over-crowded trains to Marseilles, it was the theatre of the past; and in this theatre of the past the dramatist he most read was Racine. He brooded over the possible effect that Racine's *Alexandre le Grand* might have if it were produced under the Occupation. But he decided that such a production would be out of the question. Too many similarities to the Armistice would be evoked by Porus's

> Mais encore, à quel prix croyez-vous qu'Alexandre
> Mette l'indigne paix dont il veut nous surprendre?[1]

By August, 1941 Racine was beginning to suggest to him what must have seemed then impossible dreams, like ignoring the Germans in France, and defeating them in Germany, probably in Berlin. He did not actually formulate his hopes as clearly as this; despite the acuity of his mind he may not even in the depths of his being have realised what they actually were. But their nature is obvious enough from Gide's reading to his family (in a very loud voice) *Mithridate*, and his wishing that all school children should learn by heart long sections of that part of the tremendous third act of the play in which Mithridate, king of Pont, vanquished in his own country, reveals to his sons Xipharès and Pharnace his grandiose (and totally impractic-able) plan for gathering allies and attacking Rome itself.

> C'est à Rome, mes fils, que je prétends marcher.
> Ce dessein vous surprend; et vous croyez peut-être
> Que le seul désespoir aujourd'hui le fait naître.
> J'excuse votre erreur; et pour être approuvés,
> De semblables projets veulent être achevés.
> Ne vous figurez point que de cette contrée

---

1. Porus asks what price Alexander would put on an unworthy peace.

Par d'éternels remparts Rome soit séparée.
Je sais tous les chemins par où je dois passer;
Et si la mort bientôt ne me vient traverser,
Sans reculer plus loin l'effet de ma parole,
Je vous rends dans trois mois au pied du Capitole.[2]

Rome did not fall to Mithridate, and there was never any chance of its doing so. Neither did Gide know all the roads to Berlin. But Berlin fell all the same, if not for a long time.

For Gide things were comparatively easy. Occasionally he found the trains into Marseilles from other parts of the Midi uncomfortably crowded. But otherwise he seems to have suffered little inconvenience in the early years of the war. He could dream of defiance of the invaders without being exposed either to the dangers or the temptations of men and women of the theatre who remained in Paris, and under the Occupation continued their ordinary work.

Amongst artists problems of conduct were particularly difficult. But until the autumn of 1941, after Germany had invaded Russia, the German occupants of Paris behaved with a discretion which met with a natural response from ordinary French people. Captain Ernst Junger, who was stationed in Paris for the greater part of the war, kept a diary[3] right up to the day in August 1944 when the Allied advance forced the Germans to evacuate the city. The picture he gives of his life in Paris up to the attack on Russia is that of a cultivated man enjoying the pleasures of the most cultured capital in the world in an atmosphere of quiet happiness. He wandered from one antiquarian bookshop to another, buying first editions of works on natural history. He found Paris to be a city of friendship. On his way there he was billeted for a few days in St. Michel. When he returned, his landlady, Madame Richardet, embraced him publicly in the streets, and lamented that he had been away too long; her aunt playfully warned him against falling too violently in love with attractive Parisian ladies.

This friendly spirit continued for many months after he reached Paris. In July, 1941, in the neighbourhood of the Sacré

---

2. Mithridate unfolds to his surprised children a plan for reaching the Capitol in three months unless death intervenes.

3. JUNGER, Ernst: *Journal de la guerre et d'occupation*, Julliard, Paris.

Coeur, a certain Madame Scrittore talked to him about the Holy Ghost, and then, more intimately, confided in him that her husband, though a good family man, was a poor lover. On Bastille Day, in the same year, as he was crossing the busy Place des Ternes, he felt someone touch him. He turned, and a man with a violin under his arm, whom he had never seen before, and never saw again, gave him a hearty handshake. Junger had been feeling rather depressed, and this cheered him. He formed close friendships with many French ladies otherwise unknown to history, but highly cultured and intelligent. He sauntered with them in the Bois de Boulogne, and round the shops in the Faubourg St. Honoré. He accompanied one of them to the Comédie Française. He also had casual adventures of an agreeable nature. In October, 1941 he encountered a pretty milliner. He took her to a store near the Opera and bought her a hat with a green feather in it. When she put the hat on, Junger was amused to notice that the girl was transfigured with pride, like a soldier who has been decorated. Nor did he forget his old friends, however humble. He paid repeated visits to his former concierge in Vincennes. All this was very much in the spirit of Jacques Charon.

But before Christmas, 1941, this idyllic atmosphere had begun to change. Attempts on the lives of German soldiers increased. Junger himself became secretly more and more involved in the opposition of the Wehrmacht against the Nazi Party. The Party ordered the shooting of hostages. Junger read the letters of farewell written by hostages who had been shot at Nantes. He was profoundly moved by their steadfast courage and love. He was convinced that the shooting of hostages was barbarous and wicked.

It is not surprising that Junger was affected by some of the letters written in their last hours by men condemned to be shot by the Germans. One of the most moving was addressed by Jacques Decour to his parents. Decour was with Jean Paulhan in 1941 the founder of the clandestine Resistance literary revue, *Les Lettres françaises*. This was a Communist publication of considerable aesthetic interest and value, and it flourished until the leaders of the 1968 student rising unexpectedly repudiated it. It never recovered from this totally unforeseen blow, and shortly afterwards ceased to appear.

Soon after Paulhan and Decour established *Les Lettres françaises* Decour was captured and shot. Just before his death he wrote to his mother and father a letter[4] to which for courage, patriotism, and dignity there are few parallels in literary or political history.

> Samedi 30 mai 1942,
> 6 heures 45
>
> Mes chers parents,
>
> Vous attendez depuis longtemps une lettre de moi. Vous ne pensiez pas recevoir celle-ci. Moi aussi, j'espérais bien ne pas vous faire ce chagrin. Dites-vous bien que je suis resté jusqu'au bout digne de vous, de notre pays que nous aimons.
>
> Voyez-vous, j'aurais très bien pu mourir à la guerre ou bien même dans les bombardements de cette nuit. Aussi, je ne regrette pas d'avoir donné un sens à cette fin. Vous savez bien que je n'ai pas commis aucun crime, vous n'avez pas à rougir pour moi. J'ai su faire mon devoir de Français. Je ne pense pas que ma mort soit une catastrophe: songez qu'en ce moment des milliers de soldats de tous les pays meurent chaque jour, entraînés dans un grand vent qui m'emporte aussi.
>
> Vous savez que je m'attendais depuis deux mois à ce que m'arrive ce matin, aussi ai'je eu le temps de me préparer; mais, comme je n'ai pas de religion, je n'ai pas sombré dans la méditation de la mort: je me considère un peu comme une feuille qui tombe de l'arbre pour faire du terreau.
>
> La qualité du terreau dèpendra de celle des feuilles. Je veux parler de la jeunesse française en qui je mets tout mon espoir.[5]

---

4. Quoted in ARON, Robert: *Histoire de l'épuration*, Fayard, 1975.

5. My dear parents,

   You have been expecting a letter from me for some time. But you did not expect a letter like this. And I also hoped to spare you this grief. Remember that to the end I remained worthy of you, and of the country that we love.

   You see, I might have died in battle or even in tonight's bombardments. And I do not regret giving this ending some meaning. You know that I have not committed any crime, and that you need not blush for me. I have known how to do my duty as a Frenchman; I do not regard my death as a catastrophe; remember that at this moment thousands of soldiers of every country are dying each day, carried

Paulhan's fate was very different from Decour's. After Decour's death he carried on the editorship of *Les Lettres françaises* alone, in ever increasing danger until the Allied liberation of Paris in 1944. Thereafter his career greatly prospered. His success in evading the Germans may have taught him things that were useful to him later. At any rate it has never been possible to prove irrefutably that he was or was not, the author of the most famous and, from a literary point of view, the most valuable erotic novel of our times, *Histoire d'O*. When *Histoire d'O* was first published (and banned) in 1954 the author's name was given on the title page as Pauline Réage. But no writer of that name has been discovered. What is certain is that Jean Paulhan wrote a delicate and subtle preface to the book. It is more than probable that he wrote the entire work.

Histoire d'O entered into the world of entertainment when it was made into a notorious film in the middle 1970s. This film, by concentrating on the sexual aspect of the book (which is, of course, very strong), missed out its philosophical significance. Paulhan recalls that in 1838 in Barbados the two hundred recently freed slaves of a certain Glenelg besought him to take them back into slavery, and when he refused to do so killed him. There is, says Paulhan, a deep satisfaction in absolute obedience to another, in surrendering all responsibility. This is what O experiences in her total submission to the whips and chains of her lover. The story is a parable—a startling parable —of the peace obtained by the Christian who sinks himself entirely in the will of God, or by the Communist who, like Decour (and possible Paulhan until his break with his old friends in 1953), accepts blindly and unquestioningly the dictates of the Party. As Paulhan insists, it has nothing whatever to do with either sadism or masochism. It is a study of the complete absorption of one being into another, or into a whole greater than himself.

If Junger was moved by such letters as Decour's, so were

---

away by a great wind that engulfs me also.

   You know that for two months I have been waiting for what happens this morning; I have had time to prepare myself; but, as I have no religion, I have not brooded over the thought of death; I am rather like a leaf that falls to the ground to make it fertile.

   The quality of the fertiliser depends on that of the leaves. I am thinking of that youth of France in which I place all my hopes.

other members of the German army of Occupation. The German Commandant of Paris, Von Stulpnagel, tacitly refused to carry out the orders sent to him, and was recalled to Berlin. The mood in Paris here and there became bitter to the German occupants. In August, 1942, Junger bought a notebook at a *papeterie* in the Avenue de Wagram. He was disturbed by the look of hatred in the eyes of the salesgirl who served him. This was the first sign of hostility that he had encountered amongst the ordinary people of Paris. Even to the end, however, he had friends. On the eve of the Allied Liberation of Paris Paul Léautaud assured him of his help if he needed it, and was greatly disturbed when Junger published the fact that he had done so.

It is against this background of general friendliness with the Occupying forces in the first two years that the behaviour of the leading figures of the French theatre must be judged. Junger, like many of his companions in the German army, was a cultivated man. What is surprising in the atmosphere of Paris at that time is not that some leading figures of French civilisation such as Jean Cocteau and Picasso became his friends, but that the vast majority held themselves aloof from all contact with the invaders, considerable numbers of whom, it should be remembered, were admirable and highly civilised men.

The Liberation was a time, not only of national triumph, but also a moment when many old scores were paid off. Sacha Guitry maintained that his troubles (he was arrested on 23 August 1944 by five men armed to the teeth, and accused of collaboration with the enemy) were due to the jealousy of Pierre Brisson, but the son of Lucien Guitry seems to have had no better reason for saying this than that Brisson had disliked his recent plays, and in consequence Guitry had written a satirical poem about him. But it is undoubtedly true that more than one ancient revenge was achieved at this time. In spite of the fact that, after some initial misgiving, his *Antigone* was regarded as the principal dramatic representative of the Resistance, Jean Anouilh himself encountered certain *ennuis*, largely due to jealous rivals. In fact events at the Liberation were the inspiration for his *Pauvre Bitos*, that powerful and mordant play on the settlement of old envies which provoked considerable disorder when it was first produced at the Théâtre Montparnasse-Gaston Baty in October, 1956. One of the most celebrated of contemporary French dramatists told me that at the end of the war he had been given a blank paper on which he was asked to write the names of those of his colleagues who he thought ought to be shot for their conduct during the war. He said that he returned the paper unmarked.

The purging of the world of the arts after the Liberation was very uneven in its effects. The cinema, in particular, was let off very lightly. A few cinema artists who were connected with the stage were punished. But the exclusively cinematic personnel scarcely suffered more than here and there an occasional reprimand. Newspapers, on the other hand, were treated with extreme harshness. *La Dépêche de Toulouse*, for example, was for a time brutally suppressed at the Liberation, its offices commandeered, and its capital confiscated. Yet its record during the Occupation had been beyond reproach. Fourteen members of its staff had been victims either of the Gestapo or the militia. In Paris a list of ninety-three journalists who were to be arrested was drawn up even before the Germans had left the city. Many of these had been traitors, but the list included several who had rendered great services to the Resistance.

On 28 September 1940 a list of a different complexion had been published. This was the Otto Abetz list of authors whose works were to be banned. The names included Bernstein's old enemy, Henry Bordeaux, Colette's second husband, Henri de Jouvenel, Henri Béraud, Charles de Gaulle, and, surprisingly, Adolph Hitler. But there was a great deal of confusion. Béraud, for example, was by no means a staunch resistant of the Germans. On 9 March 1942 he joined the dramatist Maurice Donnay, the novelist Céline, the Academician Abel Bonnard, and fifty others in signing an anti-Allied manifesto in *Le Petit Parisien*. Some of these genuinely believed that they were doing what was right, and in loyal disloyalty stuck to their guns to the very end. As late as 15 July 1944, hardly a month before the liberation of Paris, and when the Allied victory was already certain, there were still twenty-eight people prominent in the arts ready to sign a declaration 'that there will undoubtedly be a certain delay before the Germans inflict on the Allies a decisive defeat.' On 19 September 1944 the Liberation forces drew up a black list of artists. It is ironical that it contained the name of the unfortunate Bordeaux, who had already appeared in the Abetz list. However, he protested, and his name was withdrawn, as was that of the novelist Pierre Benoît.

Guitry, looking back on his unpleasant post-war experiences, liked to think of himself as a Talleyrand outwitting the enemies of France by guile, since even in his most exalted moments he did not claim to be another Napoleon. Nevertheless he was one of the few really famous French artists who got into serious trouble over their behaviour during the Occupation. For a short time he went to prison, but was eventually released. Defending himself he claimed, doubtless truthfully, that he had secured freedom for many French prisoners by his interventions with the German authorities, but he never succeeded in explaining exactly how he came to have so much influence with these authorities.[6]

He maintained that he had always hated the Germans, and nowhere mentions, for example, that he was on cordial terms with Junger. Junger was certainly an exceptional man, exceedingly civilised, and filled with horror at the excesses of the Nazi régime. Nevertheless at the time that Guitry and his other French friends frequented his society he was compelled, for elementary reasons of safety, to behave like any other cultured enemy of France. Junger met Guitry as a fellow-guest at the house of Brinon, the Vichy Ambassador in Paris. Later, with Colonel Spiedel, he lunched with him at his home in the Avenue Elysée-Reclus. There was an atmosphere of extreme friendliness and gaiety. Guitry behaved with none of the restraint one might have expected him to show in the presence of high representatives of the invading forces. Junger did not actually dislike him, but he found his stories of kings and himself exhaustingly exuberant. In his demonstrative amiability Guitry presented Junger with letters from Octave Mirbeau, Debussy, and Léon Bloy for his collection of autographs.

Junger noted the air of splendour with which Guitry surrounded himself. The salad was served in a bowl of silver, and the ice in a gold cup: and in presiding over it all Guitry managed his thick tortoiseshell spectacles with admirable adroitness. As soon as Paris was freed Guitry was mercilessly attacked, and his friends deserted him. But at the time that Junger knew him he was one of the idols of Paris. In January, 1942 Junger attended a matinée of one of his pieces at the Théâtre de la Madeleine. There was a great deal of applause, and the house resounded with shouts of 'C'est tout à fait Sacha!' But when he was arrested hardly anyone could be found to say

6. GUITRY, Sacha: *Quatre ans de l'occupations*, L'Elan, Paris.

a good word for him, and even some of those he had rescued from captivity denounced him.

Another great figure of the theatre besides Sacha Guitry was arrested for political reasons when the Allies entered Paris. This was the actress Arletty, who claimed that during the Occupation she had been the most fêted woman in Paris. This began, she says, when difficulties arose about getting German permission to use the château of Grosbois, which Napoleon had offered to Berthier, for the film of *Madame sans Gêne*, in which she was playing the heroine. To overcome the problem Arletty decided to 'jouer les *Boule-de-suif*'.

This was in 1941, and thereafter, until the Liberation, her social successes knew no limit. It is ironical that her most famous part should have been that of Garance in the film *Les Enfants du paradis*, for when the film came to be shown she was temporarily in a military prison. One day she had the disagreeable experience of hearing on the clandestine radio that the tribunal of Algiers had condemned her and Raimu to death. The fastidious but by no means unimpressionable Junger rather despised her. She was irrepressibly gay, and he says that one had only to utter the word 'cocu' to make her explode with laughter.

Yet another prominent figure in the world of art who was in serious danger after the expulsion of the Germans from Paris, was Céline, the author of one of the most celebrated novels of the century, *Voyage au bout de la nuit*, and a great friend of Arletty's. They had both been born in the same working-class suburb of Paris. Except Marcel and Elise Jouhandeau, Junger does not seem to have liked his famous French friends very much: he had more affection for the common people who fraternised with him. But he is not bitter about them. He accepts men like Braque and Picasso with a cold amiability. But Céline he positively hated: 'L'affreux Céline,' he calls him. Céline told him that he could not understand why, with all their bayonets available, the German Occupants did not make short work of the Jews. Junger was justly horrified.

Junger several times visited the theatre during his years in Paris. He went to the Comédie Française more than once, and was even seen at the Bal Tabarin. But in the roll call of famous men and women who gave their friendship to him, Jean Marais is the only other actor besides Guitry and Arletty whom he mentions. This fact is significant and honourable in the history

27. Jean-Louis Barrault and Georges Aminel in *Le Soulier de satin* (Palais Royal 1958). Photographs by Lipnitzki-Viollet

of the French theatre. The 'femmes nues' of the Bal Tabarin, Junger records, were watched by a house filled with German officers and officials. This could be said of many of the great performances during the Occupation. The French players played before the Occupying troops. But mostly they left it to others to fraternise with them.

Those who desired a German victory were on the whole inimical to the living forces which actuated the French theatre and cinema during the Occupation. The most outspoken of these, apart from Robert Brasillach, was our old friend Paul Léautaud. Léautaud said that the Vichy Government immediately after the Armistice ought without trial to have shot Daladier, Reynaud, Mandel and the other statesmen who had opposed Hitler. He maintained to the end of his long life that the interests of France lay in a German victory, and hoped that France, Germany, and Russia would unite to defeat England.

He spoke of the young Jean-Louis Barrault in terms almost as bitter as those he reserved for the British. He was disgusted that at the Comédie Française Barrault was entrusted with the production of *Phèdre*. He called him 'un joli sot plein de prétention.' So filled with rage was he at the emergence of Barrault into a position of the first importance in the artistic life of France, and in the country's spiritual regeneration, that he went back several years in the history of the Comédie Française to pour abuse on Bourdet, Jouvet, Copeau, Dullin and someone else (evidently Gaston Baty) whose name he pretended not to be able to remember. It was people like these, he said, who, after themselves sabotaging the French classics, made possible the work that was being done by Barrault, which in his opinion was a scandal.

He had already been totally unsympathetic to the genius of Barrault when he produced Paul Claudel's *Le Soulier de satin* in November, 1943. 'Au lever du rideau,' he wrote in his *Journal*, 'cet avis a été donné au public, par un des interprètes:

'Ecoutez bien, ne toussez pas et tâchez de comprendre:
'Et songez que ce que vous comprendrez le moins sera le plus beau, que ce que vous trouverez le plus long sera le plus intéressant, et que ce qui vous amusera le moins sera le plus drôle . . .'[7]

This was too much for Léautaud. He called it 'Vanité, puffisme,

---

7. Listen carefully, do not cough, and try to understand: Remember that what you least understand will be most beautiful, what you find most boring will be most interesting, and what you understand the least will be the most amusing.

insolence.' Yet this production of *Le Soulier de satin* was the greatest theatrical achievement of the French drama during the war, and Léautaud had once been a good and perceptive critic.

It is against a background of danger and temptation that the French theatre developed between 1940 and 1944; and, as is claimed by Dussane, the sociétaire of the Comédie Française who became a distinguished and vivid dramatic historian, it is in response to danger and temptation that in some of its major works it 'displayed an integrity and an ambition of real nobility.'

The theatre did a great deal to maintain the morale of Parisians during those difficult years. At a time when there was a great shortage of lighting and heating the physical proximity of the spectators to each other kept them warmer than they would have been at home. From time to time there were incidents in which the texts of plays were given by the circumstances of the day a new exhilarating significance that even the most vigilant censorship could not foresee. The German authorities passed for production a harmless farce of Labiche's called *29 degrés à l'ombre*. No one suspected that there could be any hidden meanings in it. Yet when one of the characters exclaimed 'M. Adolphe! l'ignoble Adolphe!' not unnaturally there was a shout of mocking laughter throughout the theatre.

Charon was right in thinking that the period of the Occupation was artistically rich for both theatre and cinema. Dussane maintains that the record of the first was better than that of the second. Both had to submit their works to German censorship. But there was nothing in the theatre like Continental Films, a German company that established itself in Paris, and did in fact find plenty of able people to work for it. This German organisation was particularly fond of the novels of Georges Simenon. It adapted his *Annette et la dame blanche*, *Les Caves du Majestic*, and *Les Inconnus dans la maison*. *Les Inconnus dans la maison* was the most famous of all, because the great Marseillais actor Raimu appeared in it. It was especially admired for its early scenes of life in a provincial city. But it concluded with a *tirade*, admirably spoken by Raimu, in which sensitive, or over-sensitive, ears heard suggestions of racialism. When I saw it in London after the war I could discover nothing sinister in it.

Between 13 August 1940, when Marcel Pagnol, the author of *Topaz* and *Marius*, resumed the production of *La Fille du Puisatier* that had begun before the defeat, and 23 May 1944,

when Pierre Billon started *Mademoiselle X . . .* (that is, during
the Occupation) no fewer than two hundred and fifty films
were made in France. Arletty was gratified that the first of
these to be completed was *Madame sans Gêne*, which owed so
much to her romantic and literary notions of self-sacrifice. Only
about seventy of these 250 films were made by Continental
Films. The rest were the work of French companies. Many were
of high quality, some, like Edwige Feuillère's *La Duchesse de
Langeais*, of very high quality indeed.

La Duchesse de Langeais, which was directed by Jacques de
Baroncelli, was very important in the development of a spirit of
hope and resistance in both theatre and cinema. Along with
Claudel's *Le Soulier de satin* and Robert Bresson's *Les Anges du
péché* it is one of the great French achievements of the Occupation. The script was written by Jean Giraudoux from a story by
Balzac, and its success made people realise with something of
the shock of a revelation that the temper of the Paris public had
risen out of its first despondency to a height where it could
appreciate the challenge of a high literary style.

The critic Roger Régent considered 1942, when *La Duchesse
de Langeais* was shown, as the annus mirabilis of the modern
French cinema. It was the year not only of Madame Feuillère's
film, but also of *La Nuit fantastique*, directed by Marcel
L'Herbier, and of *Les Visiteurs du soir* (Marcel Carné). It seemed
to Régent that the combined efforts of certain authors, directors, players and critics had succeeded in making baseness contemptible and quality estimable. He felt that by the beginning
of 1943 the battle for distinction in the French cinema was
taking on the allure of a revolution. People who two years
earlier had spoken with mockery of everything pure and noble
began to refer to Giraudoux with respect, and there were long
queues in the Champs-Elysées for *Les Visiteurs du soir*.

Cinema companies now began to seek the services of writers
of quality. Cocteau was solicited for scripts, and Giraudoux,
with the Reverend Father Bruckberger, wrote the scenario for
Les Anges du péché. This script was an act of faith, an affirmation
of belief in the future, one of the finest films of the Occupation period, and it had a particularly exalted theme. The nuns
of the order of Bethanie, founded in 1862 by the Père Lataste,
brought thieves and criminals from prison to live with them in
the hospitality of their convent. They believed that good conquers evil, that purity and not corruption is contagious. In this

film Giraudoux proved again what he had already done in *La Duchesse de Langeais*: he established anew that a man of letters, a man of highly civilised and intricate mastery of language and thought, could make films that attract the public. Roger Régent goes so far as to say that had Giraudoux not died in January, 1944, he would have transformed the art of the cinema. Perhaps this would not have been as desirable as Régent supposed. It is very questionable whether the art of the cinema depends to anything like the same degree as that of the theatre upon the written word. Nor is it by any means certain that the written word of Giraudoux does not contain subtle falsities and pretentions.

Nevertheless in its influences and repercussions in the theatre the films written by Giraudoux had great importance. Their principal result was that *La Duchesse de Langeais* transformed the career of Edwige Feuillère. When Julia Bartet, the unrivalled Bérénice of the Comédie Française, saluted her after her prize at the Conservatoire, she said 'You will be a great actress.' But nothing in the treatment she received from the Comédie suggested that it shared Bartet's opinion. Robert Kemp thinks that no one in the Comédie perceived that here was a 'grande dame', an actress of majesty and splendour. Indeed no effort seems to have been spared to vulgarise her, to make it impossible for her ever to reach the glory which she later achieved in *Partage de midi*. Her most striking role at the Comédie was that of the typist in Sacha Guitry's *La Jalousie*, and in this she was made up with a heavy cold and a red nose, short-sighted and silly.

The cinema did at least avoid the mistake made by the Comédie Française. From the earliest days it did not regard Edwige Feuillère as a figure of fun. It at once perceived that she was an actress of glamour, and proceeded to exploit this glamour in its own way. In 1936 she played the principal part in Abel Gance's *Lucrèce Borgia*, in the most famous scene of which she stepped naked into a Renaissance bath. She again appeared nude in Max Ophuls's *Sans lendemain* in 1939. In the later days of her dazzling fame as a great and serious actress Edwige Fueillère was never allowed to forget these two memorable episodes in her career. As a matter of fact, in any proper study of her art and achievement, there is no reason at all why she should not remember them with pride and satisfaction. Before she could bring about her triumph in Claudel, whom with

28. Edwige Feuillère in *Partage de midi*. Photographs by courtesy of Harcourt, Paris

Barrault she established as one of the peaks of twentieth-century theatre, it was necessary that she should be recognised as a desirable and seductive woman. And it was to the cinema, not to the theatre, that she owed this recognition.

Though she is incontestably beautiful, Edwige Feuillère was from her first days in Paris worried, though unnecessarily, about her looks. She had a very unfortunate experience whilst waiting with scores of other candidates for her entrance examination to the Conservatoire. She overheard someone say, 'What a pity it is she is ugly,' and the reply, 'Réjane was ugly, too,' was hardly reassuring. These remarks had a profound effect upon her. Thus the fact that the films in the 1930s considered her seductive enough to play without clothes, far from being an insult to her dignity, was psychologically of great benefit to her. It did infinitely more for her than the Comédie Française, with its red nose and swimming eyes, and its failure to see that it had in Edwige Feuillère a perfect Bérénice, an incomparable Célimène, had ever done.

Yet the anxiety caused by those few thoughtless words at the Conservatoire never entirely disappeared. In Giraudoux's *La Folle de Chaillot* she had to make herself up as an ugly old woman. When her performance was over she said that when she looked in the mirror after taking off her make-up, 'Pour la première fois de ma vie je me trouvai vraiment belle.' Had there not been films like *Sans lendemain* and *Lucrèce Borgia*, with its uncomfortably shallow pool, and its nude scene that had to be shot nineteen times (for, as Madame Feuillère herself slyly remarked, the technicians did not hurry their work), it is doubtful whether the damage inflicted by the gossip of the Conservatoire would ever have been sufficiently repaired to make it possible for her to play Ysé in *Partage de midi*.

What made *Partage de midi* possible was the converging of two lines of influence and development. The first was the resounding entry into the theatre of Jean-Louis Barrault. He had joined the Comédie Française in 1940, soon after his marriage to Madeleine Renaud, the youthful and adorable *doyenne*. Barrault had a consuming passion for the plays of Paul Claudel. As early as 1942 he was absorbed in the intricate and difficult rhythms of *Le Soulier de satin*. In May in that year André Gide met him in Marseilles. Barrault had come to that city to read selections from the play on the radio. He made an immense impression, as also did Madeleine Renaud, on Gide, when all three lunched together in a restaurant near the Avenue du Prado.

Gide had in him none of the sour bitterness of Léautaud. 'An admirable face,' he wrote of the young Barrault, then only thirty-two years old, 'breathing enthusiasm, passion, genius. Beside him Madeleine Renaud effaces herself with an exquisite modesty. Her grace and naturalness immediately put me at ease.'[8]

Claudel, however, was not popular with the Germans. To champion him in the fanatical fashion of Barrault, was a considerable act of defiance to the Occupying authorities. It was the policy of the Germans, an enlightened policy in its way, to treat eminent representatives of Parisian cultural life with deference and favour. As we have seen, not all leading French artists were proof against this flattery. Claudel however was obstinate. The Germans attempted for a long time in vain to tempt him to return to Paris from his chateau of Brangues. But he insisted on remaining there, an isolated and implicitly protesting figure.

The play was, however, produced in November, 1943, with a cast—Madeleine Renaud, Jean-Louis Barrault, Aimé Clariond, Jean Yonnel, André Brunot, Pierre Dux, Jean Chevrier, Jacques Charon, Marie Bell, and Mary Marquet— that recalled the legendary Comédie Française of Mounet-Sully. The Germans gave permission for the production of *Le Soulier de satin* because they assumed that the play was too involved and complicated in expression to run for more than a few performances. When it proved highly popular they were embarrassed by the permission they had given, but allowed it to be presented more than sixty times before bringing it to a close. Some of their sympathisers at once perceived its danger. Within a week of its opening the collaborationist journal *Je suis partout* said ominously, 'Because the Comédie Française has decided to play *Le Soulier de satin*, which was to be the *clou* of the Liberation, M. Claudel has agreed to become a Parisian again.' The suspicions of *Je suis partout* were well founded. In its spiritual effects *Le Soulier de satin* became the principal Resistance play of the Occupation period, more so even than Jean Anouilh's *Antigone*, about which there was a greater ambiguity than it is

---

8. GIDE, André: *Journal*, Bibliothèque de la Pléiade, Editions Galli-mard, Paris.

fashionable to suppose in England. In 1943 French families were already beginning to be broken up by the war: and the heroic sacrifice of Prouhèze and Rodrigue became, says Dussane, the echo and symbol of all those sacrifices that could not be spoken of openly.

It is my impression that Barrault considers *Le Soulier de satin* as Claudel's masterpiece, and his own production of it as the best thing that he himself has done. But personally if I were asked to name the play which for text, production, and performance was the best I have ever seen, either in France or anywhere else, I should choose *Partage de midi*.

As soon as the curtain rises an incomparable spectacle is presented before the eyes of the audience: the deck of a ship; the dazzling sunlight rippling on the waves reflected in the white awnings; whiteness everywhere; in the sails; in the ship's appointments; in Edwige Feuillère's dress as she exclaims 'Qu'il fait chaud' in the intense, still heat of midday, a stillness broken only by the peal of the ship's bell which breaks the silence as dramatically as the ringing of the bell at the Elevation of the Host; in Barrault's tropical suit as he stands drawn and immobile in the knowledge that he has offered his heart to God and God has rejected it; pure white, clothing murder and betrayal and the impenetrable coldness of the spirit. This is something the like of which, in its enduring and terrible beauty, I have not seen in any other play. It was Edwige Feuillère's performance as Ysé in *Partage de midi* that made me recognise her as the greatest actress in the world.

It has been said that it was difficult for Madame Feuillère, a Christian brought up exclusively on the Bible, who in her youth had played the organ in the Protestant church in Dijon, to comprehend the almost hysterical mysticism of Claudel's Catholicism, which sees the salvation of a soul resulting from a crime like that of David in respect of Uriah the Hittite: for Mesa sends Ysé's husband de Ciz deliberately into a part of China where he is certain to die. Robert Kemp admired the passion and sincerity with which Feuillère accomplished this ascension, and declared that in playing Ysé she took her place in the history of the French theatre.

The second line of development and influence which I described as making possible the conquest of the stage by *Partage de midi* is in fact that which brought Edwige Feuillère to the point where she was capable of playing Ysé. There can be little doubt that the decisive step was taken when she played the fickle and tormenting heroine in the film of *Duchesse de Langeais*. Previous films had indeed established her—and this was a necessary preliminary—as a woman of extreme seduction, but seductive chiefly in a light and frivolous way, so frivolous indeed that the film critic Jacques Siclier once dismissed her as merely provocative and piquant.

Even in the Duchesse there was a little of this frivolous spirit: Balzac in a curiously exasperated phrase on one occasion calls her 'one of these skirt-carriers ("porte-jupes")'. But there was also something deeper and more resonant than was to be found in *Mam'zelle Bonaparte* or *Lucrèce Borgia*. There is in the first place the solemn and anguished tone established by the setting of the opening and closing scenes, memorable like the opening of *Partage de midi*: the sea-girt convent on the small Spanish island; the resounding echo on the flagstones of the boots of the love-tortured and torturing general, the luscious Te Deum on the organ, that grandest and most sensual of instruments; all combine to create a conception of love hysterically united with religion, a religion expressed in sexual terms as when Balzac describes the convent to which his heroine has fled as the tomb in which women are reborn as the brides of Christ. From this it is not a long step to the mysticism of Claudel, a perhaps evil mysticism. (At a conference in Oxford one of his daughters interrupted an address to exclaim, 'My father was an evil man').

Secondly, in the Duchesse de Langeais piquancy and provocativeness pass into a demoniac power to drive men into frenzy. ('I love to play monsters,' says Feuillère) Ysé also drove Mesa into frenzy, as the Duchesse brought madness to the Marquis de Montriveau. But in Mesa's case it was a frenzy that led to salvation.

However, there is in *Partage de midi* something not to be found in *La Duchesse de Langeais*. *La Duchesse de Langeais* may have made *Partage de midi* possible; but in *Partage de midi* in its second act where Mesa meets Ysé in the deserted cemetery there is a passionate ecstasy of lyrical love not even hinted at in Balzac's story. Barrault standing behind Edwige Feuillère, with his hands flickering up and down from her breasts to her waist without ever touching them, whilst both players pour out a chant of love as reckless as the Song of Solomon, created a union of eroticism and beauty quite unrivalled in drama, and rivalled in opera only in *Tristan and Isolde.* The effect of this scene was so powerful that Claudel for many years would not allow *Partage de midi* to be produced. He finally gave way to Barrault's persuasions only when he was assured that the play would lead —had in reading in fact already led—to many Catholic conversions.

Partage de midi did not produce the same difficulties for Barrault as it did for Feuillère. He is after all an orthodox Catholic believer, proud of having the same birthday as the Virgin Mary. He entered into its mystical spirit with the enthusiasm of one to whom such a spirit is entirely congenial. 'This drama,' he exclaimed, 'is the struggle between the flesh and the spirit. It is to Claudel what *Bajazet* is to Racine. Like Racine, Claudel envelops a very ordinary theme in a crime. But Claudel raises it to a higher level, because he adds a fifth character who is God himself. *Partage de midi* is the most magnificent descent into the impenetrable depths of sin out of which it is possible to rise victoriously holding the Cross aloft.'

When *Partage de midi* was produced at the Marigny Theatre in 1948 Claudel had been writing plays for nearly half a century. Some of them, such as *Tête d'or*, had been avant-garde successes before the 1914–18 war. *Partage de midi* itself was many years old. It was not only Claudel's moral objections that so long delayed its presentation to the public. It is written in a form of verse which no one before Barrault had been able to speak effectively on the stage. This verse of Claudel's is heightened, exalted, passionate, and exultant. Its lines have a strange inequality of length, and their syntax is so odd that they sometimes separate the definite article from its noun. Its difficulties, and also its opportunities, can be seen in Ysé's canticle of love in the Chinese cemetery in which her lover decides to send her husband to his death:

> Tu ne sais pas ce que c'est qu'une femme et combien
> merveilleusement, avec toutes ces manières qu'elle a
> Il lui est facile de céder et tout-à-coup de se
> trouver abjecte et soumise et attendante;
> Et pesante, et gourde, et interdite entre la main
> de son ennemi, et incapable de remuer aucun doigt.
> O mon Mesa, tu n'es plus un homme seulement, mais
> tu es à moi qui suis une femme,
> Et je suis le double de toi avec moi, et tu es le

double de moi avec toi, et nous nous sentons battre
dans la chair l'un de l'autre le même coeur.[9]

It is also, when the occasion demands it, carnally and triumphantly metaphysical. In the end Mesa and Ysé, who had thought
herself cast aside as the instrument of salvation, die together in
regret for the wafer of absolution that has not been given them,
but with a dizzying confidence in the divine mercy. As Mesa
speaks his last exultant words the stage opens up to show a night
brilliant with stars, and in the distance can be heard the explosive sounds of the Chinese rebellion:

> Par quelles routes longues, pénibles, distants, encore
> que ne cessent de peser l'un sur l'autre, allons-nous
> mener nos âmes en travail.
> La vigne! le signe, le signe bon gré mal gré que nous
> avons été l'un pour l'autre.
> Le mien ce n'est pas de vains cheveux dans la tempête
> et le petit mouchoir un moment,
> Mais toutes voiles dissipés: moi-même
> La forte flamme fulminante dans la gloire de Dieu
> L'homme dans la splendeur de l'Août,
> L'Esprit vainquer dans la transfiguration
> de Midi.[10]

In all my theatre-going experience Barrault's delivery of these
lines is the most sublime moment I have known. It is a moment
when earthly love is translated into the divine, and the purged
heart is filled with eternal trust. I know nothing like it in any
other play, in any other performance. The achievements of
Feuillère and Barrault in *Partage de midi* were, I think, beyond
the range of the English theatre, whose peculiar excellence lies
in another direction than rhetoric. Claudel's dialogue is in a
different world from that of the everyday. It is not to be spoken
like the dialogue of Porto-Riche or Bernstein; it does not, says

---

9.   Ysé speaks of how easy it is for a woman to surrender, to find herself
     abject and submissive, incapable of moving even a finger. Mesa and
     she are the double of each other, and the same heart beats in both
     bodies.
     CLAUDE, Paul: *Partage de midi*, NRF Gallimard, Paris.

10. Mesa comes to God in the flaming splendour of August, the spirit
     conquering in the transfiguration of midday.

Robert Kemp, belong to a *garçonnière* a few hundred yards from the Madeleine, and Feuillère did not so much speak it as chant it.

So far as France is concerned it is customary to place the great change which came over the theatre after the war in 1953, when Roger Blin, later to be closely associated with Barrault, and one of the few people who notably stood by him in 1968, produced Samuel Beckett's *En attendant Godot*. In actual fact it came several years earlier, and stemmed from the year 1946 when Barrault and his wife left the Comédie Française, and formed the Renaud–Barrault company.

The formation of this company was a logical development of the creative, restless, urgent side of Barrault's character; for Madeleine Renaud it was an act of extraordinary courage and devotion, to which Barrault himself has paid a touching tribute. Madeleine Renaud was at the summit of her profession, with an assured and comparatively wealthy future at the Théâtre Français to the end of her career, which would itself be followed by an opulent pension. She left all this to follow her husband into a world of competition, chance and uncertainty. Other players left the Comédie at the same time. These included Marie Bell, Renée Faure, Maurice Escande, Aimé Clariond, Jean Debucourt, and Jean Chevrier. Béatrice Bretty recounts with some glee that not all these did well outside the shelter of the Comédie: under the new Administrateur, Pierre-Aimé Touchard, all except Barrault and Renaud returned.

The Renaud–Barrault company leased the Marigny Theatre. Barrault himself says that the floor of the stalls is not raked, and this is presumably true, and a considerable disadvantage. Nevertheless, standing just off the Avenue des Champs-Elysées half-way between the Place de la Concorde and the Arc de Triomphe, the Marigny is a delightful theatre: and on Sunday afternoons, when the weather is fine, a charming open-air stamp market is held under the trees that shade its door. It was here that the great Renaud–Barrault adventure began, the most remarkable achievement in the history of the twentieth-century European theatre. It has taken the company all over the world: it has associated it with players like Edwige Feuillère, Jean Desailly, Simone Valère, Pierre Bertin, Marie Bell, and Pierre Brasseur: it has given to the world new work by André Gide, Samuel Beckett, Marguerite Duras, Jean Genet, Albert Camus, Henry de Montherlant, Jean Anouilh, Armand Salacrou, and a host of others. There is nowhere in any theatre a record comparable with this record: for catholicity, for adventurousness, or originality of production, and for an almost unbelievably high standard of acting.

There is only one eminent name missing from the roll-call of the Renaud–Barrault company. It is that of Jean-Paul Sartre, a man with whom one would imagine that Barrault has an instinctive sympahy, at any rate upon social, if not upon religious, grounds. The years immediately after the war were a time of great mental disorganisation, of re-examination of principles, of revenge and retribution. In this disordered atmosphere Sartre appeared to be the coming dramatist.

The most vivid picture of the time is given by Léautaud in the almost daily records he kept in his diary. It was a period both of hope and of self-contradiction. There were no certainties any more. Some of the greatest figures went in danger of disgrace and death. The proud and boastful Montherlant, by many considered to be the greatest living stylist, renowned both as a dramatist and a novelist, was forbidden to publish anything for a year, because of an incident that had occurred in October 1945. The novelist Pierre Benoît, the author of *L'Atlantide*, a sensational French version of Rider Haggard's *She*, about a fantastic and fatal woman in an unknown oasis in the Sahara, was condemned to silence for twice as long by the Comité National des Ecrivains.

The divisions in the French nation were reflected in Léautaud's mind. Moreno, now well over seventy, had had a great success in Giraudoux's *La Folle de Chaillot*, and was also famous as a film star. She was far better known in the late 1940s than she had been when Léautaud had frequented her dressing room at the Comédie Française. Léautaud decided that he could make a deal of money if he published the extracts from his Journal which described her taking off her clothes in his presence in the days of her youth. He also reflected that if he did so the old lady would probably be very annoyed. But he thought she would be very silly if she objected to the publication of such an old story. Anyway nowadays he was making quite a lot of money. If only he could have made as much, he thought sadly, when he was sixty (he was now nearly eighty).

His mind was divided, as was the country, on more serious matters than that of scandalous stories about an actress who had waited until the eighth decade of her life, after she had been upon the stage for half a century, before achieving the biggest triumph of her career. He mused regretfully over the days of the Occupation. He recalled seeing during the war a small group of German soldiers, young and pleasing, singing as they marched down the rue Corneille. It is almost the only happy memory he seems to have had. He wishes they were in Paris now (April 1948). There was nothing provocative in their singing: it was wonderfully 'prenant', nostalgic, like a profound reverie. With incredible misjudgment he said all this at a more or less public luncheon, and was very unpopular for doing so.

Yet much as he wished that the Germans had won the war he thought that England was the greatest country in the world. His literary country, he says, is France, but in politics, society, and customs England. But soon after this he meets a young English student at the Cité Universitaire, and is back on his old tack. He declares that this girl is not duped by the theory that Hitler was the aggressor; it was England and France who started the war. Nevertheless the only really great nation in the world is England. Though it fights wars with the blood of others it is the only country left where civilisation still exists. It is the only country he has ever wished to know, and he will always regret not having been able to visit it.

This confusion of mind was not confined to Léautaud. No one in France or indeed anywhere else more bitterly resented the German Occupation than did André Gide. He was normally the most serene of men, a man to whom happiness was the natural state of existence. Yet throughout his Journal of the war years there is a savage anger and sorrow for the things that have befallen his country. But he combines this sorrow and anguish with a portrait of the German army just as attractive and admiring as Léautaud's. When he met Barrault in the restaurant in Marseilles, where Barrault asked him to make that translation of *Hamlet* which the Renaud–Barrault Company brought a few years later to an early Edinburgh Festival, he was on his way to Tunisia. He was in Tunis all the time of the Allied advance against Rommel. He was thus surrounded during the period of the bombardment of the city by German and Italian troops. For the Italians he has nothing but contempt. They were inefficient, insolent, and overbearing. But the Germans in contrast were young laughing Apollos, always well shaved, neat in their shapely uniforms, and courteous to the local population.

Gide's friend Dr. Ragu said that if an English prisoner

needed an urgent blood transfusion, six German soldiers immediately volunteered. But no one awaited their defeat more anxiously than did Gide. He dined by candlelight at six o'clock, went to bed at seven, got up several times during the night to watch, with a mixture of fear and delight, the firework display of the Allied bombs, rose at five, read both parts of *Henry IV*, meditated *Hamlet*, and could not understand why the Allied advance was not quicker. This division of mind, this desire (at least on the part of Gide) for liberty, contradicted by, yet entertained alongside an admiration for the military product of totalitarianism, is reflected in a clarified and sharpened form in Jean Anouilh's *Antigone* (1944), the most famous of all the French plays actually written during the war.

In the period of confusion that followed the end of the war the now defunct Paris newspaper *Combat*, which used to carry a banner across its front page proclaiming 'From the Resistance to the Revolution', asked its readers to vote on who were the greatest living French writers. Not all those chosen, of course, were dramatists, but a considerable proportion were people who had been at some time or other connected with the theatre. The result showed that the top three authors in the estimation of *Combat* readers, who in general were members of the intelligent liberal Left, were Gide (423 votes), Albert Camus (342), and Jean-Paul Sartre (324). They were followed in fourth place by André Malraux. In the fifth came Montherlant (290 votes against Malraux's 298). It was something of a triumph for Montherlant, so soon after his public disgrace, to come in top of all the wholly professional dramatists, even in the judgment of a newspaper of the Left.

The next three were Claudel (256), François Mauriac (243), and another dramatist, Jules Romains (191). Then came Gide's friend, Martin du Gard (180), and, surprisingly low, Colette (172). Georges Duhamel, a popular novelist whom Léautaud particularly despised, got 169 votes, and Anouilh, already a figure of bitter controversy, no more than 141. Marcel Aymé, a novelist and short story writer of high talent whose conduct during the war had been much criticised by the Resistance, obtained 128 votes, considerably more than the 107 and 99 respectively given to the surrealists Paul Eluard and André Breton. The remarkable Provençal novelist Jean Giono led Jean Cocteau by 97 to 93. The only music hall writer to appear in the list is Jacques Prévert, who received 90 votes.

His presence is neither surprising nor undeserved. Prévert is the author of the harrowing song, *Barbara*, which quickly became one of the most famous items in the repertoire of Les Frères Jacques, five French music hall artists who dress in clinging black like Musidora in Louis Feuillade's *Judex*, with the addition of black capes that make them resemble bats. They leap about the stage in the gathering darkness, and are capable of astonishing vocal orchestrations, and of probably the fastest, most compulsive utterance known to man. Barbara is a young girl in the streets of Brest one night when the city is bombed. Without a full stop, without a comma, without pause or punctuation of any kind, Les Frères Jacques race through this poem to its annihilating climax, giving to its final word 'Rien' the emphatic thud of one who has crashed into a brick wall at a hundred miles an hour, a total destruction to which the whole universe seemed to be moving, as to an inevitable goal.

> Oh Barbara
> Il pleut sans cesse sur Brest
> Comme il pleuvait avant
> Mais ce n'est plus pareil et tout est abimé
> C'est une pluie de deuil terrible et désolée
> Ce n'est même plus l'orage
> De fer d'acier de sang
> Tout simplement des nuages
> Qui crèvent comme des chiens
> Des chiens qui disparaissent
> Au fil de l'eau sur Brest
> Et vont pourrir au loin
> Au loin très loin de Brest
> Dont il ne reste rien.[11]

In any history of the modern French theatre this poem, and this performance should not be forgotten.

Prévert was followed by the Communist poet and novelist Aragon with 87 votes. Aragon was later the editor of the

---

11. In this magnificent poem, through which rush the terror and destruction of war with the uncontrollable force of a mighty wind, the bombs rain down and totally destroy Brest, whilst a young girl, panic-stricken, vainly seeks refuge.
    PREVERT, Jacques: *Paroles*, Le Livre de Poche, NRF Gallimard, Le Point du Jour, Paris, 1949.

independent Communist literary weekly, *Les Lettres françaises* and, like so many others in this book, he ended his life in disillusion and disappointment when both he and Barrault were repudiated in the student rising of May 1968.

After André Maurois (82), Michaux (77), Alain (71), Queneau (58), the author of a book *Mon ami Pierrot*, which greatly influenced the early novels of Iris Murdoch, Supervielle (47), came the wretched Céline with 46 votes. Valéry Larbaud obtained 29 votes, and Julien Green 28. Salacrou had 28, a figure that must have caused great heart-burning in the grand apartment in the Avenue Foch. Léautaud's 25 however must have been a pleasant surprise, since Léautaud had never engaged in any of the forms of writing, such as the theatre or the novel, which bring widespread renown.

At the bottom of the list there is much crowding: Dorgelès (25), Carco (24), Gracq (23), Maurras (22), Lacretelle (22), Daniel-Rops, the historian of the cathedrals, (21), Herriot (21), and the theologian Jacques Maritain (21). A surprise is reserved for the very end. Simenon ties with Peyrefitte for the lowest place of all, with no more than 20. This is a disconcerting position to be held by a man whom the writer at the top of the list, André Gide, regarded as one of the very greatest of living authors: as in fact a novelist who brought to the attention of his readers, casually and without pretension, moral issues of deeper significance than are to be found in the works of more ponderous writers.

The omissions are significant. The leading dramatists of the pre-war period seem to have been entirely forgotten. There is no mention of Jean-Jacques Bernard or of Marcel Pagnol, famous both on stage and screen for such dramas of Marseilles life as *César* and *Fanny*; nor of Steve Passeur, whose *L'Acheteuse*, about a rich woman who dominated her husband, had achieved great success in 1930. No one remembered Mazaud, nor Bernstein, nor Vildrac. A certain almost sordid melancholy clouded the past. Léautaud met Vildrac at a funeral in 1948, and found his appearance vulgar and unprepossessing. He had a straggly moustache and beard, and looked as if he had just got out of a bath, and was still wet. Léautaud remembered him when he and his wife had had an art gallery in the rue de Seine. But he admits that Vildrac had real talent as a playwright, and a very personal choice of subject.

This is more than he can say for Bernstein, the great savage luminary of the early years of the century. Bataille had been dead for many years, but Bernstein was still writing busily. Yet Léautaud recalls him only as a *coureur de jupes*, boastful of his supposed conquests, but not, in Léautaud's opinion, really successful. Guitry, one of the few men whom Léautaud admired with genuine warmth, had slipped into complete oblivion, although he lived until 1957. The days of the domination of the middle class had passed away; also those of light-hearted, fashionable frivolity, and of gentle, Chekhovian, tender regrets. There were to be plenty of regrets in Anouilh, but they were to be fierce, and resentful, and appalled.

For a few years, in fact, the stage was to be dominated by politics. From the end of the war until the plays of Samuel Beckett and Eugene Ionesco finished off all hope of salvation by political or indeed by any other activity, the *théâtre engagé* reigned supreme, and, after it was dead in France, exerted great influence in Britain. Marshal Pétain had encouraged the production in France during the war of films with a political message, lauding the Nation, and Family, and Work. These films were few in number, and were neither notable, nor successful. Balzac's Duchesse shook their foundations with the implications of her cynical observation, 'La religion sera toujours une nécessité politique.' It was becoming clear that an awareness of the importance of political and social dynamism was invading the world of entertainment. This urgent sense was what Antonin Artaud (1896–1948) wished frantically to bring into the theatre. He had been trying to do so ever since the 1920s, when he produced Roger Vitrac's *Victor* (1928), the best modern play that ever entered his repertory. Ida Mortemart's uncontrollable explosion of wind on a social occasion in that play symbolised for Artaud the explosion by which he hoped to blow up the ordinary theatre. Like Jouvet, he believed in the domination of the director. Where he differed from Jouvet was in his attitude to the text. He despised the text. He preferred 'le cri' to 'l'écrit'. For coherent speech he substituted cries, screams, shrieks, and incantations.

Despite the enormous efforts he made with his adaptation of *The Cenci* (1935) Artaud never successfully demonstrated his theory of the Theatre of Cruelty. His work was a delayed action bomb that had to wait for its full effect until his theories were triumphantly put into practice by Peter Brook in *US* and *The Marat/Sade*, and by Jérôme Savary in *Le Grand Magic Circus*. For a period in the 1960s and 1970s the Theatre of Cruelty exercised both in France and in England an influence out of all proportion to its influence during Artaud's lifetime.

The theory of political dynamism was explicitly stated by Jean-Paul Sartre in 1946 in a commentary on Jean Anouilh, a dramatist with whom he is generally thought to have little in common. An approach had been made towards it by André Gide in his North African Journal in 1943. Gide, as we have seen, was to a certain extent troubled by his admiration for the German soldiers he encountered. He certainly did not, as Léautaud did, desire a German victory. His patriotism, his love of France could not be questioned. But the fact remains that until he met the 'glorious Eighth Army' under Montgomery he did not find any soldiers morally comparable with the Germans, and he protested against the vilification of the enemy which took up a large part of both German and Allied propaganda.

But then he reflected that the vital question is not really whether one can find individual good men in the enemy country or party. The real question which should decide one's attitude is not the moral worth of individuals but the principles and ethics that animate them. For the principles and ethics of Hitler, Gide had an absolute hatred. They weighed down on his head and chest, he said, so that they almost prevented him from thinking and breathing. Character was not the thing that really mattered.

Three years later Sartre took these feelings of Gide and constructed out of them a theory of what the modern theatre should and would be. He concluded that the theatre of characters had nothing more to give to the world. There was no longer any room for character delineation, such as Bernstein had given to his masterful capitalists, or Vildrac to his timid young men, or Jean-Jacques Bernard to wistful, inarticulate girls like Martine, or Montherlant to ascetic grandees like the Master of Santiago, or Salacrou to eccentrics like Patchouli. In the modern world it was necessary to replace the conflict of characters with the conflict of rights.

People who defended the right were not necessarily good: people who defended the wrong were not necessarily wicked. Their individual worth was no longer of any importance. Sartre would have no sympathy with the view often expressed in the 1970s in the productions of the Royal Court's Theatre Upstairs, that it is sufficient to see a man get out of a Rolls-Royce to know that he is personally evil. It was not a question of opposition of characters between a Stalinist and a Trotskyist; it was not an opposition of character that opposed an anti-Nazi to an SS in 1933; the difficulties of international politics do not arise from the personal characters of the men who govern us; and strikes do not reveal differences of character between employers and employed. In each of these cases it was Sartre's principle that in the last analysis the real question was one of an opposition of values and morals.

Sartre's theory is obviously far too simple. The personal character of Richard Nixon was quite as powerful an influence on the history of the United States in 1973 and 1974 as were the principles of the Republican Party. Nevertheless this theory had considerable influence on the early post-war theatre in France. Sartre claimed that every individual, when faced with a clash of values, was free to choose those to which he would adhere. His choice was not determined by his character: it was his character that was determined by his choice.

This is the basis of Sartre's best plays. In *La Putain respectueuse* the heroine betrays her lover because she chooses to respect the dictates of society. Sometimes in his work it is almost impossible to tell which side Sartre himself is on. *Les Mains sales*, the story of a young Communist who cannot always bring himself—and in this he resembles Sartre—to accept the instructions of the Party, illustrates the conflict between conscience and cause. Most audiences conclude, though rather uncertainly, that Sartre is for the man who obeys his conscience, but he himself says that this is a mistake. He has even stopped the production of the play at times and in places where the popular interpretation of it might injure the Communist cause.

But Sartre's formula has not held for subsequent French drama. The best later dramatists—Samuel Beckett, Jean Genet, Marguerite Duras—do not show the clash of rival truths. They seek only to establish their own. But so long as his theory held the field—actually in fact before it formally entered it—Sartre found its perfect exemplification in *Antigone*. It is fascinating that Sartre's best play should have been written by Anouilh!

When American audiences first saw *Antigone*, which came to them with the enormous reputation of having been the play that most vividly encapsulated the spirit of the Resistance, they were disappointed with it. Antigone is very conscious of being young, and knows that she will never see old age: she is aware that she is not as pretty as her elder sister Ismène: to make herself as beautiful as possible she wears a ball dress, and powders her face, and puts rouge on her lips so that her fiancé Hémon, the son of the tyrant of Thebes, Creon, shall not be disappointed in her: she is deeply attached to her little dog. Nevertheless those who saw the play in New York felt that she was not a real character, but a wraith whose only mission was to say No to the oppressor. Sartre agrees with this. It is why he admired the play, and it is what gave him the occasion to formulate his theory of the new contemporary drama.

The first reaction to *Antigone* in Paris in 1944 was one of indignation on the part of those sympathetic to the Resistance. The word ran round that *Antigone* was a Nazi play. It was thought in the arguments between Antigone and Creon that Creon made out the better case. In fact at one point Antigone admits this, and agrees to accept the mercy that Creon offers her. And then, for no particular reason, public opinion changed. Antigone's brothers, Etéocles and Polynice, had been defeated in their revolt against Creon, who had buried the first with honour, and decreed that the body of the other should be left exposed to be pecked at and ultimately devoured by birds. This was the voice of authority, and Antigone defied it. Frail, timid, frightened and shrinking, but nevertheless driven on by some irresistible impulse inside her, she had, in full view of the guards placed round the body of Polynice, flung earth upon the corpse of her brother, in accordance with the imperative rites of her religion. After a comparatively small number of performances Creon became identified in the popular view with the German Occupants: and to these Occupants Antigone was the indomitable rebel who, though routed in argument, still resolutely said No. Even before the end of 1944 the legend had become firmly established that in writing *Antigone* Anouilh had deliberately intended to present to the public a Resistance play.

Now that the passage of time enables us to see *Antigone* in perspective, it is its dramatic merits rather than its ambiguous political significance that makes the deepest impression. *Antigone* does not owe its immortality to the fact that like Hugo's *Hernani*, it was at one particular point in history (largely through misunderstanding) a document of high social significance, but to the other and more important fact that it is a living and breathing play, instinct with that spirit of bitterness and regret, of poetry and disgust, of horror at the contrast between what life could be and what life is that makes Anouilh the most deeply searing as well as the greatest of modern French dramatists: indeed one of the very greatest dramatists in the whole of European history. No other French dramatist passes through such torments as Anouilh: no other dramatist has so poignant a vision of such soaring heights. He is, like Terence Rattigan, anima naturaliter dramatica.

The theatrical vitality of *Antigone* is undeniable, from the disenchanted *désinvolture* of the Prologue's casual acceptance of ruin and death as things inevitable and the tenderness of Antigone's asking the nurse to talk to her dog if for one reason or another she cannot talk to it herself, to the play's great scene when Antigone forces Creon to kill her against his will. The critic Gabriel Marcel rightly called this the most powerful that Anouilh had yet written, and one of the finest in modern drama. Here, if anywhere, the play has an intended political significance: what Anouilh is telling us is that it is he, the king, the master, not the weak and trembling Antigone, who is not free, who is the prisoner of power.

It was, of course, absurd to say that *Antigone* was a Nazi play. Anouilh, except in occasionally a personal sense, has little or no interest in politics. But the nature and quality of Antigone's famous No has been questioned even by critics who have devoted long and serious consideration to the play. Neither Gabriel Marcel, who admires it, nor Clément Borgal, who does not, accepts that this No is the defiance of oppressive authority that it is now universally taken to be.

They maintain that this No is not an assertion of freedom, but a denial and defiance of life itself. Antigone is determined to die, not because Creon represents a principle of life that is evil, but because she is afraid of life itself. Life is what has made Creon old and sucked from him all satisfactions and joys and has put wrinkles into his face; and it is because of this, not because authoritarianism is evil, that she is resolved to die.

The world which Anouilh offers us, says Marcel, is ignoble in *Antigone*, as it was to be said to be ignoble, and even disgusting, in *Ardèle* and in *La Valse des Toréadors*. When Creon proves to Antigone that the brother for whose honour she is dying, for the safety of whose soul she is sacrificing herself, was nothing but a heartless, worthless pleasure-seeker, she can find nothing to reply. Nor is her other brother, Etéocles, whom Creon had buried with ceremony, any better. Both of them, if he had remonstrated with them when they came home drunk and reeling, would have struck their father Oedipus, himself guilty of incest, in the face. A final touch of sordidness is added when Creon says that in battle the bodies of Etéocles and Polynice were so mangled and disfigured that he really does not know which is the one that has been left exposed, and which the one that is honourably buried. Borgal criticises this vision of the world because it has no gleam of Christian hope, which seems irrelevant, since Anouilh has never claimed to be a Christian dramatist. But Marcel, who is above this sort of absurdity, also condemns it as being altogether too savage, brutal, and degrading.

Some colour is given to these accusations by the vocabulary which Anouilh chooses to employ. He cuts across moments of the greatest tenderness with expressions which, at the time that he first used them, were unknown in the theatre, whatever they might be in private life. Thus when Antigone is thinking so sadly of her dog's loneliness when she is dead, and asks for it to be cared for, the nurse interrupts with brutal realism, 'Et si elle pisse sur mes tapis?'[12] Within a few years Anouilh was to carry this freedom of expression much further.

Jean-Jacques Gautier, the most outspoken and trenchant of Parisian critics, was moved to desperate protest by the language which the wife of the General St. Pé uses to her abject and pitifully heroic husband, who sets before himself an ideal of loyalty to the bed-ridden and wretched woman which he cannot possibly sustain. Gautier describes as abominable the scene in *La Valse des Toréadors* (1952) in which this tormented and terrible creature rises from her bed, and denounces the General's humiliating lecheries. 'I think,' says Gautier, 'of the atrocious words which she employs.' 'Je l'entends lui cracher à la figure avec volupté toutes sortes d'abjectes précisions. "Pour moi tu es ceci, tu es cela . . . Tu es ma *boîte à ordures*".'[13] Gautier goes on to wonder how much longer the public will continue to endure Anouilh's paroxysms in the display of dirty linen. 'After excess, the excess of excess, and then what? And then tomorrow?'

---

12.   And if she pisses on my carpet?

13.   I hear her relishing spitting in his face all sorts of abject insults. 'For me you are this, you are that . . . You are my chamber-pot.'
      GAUTIER, Jean-Jacques: *Deuç fauteuils d'orchestre pour Jean-Jacques Gautier et J. Sennep*, Flammarion, Paris.

Tomorrow brought a surprise. Anouilh's next play was *L'Alouette*, which was produced on 14 October 1953 at the Théâtre Montparnasse-Gaston Baty, under the direction of Marguerite Jamois, with Suzanne Flon as Joan of Arc and Michel Bouquet as the Dauphin. This play is unique in Anouilh's work in that it ends in a blaze of sheer triumphant uncomplicated and unquestionable joy. Rarely has there been seen upon the stage such an ecstasy of victorious happiness as when the Dauphin interrupts the scene of Joan's burning with the words, (to which the actor Michel Bouquet communicated an overwhelming excitement), 'La vraie fin de l'histoire de Jeanne est joyeuse. Jeanne d'Arc, c'est une histoire qui finit bien!' and the whole company flung themselves into the task of dismantling the fagots and the stake, and replacing them with an altar; with lights streaming through stained glass windows, whilst organs and bells peal out, and Joan stands erect, holding her standard aloft, smiling, and everyone else kneels, and the Archbishop places the crown on the Dauphin's head, and the curtain slowly falls. *L'Alouette* is a happier play than any of the 'Pièces roses' such as *L'Invitation au château*, which have disturbing undertones, and its ending with the Dauphin's coronation instead of Joan's execution, in defiance of logical time but with complete emotional truth, is Anouilh's first and simplest demostration of the amazing theatrical dexterity he later manifested in *Ne réveillez pas madame* (1970).

Anouilh's critics however are never satisfied. Borgal had lamented the lack of hope in *Antigone*. *L'Alouette* is full of hope; nevertheless Borgal dismisses it, this time because it does not formulate the opposition between rival political and moral systems that had been at the base of *Antigone*.

For the same reason he is less than enthusiastic about *Becket* (1959). Anouilh's *Becket* does not show the struggle between Church and State which is described with care in T. S. Eliot's *Murder in the Cathedral*. It is a private, not a public drama and, despite Sartre, is built on character. On the one hand there is the proud, cold, elegant Becket, incapable of affection, able in a single moment to switch from one absolute loyalty to another, the incorruptible mercenary of honour: and on the other the bewildered, loving Henry, who cannot comprehend why Becket in the flash of an eyelid turns utterly against him.

Both men grope towards an understanding of this in one of the most splendid scenes in modern theatre, that in which on the cold seashore they talk to each other on their restless horses, Henry longing for some assurance of even past affection, Becket for the first time recognising the one thing wanting in his nature. When Henry despairingly asks whether Becket had ever loved him, there is a world of desolation in the reply of the implacable archbishop: 'Insofar as I am capable of love, yes.'

Gautier handsomely recognised *Becket* as a masterpiece, played with turbulent passion by Daniel Ivernel as the king, and by Bruno Cremer as Becket with an exalted grace. The Royal Shakespeare Company's production of the play in London was disappointingly inadequate.

If *L'Alouette* and *Becket* were attacked (wrongly) because they had too little to do with politics, *Pauvre Bitos* (1956) was denounced, and with even greater vigour, because it had too much. Gautier, whilst admitting that it had several moments of quality and some penetrating observations, said that it made hatred current coin. The first performance, at the Théâtre Gaston Baty, almost provoked a riot, since it was taken by the audience to be a slander on the Resistance. The suggestion in most of the reviews I read was that no patriotic audience could be expected to sit through it peacefully, and I went to the next performance after these reviews appeared with some trepidation. I cannot decide whether I was more relieved or disappointed that the evening passed off in perfect calm.

Pauvre Bitos arose out of a conflict of emotions and a state of great bitterness in Anouilh's mind. It is the most direct expression that he has given to the disturbing fact that the drama of a country flourishes when that country is in a state of mortal division and distress. The great age of Greek drama coincided with the disaster and defeat of the Peloponnesian war. The triumphs of the Elizabethan and Jacobean theatre resulted from the ambiguity and stress of emotion following on the disillusion and rebellion that succeeded the routing of the Armada. The highest peak of French drama was reached on the eve of the defeats of Louis XIV. Solid achievement and national content breed a mood of complacency whose consequence in the theatre is the monolithic dullness of Soviet drama or the childish chauvinism of *Where the Rainbow Ends*. Anxiety and distress produce a vividness of response, an ambiguity of attitude, an inability not to see the merits and defects of conflicting values, even perhaps an incapacity to choose decisively between them that give permanent life to the drama.

29. *Pauvre Bitos* with Michel Bouquet (Théâtre Montparnasse 1956).
    Photograph by courtesy of Lipnitzki-Viollet

This mood of a magnificently divided soul was widespread in
France during the war, and in the years that immediately followed it. It is the principal source of the greatness of the French
theatre between the defeat of 1940 and the accession of General
de Gaulle in 1958, with the subsequent restoration of French
prosperity and international prestige.

It can be seen plainly enough in individual lives. Georges Suarez was the biographer of Clemenceau, and a supporter of the moderate government of André Tardieu. He vigorously op-. posed the reactionary Right wing policies of the Action Française. But when the Right made its celebrated and abortive attempt on 6 February 1934 to overthrow democratic govern- ment ('Better Hitler than Blum' was its slogan) he changed sides, and he was the first journalist to be shot for treason after the Liberation of Paris. In Claude Roy, who has written drama criticism of great delicacy and perception, there was a move- ment in exactly the opposite direction. He wrote for *L'Action Française*, and before the war was the youngest member of the staff of *Je Suis Partout*. His interests were primarily literary, and he shared to the full the overwhelming enthusiasm which French collaborationists felt for Margaret Mitchell's *Gone With the Wind*.

This was accepted as an entirely Fascist work because, in the collaborationist view, it showed the destruction of American civilisation of the south by barbarian democrats of the north. The only foreign writer whom collaborationists regarded with an admiration equal to that they felt for Margaret Mitchell was Hilaire Belloc. The favourite French writer of *Je suis partout* after it became the most powerful and literate of all the French journals which campaigned for the victory of Germany, was Jean Giraudoux.

Claude Roy exerted a considerable influence on French literary taste both before and after he escaped from being a prisoner of war. He succeeded in reaching Vichy, where he wrote for the Vichysoisse press, and took part in the artistic activities of the 'Compagnons de France' and of the group 'Young France'. But in 1943 he rallied to the cause of Com- munism, and at the Liberation was a member of the extreme left Comité National des Ecrivains. I have noticed earlier a similar conflict of feeling in André Gide and in Paul Léautaud. Léautaud admired England, yet wished for her defeat; Gide desired the defeat of Germany, but admired the German army. Anouilh was a man to understand the ambiguity of both Gide and Léautaud. Though he wrote what quickly came to be regarded as the definitive play of the Resistance, he published one of his works, *Léocadia*, in *Je suis partout*.

It was this association with *Je suis partout* which produced both *Pauvre Bitos* and Anouilh's only direct intervention in

politics. For the editor of *Je suis partout* at the time of *Léocadia*
(1942) was the critic Robert Brasillach. Though he was undoubtedly brilliant and in many ways engaging, Brasillach during the Occupation wrote unforgiveable things. He demanded
the summary execution of men like Daladier and Béatrice
Bretty's friend, Georges Mandel, who was in fact assassinated.
Now in the early days of the war the majority of French people
were convinced that the Germans would win. In August 1940,
only 98 French officers, 113 non-commissioned officers, and 716
men decided to stay in London with de Gaulle. By the end of
that year 21,000 men of the military marine, 2000 merchant
seamen, and between seven and eight thousand soldiers had
taken the option of being repatriated to France. Brasillach at
this time fully shared the confidence of ordinary French people
that Germany would be victorious. Neither the invasion of
Russia nor the entry of the United States into the war altered
his belief in Germany's invincibility. It was against this background that he was able without misgiving or fear of personal
consequences to express his virulent hatred of Jews and of the
Socialist politicians who had failed to avert the war. He also
denounced both Claude Roy and his wife.

But on 25 July 1943 he seems to have received some sort of
shock. It was on that day that Mussolini fell. The fall of Mussolini appears to have affected French collaborationists much
more than it did the British people, who, delighted though they
were, hardly regarded it as the decisive turning point of the war.
That they would have placed at Lord Montgomery's victory at
El Alamein. But the news of Mussolini's dethronement put the
cold hand of fear on Brasillach's brow. All his confidence
drained from him. He wrote in panic to a friend that in 1938
he and his associates had refused to board the sinking ship of the
Czechs, and that in 1939 they had laughed at those who were
ready to die so that Danzig should remain Polish. And now shall
we die for Danzig to remain German? 'I reply no!'

He brought his association with *Je suis partout* to a sudden
end, thereby incurring the scorn of several of his fellow-
contributors, including especially Lucien Rebatet and Pierre-
Antoine Cousteau, whose father had vainly tried to persuade
him to come to London to support de Gaulle. Either from
principle or because they felt that they had already gone too far
to draw back, these men supported Hitler until the very end,
when they fled to Germany before the advancing Allied forces

of the West. They were eventually captured, put on trial, and condemned to death, but subsequently pardoned. At his trial Cousteau behaved with great composure, but Rebatet went completely to pieces.

Not so Brasillach. As the prospect of a German victory decreased he experienced a great renewal of courage. Almost alone of the staff of *Je suis partout* he refused to seek refuge in Germany after the Liberation of Paris. He wandered round the rejoicing city, a hunted man. When he heard that his mother (who was later released) and his brother-in-law, Maurice Bardèche, with whom he had written an impressive *Histoire du cinéma* had been arrested, he gave himself up. At his trial he defended himself with remarkable coolness and skill, and the jury was momentarily shaken. But it returned a verdict of guilty, and he was condemned to death.

Whilst waiting for the sentence to be carried out he continued to write. On 1 February, five nights before his execution, his mind returned to the beginning of his political activity, and he wrote his last poem:

> Les derniers coups de feu continuent de briller
> Dans le jour indistinct où sont tombés les nôtres.
> Sur onze ans de retard, serai-je donc des vôtres?
> Je pense à vous ce soir, ô morts de février.[14]

It is evident that he knew that a petition was being organised to save his life; he did not yet regard his death as certain. But the petition failed, and he was shot at the fort of Montrouge on 6 February 1945, eleven years to the day after the attempted Right-wing *coup* of 1934. Brasillach was thirty-five years old. Claude Roy, who did not like him, and had suffered at his hands, says that he died bravely, and this is indeed generally accepted. No other important drama critic has suffered so sensational a fate as he, and since his death a society has been formed called *The Friends of Robert Brasillach*. It is ironical that Rebatet and Cousteau died peaceably in their beds many years after the end of the war. Bardèche received in 1971 the *Grand prix de la critique littéraire* for a study of Marcel Proust.

It has been said that Claude Roy refused to sign the petition

---

14. Brasillach remembers those who died in the attempted *coup* of 1934. Quoted in DIOUDONNAT, P. M.: *Je suis partout 1930–1944*, La Table Ronde, 1973.

designed to save Brasillach's life. This is not true. Roy is a man who remembers kindnesses more vividly than injuries. When presented with the petition he signed it immediately, to the consternation of friends who considered that Brasillach had done him irreparable injury. Brasillach, though a critic (and Anouilh is not fond of critics) had done no injury to Anouilh, who remembered his old editor in his hour of distress. Despite his retiring nature, his shrinking from all contact with political and public life, Anouilh strove to secure a commutation of the sentence of death. He was joined in his efforts by the future Academician Thierry Maulnier, and by the novelist François Mauriac, whose play, *Asmodée*, was one of the Comédie Française's great successes.

The incident of Brasillach's execution permanently embittered Anouilh. It has soured all his memories of the Resistance. It is what makes his *Les Poissons rouges* (1970), in the words of the critic François-Régis Bastide, 'sweat with hatred of the people'. 'Everyone.' says Bastide, 'knows that there are two important dates in the life of Jean Anouilh: that of the death of Louis XVI, on, I think, a certain 21 January, and that of the Liberation of France, in 1944. About this second date I know even less. I was then so young that I took great pleasure in entering Germany in the uniform of the spahis of General Leclerc, a crime for which Jean Anouilh will not forgive me.'[15]

Bastide is a great admirer of Anouilh, and these words have a touch of irony. But they bear witness to the fact that a great dramatist is more likely to be a rebel than a conformist. Certainly Anouilh has always swum hard and guilefully against the tide, and never more so than in his attitude to the Resistance. This is what has led to such fierce division of opinion about his work, to such misunderstandings and undeserved condemnations; and also to such strange results that his *Antigone* was taken not only in England, but also in France, to be the greatest of all Resistance plays, and yet was inordinately praised by the 'équipe atroce' of *Je suis partout*.

Pauvre Bitos is the most bitter of Anouilh's plays, and its fundamental assumption is that the Resistance was not a thing to be proud of, something that restored the dignity that France had lost through the Vichy Government of Marshal Pétain and Pierre Laval, but that it was little more than a sordid settlement

---

15. BASTIDE, F. R.: *Au théâtre certains soirs*, de Seuil, 1972.

of old scores. It attacks both the Resistance and those whom the Resistance punished at the *épuration* after the Liberation.

The scene of *Pauvre Bitos* is a fancy dress dinner, with all the diners representing a figure from the French Revolution, Bitos himself coming as Robespierre. The dinner is given by his old school-fellows, who in his youth had persecuted and ridiculed him for his poverty. Since the Liberation Bitos has become a magistrate, and as a magistrate has gravely injured some of his former tormentors, and not his tormentors only. It is the intention of the survivors of these that he shall not leave the dinner alive.

Whilst they are waiting for him they recount a recent incident in his life. He has requisitioned for his sister an apartment on the very same day that he demanded the head of its occupant for collaboration during the war. One hardly knew which he wanted more—the apartment or the head. Bitos had himself been a childhood friend of the *milicien*, but he insisted on being present at the execution. The *milicien*, scarcely knowing what had happened but wishing to rise to the occasion, asked to shake Bitos by the hand. There was a scene of mutual forgiveness, and before the fusillade the *milicien* murmured 'Vive la France', and was himself allowed to give the order to fire.

Bitos was very pale. It was noticed that he wanted to speak. As soon as his friend dropped to the ground he took out his watch and observed, 'Dead on time.' Just like a station master. 'That night Bitos broke down, and sent a doll to the *milicien's* little girl. As a replacement, no doubt. A very expensive doll. That is what is so touching, for Bitos is poor. It cost him more than half a month's salary as a magistrate. A doll that shut its eyes, said papa and mama, and made water. Also it was a German doll, for if executions were still going on, trade must not be interfered with.'[16] All this is very Robespierre.

Now it is to be remarked here, what was overlooked in the fury of the play's reception, that it is not only Bitos who revenges himself for the hardships and the insults of his youth. His hosts at the *diner de têtes* are as vindictive as he is, and in fact they seem in Anouilh's eyes still less excusable. The second act of the play goes back to the time of the real Robespierre and it contains a remarkable scene in which Robespierre as the cleverest child in his religious college says no with an unflinching obsti-

16. ANOUILH, Jean: *Pauvre Bitos*, La Table Ronde, Paris, 1956.

nacy, a cold determination, a resolution to accept no quarter, even the quarter his enemies are anxious to give him, that goes beyond that of Antigone herself. It is hard not to feel here that for Robespierre, and therefore for Bitos, Anouilh had a certain admiration. Despite the condemnation of critics like Jean-Jacques Gautier and Marc Begbeider, *Pauvre Bitos* is of astonishing vigour, and remarkable sardonic humour.

The bitterness of Anouilh is well known, but had he lived in a less bitter time it is likely enough that it is the seeds of tenderness in him that would have grown instead of those of rage and disgust. It is the tenderness of his work, crossed and frustrated though it is, that makes the most permanent if not the most immediately sensational impression. When in *Antigone* all have died, Hémon by Antigone's side, and Eurydice, Creon's wife, has quietly, composedly, as she did everything quietly, composedly, killed herself, Creon is left alone with his young page, to whom he says sadly, 'You wish to grow up?' and eagerly the little page replies, 'Oh oui, monsieur', to which Creon answers 'Tu es fou, petit. Il faudrait jamais devenir grand.'

This regret for lost childhood haunts all Anouilh's work; it is more poignant than any other quality in his plays. It is strange to reflect that Anouilh, so famous for his uninhibited savagery, might, in other kindlier ages, have been one of the most heart-melting of writers. He might have written exactly the sort of play which critics said, in protest against the fierce egotism of Bernstein, would meet with the instant approval and gratitude of the general public, which they mistakenly thought yearned for the good, the beautiful and the true.

In their view of the desire of ordinary human nature for gentleness and spiritual reassurance, they seem to have been wrong. Mazaud answered perfectly to their specifications, and Mazaud quickly became forgotten, even though presented with all the intellectual and avant garde prestige of Copeau, and welcomed by the enthusiasm of Léautaud. It is the wickedness, the evil, and the cruelty of our time that have preserved Anouilh from being another Mazaud. The theatre has gained from the world's loss.

There is a feeling of surprise when one contrasts the gravity and even pessimism of the French theatre in the late 1940s with the euphoria of the British drama of the same period, when it seemed to be breaking the bonds of naturalism with the joyous poetic spirit of Christopher Fry and the, admittedly less resilient,

theatrical verse plays of T. S. Eliot. But Britain was then a
united country, entering with some degree of enthusiasm into
the new age expected of the Welfare State. France, on the other
hand, was not united.

Almost all Frenchmen had come to agree that the expulsion
of the Germans was a national advantage. But they had very
different reasons for thinking this, the sole point on which most
of them were agreed. Even the Resistance itself was not at one.
Some believed in democratic government as exemplified by the
Third Republic. But certain amongst them wanted to overthrow it, and others saw the Liberation as a means towards the
complete destruction of the existing social and economic order.
On 26 August 1944 General de Gaulle rode in a triumphal
procession from the Arc de Triomphe to Notre Dame. Vast
crowds of excited citizens acclaimed him the whole length of
the route. But on the square in front of the cathedral there was
a mysterious burst of gunfire of which no satisfactory explanation has ever been given.

There were very good reasons why the French nation during
these years had little or no cause to look upon either the present
or the future with pleasure or with hope. Immediately after
the Liberation the condition of France was desperate, and
weighed upon the spirits of everyone in the country who was not
of an irrepressibly optimistic nature. During the war there had
been heavy loss of life, not, it is true, on the Russian or the
German scale, but enough to throw the existence of the country
into disruption. In the army 149,954 men had been killed. A
hundred and fifty thousand had been deported, and 188,000
civilians were killed in the Allied bombardments which prepared the way for the Normandy landings. Thirty thousand
men and women were shot, and 38,000 prisoners of war died
in captivity. Fifty-one thousand others were killed or disappeared.[17]

The material damage was on an even greater scale. Nearly
all the bridges, stations and locks had to be rebuilt. Two million
homes were damaged, and 200,000 of them were entirely destroyed. Half the vineyards had to be replanted. The machinery
both for agriculture and for industry had been destroyed. In
1938 France had been 87 per cent self-sufficient; in 1945, it was

17. FRANÇOIS, Michel: *La France et les français*, Bibliothèque de la
Pléiade, Paris.

not more than 65 per cent. But though France had to buy more from abroad than ever before, she had less money to do it with. During the Occupation the Germans had exacted from France more than 300 milliards of francs, and internal expenses had enormously increased. In 1913 the budget had been five milliards. In 1946 it was 600 milliards. In that year the budget deficit was 215 milliards.

On the other hand France had had much to be proud of during the war. Dunkirk was an especial point of glory. It was largely the voluntary sacrifice of the French divisions under General La Laurencie that enabled 260,000 English and more than 100,000 French to reach the shores of England. During the early weeks of the campaign in Tunisia in 1942 which made so poor an impression on Gide, the French troops were almost alone in standing up to the Germans and Italians.

There were a few dramatists of exuberant temperament who responded to facts like these more readily than to the graver considerations that depressed the greater playwrights of the time. They were, naturally enough, boulevard writers, for it often seems that commercial dramatists have a more robust morale than those who enjoy a higher regard. They are more cheerful in adversity; they are less ready to accept defeat. Amongst the light-hearted plays of the period were Jean Luc-Bernard's *Le Complexe de Philémon* in the season 1950–51; Albert Husson's *La Cuisine des anges* (1951–52); Gabriel Arout's *La Dame de Tréfle* (1952–53), which in a small but significant degree anticipated future developments in the work of dramatists like Pinter and Duras by leaving the identity of one of the characters unexplained; and Alexandre Rivemale's charming fantasy about an elephant, *Azouk* (1953–54). Best of all were Alexandre Breffort's haunting portrait of a simple-hearted, transparently sincere and touchingly conscientious prostitute in *Irma la douce* (1956–57), set to ravishing music by Marguerite Monnot, and the playfully daring comedies of André Roussin (now a member of the Académie Française) *La Petite Hutte* (1947–48), *Les Oeufs de l'Autruche* (1948–49) and *L'Amour fou* (1955–56).

Roussin was particularly successful. When Anouilh was accused not very seriously of being a popular dramatist he shook his head rather sadly, and said, 'No, I am nothing like so popular as Roussin. My plays don't run for a thousand nights.'

Anouilh is a man who notices such things, and there have

been many such things to notice. On his way to the Comédie Française to read his play *Becket* to the selection committee, he was observed by the critic Bastide to go into a bookshop to buy a text of the play. When he asked for *Becket* the bookshop attendant handed him a copy of *Waiting for Godot*. Life is full of such irritations, and Anouilh does not always take to them kindly. As a young man Anouilh took a play to Charles Dullin. When he had read it Dullin said, 'I am going to please you. I shall put your play on the stage. Tear the manuscript into small pieces, and I'll use it as snow.' Incidents like these make a deep impression on Anouilh; and they are not lessened in their impact by the fact that this particular incident, for example, was made public, not by Anouilh himself, but by his fellow-dramatist, Marcel Achard. It is hardly surprising that it has been said of him that he 'has deceived many with his solemn glasses and studious air. This little man was born with a passion for justice. It is a formidable weakness. So that he should not die stifled, he has once a year to seek relief in a scream in three acts.'[18]

It was in the 1953–54 season that the mime Marcel Marceau began giving the solo performances that have made him almost as famous in Britain as in France. The Renaud–Barrault Company led the extraordinary renaissance of Georges Feydeau with its production of *Occupe-toi d'Amélie* (1948–49), and it was about this time that the high talents of Madeleine Renaud became fully appreciated. Even when she had been a senior Sociétaire of the Comédie Française her physical charm and piquancy and her well-shaped legs had been what had struck critics most powerfully. She was put at the top of the league, but the league chosen for her was not the highest.

Towards the end of the 1940s all that changed. The newer generation of critics, led by Jean-Jacques Gautier, recognised in her performances a more serious quality than had been perceived before, though doubtless it had always been there. Beside the mischievous provocativeness and saucy charm which had hitherto been seen in her more or less exclusively it was now acknowledged that she had an incomparable radiance and joy. Her presence on the stage, quiet, still, and unobtrusive, illuminated the theatre with light of the rarest quality. She

18. BASTIDE, F. R.: *Au théâtre certains soirs*. Seuil, 1972.

entered the ranks of the world's very greatest actresses, not only
of the present day, but of all time.

During this period the Comédie Française exactly mirrored
the conditions of the nation. It was divided against itself. In
1947 a journalist, Pierre-Aimé Touchard, became its Administrator, and remained in the post until the intrigues and down-
right hatred of some of the older Sociétaires forced him to
resign. When Barrault and Renaud, accompanied by Marie
Bell, Renée Faure, Maurice Escande, Aimé Clariond, Jean
Debucourt, and Jean Chevrier, left the Comédie in 1946 those
who remained behind were well content. For Barrault and
those who thought like him were supporters of the ideas of the
Cartel: and the Cartel had shaken the Théâtre Français to its
foundations.

Until 1936 the Comédie had been essentially a society of
actors. We all acted as superlatively as we could, said Béatrice
Bretty, and that was that: we did not bother about a *metteur en
scène*. This was what the Cartel changed, and the dissidents of
1946 were those who agreed with its new conception of theatrical production. The old guard amongst the Sociétaires—
Béatrice Bretty, Jean Yonnel, Denis d'Inès—were not at all
sorry to see the dynamic young Barrault and his friends depart.
They hoped that their departure would clear the way for a
return to the old days when the player, not the director, was
supreme.

This is undoubtedly what would have happened if the new
Administrateur had not been himself a believer in the methods
of the Cartel. It might have happened anyway if Touchard,
who was not a strong man, had not found to support him that
remarkable director and actor, Jean Meyer. Touchard aroused
the contempt, and Meyer the virulent hatred, of Béatrice
Bretty, whose strength of character and bitterness of determination were belied by her buxom bourgeois appearance and her
famous cascading laugh. The Comédie was rent in twain between these three, none of whom permanently triumphed.
Touchard's nerves were worn to pieces by 1953, when he
resigned. Soon afterwards Bretty was put into retirement, and
in 1959 Meyer sensationally followed as the direct result of an
astounding political situation in which his work was found to
be superlatively good, highly successful, and altogether
unsatisfactory.

In the midst of this confusion and mutual recrimination

Gaston Baty in 1949 began to direct Armand Salacrou's *L'Inconnue d'Arras* in what was considered an old-fashioned Expressionist manner, and Salacrou withdrew the piece fifteen days before the projected first performance. Responding to Baty's impassioned appeals, Salacrou gave way, but he stipulated: 'I will give you my piece on condition that you invite the President of the Republic.' The invitation was duly and properly given, but on the night of the first performance the President went instead to the Athénée for the twenty-fifth anniversary of *Knock*. It was a sad blow to the pride and prestige of the National Theatre, and seemed to be a declaration of an official feeling that the function of the theatre was to make people laugh rather than to harrow their feelings. It is possible that Jean Meyer, whose power in the Comédie Française was to go on increasing for some years, made this interpretation of the President's action. If he did so he was grievously misled.

Through Meyer's influence some of those who had left returned, and there were several illustrious productions: Pierre Dux in *Le Légataire*; Marie Bell in *Le Soulier de satin*; Debucourt, of whom Meyer exclaimed, 'One ought to pay him merely for walking down the corridors.' There was in those days, said Touchard, an air of passionate resurrection about the place. He spoke emotionally of the extraordinary rigour of Meyer's productions, a rigour the London public was able to appreciate when Peter Daubeny's World Theatre Season brought Montherlant's *La Ville dont le prince est un enfant* to England: of the enthusiasm with which he was charged as if with an explosive: of his passionate devotion to the Comédie: and of his joyous optimism. If only the Comédie had had three or four like him, Touchard lamented, it would have been spared all its troubles.

A couple of months after the failure of the revival of *L'Inconnue d'Arras* there was abundant compensation in Marie Bell's *Phèdre*. Touchard was a great admirer of Marie Bell. He evidently regarded her as a convincing reply to the charge that the Comédie in the years after the war had no players of either sex comparable with Mounet-Sully or Julia Bartet. When she was tired it seemed as though she carried through her performances only as a sort of mechanism. But at all other times she gave herself wholly to the character she was playing, and on the stage was transformed. Whilst rehearsing a revival of *Le Soulier de satin*, Touchard declared that he came to understand

30. Marie Bell and Aimé Clariond in *Le Soulier de satin* at the Comédie Française (1949). Photograph by courtesy of Lipnitzki-Viollet

why Claudel looked on Marie Bell as a saint. In the part of Dona Prouhèze she rediscovered a state of childlikeness, in

31. Béatrice Bretty and Jean Meyer in *Les Caves du Vatican* at the Comédie Française (1950). Photograph by courtesy of Lipnitzki-Viollet

which humility, purity, a gentle confidence and a sense of grace brought audiences to the verge of tears. And herself also. Yet this was not like her ordinary bluff, outspoken, everyday character. One day, as she came off the stage after playing a scene in *Phèdre* he found her weeping in the wings. 'What a hell of a job,' she exclaimed. 'I'm blubbing.' Touchard said that he had never heard an actress say anything more beautiful.

André Gide's *Les Caves du Vatican* won a certain renown in 1950, and in the same year so did a production of *Le Conte d'hiver*, in which Leontes showed his mental disequilibrium by passing distractedly backwards and forwards, in and out of a display of giant banners and flags which filled the entire stage. But rapidly it became clear that such triumphs as the Comédie was to have in the next ten years were to be in the realm of more light-hearted entertainment, even of farce, and it was this that brought about the unmerited downfall of Jean Meyer.

Meyer survived the inveterate hostility of Béatrice Bretty, and his production of Feydeau's *Le Dindon* made the Comédie one of the most popular theatres in Paris. Meyer, following the trail first blazed by Barrault, created an immense public for Feydeau. In the terrible years of the Indo-China war in the early 1950s Meyer, reacting strongly, as we have seen that Roussin did, against the universal defeatism and depression, made the French National Theatre a refuge for laughter and joy. The influence of his work there eventually spread to the World Theatre Season; and this in turn led to John Mortimer's memorable translation (*A Flea in Her Ear*) of *Une Puce à l'oreille*, which became a celebrated production in 1966 at the English National Theatre.

The whole trend of Meyer's work was to make France known again as the nation before all others representative of civilised gaiety. This was a great patriotic service, but General de Gaulle, when he came to power in 1958, did not look upon it as such. The General did not want the French National Theatre to make the world laugh; he wanted it to make the world look upon France with wonder and awe. He shuddered at the thought of Feydeau, but the mention of Racine caused him to glow with pride. Unfortunately the Comédie was not well equipped to play Racine, since it was lacking in great tragic talents. But under de Gaulle the grandeur and splendour of France had to be kept constantly in mind, and in order to do so Jean Meyer produced *Phèdre* in December, 1959.

This production was a disaster. Marie Bell, as we know, for we have seen her in London, could play Phèdre, but by 1959 she had again left the Comédie Française. Edwige Feuillère also could play Phèdre. She had done so in London in 1957, when Jean-Jacques Gautier says that she was 'justly rewarded by triumph itself, by interminable applause, by innumerable recalls, and her brilliant performance was greeted by acclamations without end.' But, like Marie Bell, Feuillère was not available to the Comédie Française, which instead had to make do with the personable but unpassionate Annie Ducaux.

The piece was prettily presented in the costume of the courtiers of Louis XIV. The playing was polished, smooth, unctuous, and slow. This *Phèdre* was universally condemned, Meyer departed from the Comédie Française, and a brilliant period in its history, but with a brilliance that General de Gaulle did not appreciate, came to an end. Later in his career, in *La Ville dont le prince est un enfant*, Meyer showed by the vertiginous but always unconfusing speed and austerity of his production that he really had the power to rise to the intensity of tragic feeling. But no doubt the General liked this play no better than Feydeau. Did it not show French schools, even French religious schools, to be tainted with moral perversity?

I am sorry to have seen Meyer dismissed from the Théâtre National. Its *élan*, its vitality went with him. But it may be said that I am prejudiced. For I know M. Meyer personally, and have always found him a man of perfect courtesy and friendship, helpful and discreet, frank where frankness is compatible with kindness, but even under great provocation saying no word against his enemies. If one leaves aside Edwige Feuillère and Marie Bell (a rather cavalier way of treating two such superlative actresses), this is a kindness I have encountered in no other member of the Comédie Française, an institution unparalleled in my experience in the disagreeable art of freezing foreign drama critics with its unconcealed contempt.

But the principal dramatists of the post-war period were neither oblivious of the state of the nation nor absorbed in their own private difficulties and disagreements. Some, like Anouilh, found their temperaments directed by events into the ways of distress and even despair. But there was at least one other whose savage view of the universe, though it may have been reinforced by the circumstances of the time, derived from philosophic and religious conviction. This was Jacques Audiberti (1899–1965).

Audiberti was a fully subscribing Christian, and as such was vividly conscious of the existence of sin and evil in the world. He haunted religious places: his steps constantly took him to brood in the Parisian churches of St. Sulpice and Saint-Sebastien. In this latter church he was immensely impressed by a sermon preached by the curé. As soon as he entered the pulpit

this curé, a Franciscan, engaged Audiberti's attention by re-
moving the violently coloured carnations that decorated the
altar.

Then his eloquence enchanted and transported Audiberti.
Original sin, cried the preacher, that detestable present which
Adam left to his descendants, we wallow in it. Moreover, we
cannot discern the slightest sign that in this world there is any
hope that this metaphysical, transmitted, and transmissible
plague will be cured. The world is an organisation of murderers
who will one day themselves be murdered, and its cruelty
derives from man's initial disobedience.[19]

This view of the overwhelming power of evil saturates Audiberti's most remarkable play, *Le Mal court*, directed by Georges
Vitaly (1947). At its first presentation the critic André Frank
speculated that it might one day come to be regarded as
amongst the masterpieces of the French theatre. But Jean-
Jacques Gautier, because of the vigour of his style and his position as the drama critic of *Le Figaro*, a much more influential
writer, received it in a mood of only tepid appreciation. He was
much more excited by the appearance of a new, young actress,
Suzanne Flon (alert, pretty, with beautiful hands, an agreeable
and confident voice, and plenty of temperament: with, moreover, humour, movement, authority, and wit) than by the
emergence of a new and middle-aged author.

Nevertheless Audiberti was a dramatist of the first order,
strong in conviction and highly original. In *Le Mal court* he took
a cloak and dagger costume drama, which might have been of
little greater value than *The Scarlet Pimpernel*, and made it a
powerful and ironical denunciation of the world in which he
lived. This strange and impressive play is, or begins like, a
historical bedroom farce set amongst royal personages in the
lands of the Elector of Saxony, where the Princess of Courte-
lande, Alarica, is on her way to be married to Parfait, seventeenth of that name, king of Occident, Burgundy, and the
Vascons.

There bursts into the Princess's bedchamber an irrepressible
young man, as voluble as Mr. Jingle, but with a greater mastery
of long and involved sentences. The Niagara of controlled
verbosity, picturesque and ardent, that flows from this imposter

---

19. AUDIBERTI, Jacques: *Dimanche m'attend*, NRF Gallimard, Paris,
    1965.

pretending to be the king, and with the utmost sang-froid jump-
ing through the window when he is found out, is typical of the
richness of style for which Audiberti is famous. No other French
dramatist of his time commanded such an unstaunchable tor-
rent of rhetoric as Audiberti. The words poured out of the
mouths of his characters like a cascade of glittering jewels: there
was no end to their pomp and splendour.

> 'Mais vous, Alarica,' exclaims the athletic intruder, 'vous,
> chair de ma vie, pensée de ma chair, vous que je sais, vous
> que je sens qui m'écoutez de toutes vos bouches, qui me
> saisissez de toutes vos boucles, vous dont le coeur bondit
> d'amour et de douleur, de quel oeil oserez-vous me
> regarder quand, aujourd'hui même, ce soir, non loin du
> fleuve, devant la cathédrale, nous nous rencontrerons dans
> la présence de nos ministres et de nos tabellions?'[20]

Speeches like these immediately struck the imagination both
of audiences and of critics. But, though not in *Le Mal court*,
there were too many of them. They dragged out plays like *Les
Naturels du Bordelais* to inordinate lengths, and eventually deprived Audiberti of his public. Praised at first as the distinctive
mark of his style, they eventually led to his downfall.

But it is as a fierce moralist, as a dramatist preaching the
doctrine of the curé of Saint-Sébastien, and not as a stylist, that
Audiberti ranks amongst the leading writers of his day. He does
in fact add to the apparently illimitable profusion of his words
and a heightened style thick with expressions of nobility and
chivalry an in-built mockery that saves them from pretentiousness. He pours them out with a volubility that makes them
appear to be entirely spontaneous, and employs them almost
entirely to drive home his terrible conviction that mankind has
never recovered from the Fall.

In the Princess's bedchamber, out of these iridescent clouds
of eloquence, two images are repeatedly evoked: the cold land
of desolate plains which is her father's poverty-stricken kingdom

---

20. But you, Alarica, flesh of my life, thought of my flesh, you whom I
     know, you whom I feel listening to me with all your ears, who bind me
     with every lock of your hair, whose heart leaps with love and grief,
     with what an eye dare you look at me when, this very evening, we
     meet again, not far from the river, before the cathedral, in front of our
     ministers and their clerks?

that she is leaving is set against the rich country of splendid harvests and pealing church bells to which she is going. But this smiling and prosperous future is dashed from her hands. The night on which the play takes place is a night on which Alarica is multiply betrayed. The proposed royal marriage is a trick: her governess, who had brought her up from childhood, is in the pay of her enemies: even her father has been bribed to accept her betrayal.

But Alarica, unlike Antigone, is not a girl who says no. On the contrary she says yes. She joins the party of Creon. If the writ of evil runs, then run with it. In the last few moments of the play, in a determined reversal of all that has gone before, she herself turns traitor.

'Jusqu'ici,' she cries, still with the great Audiberti flux of words, 'Jusqu'ici, elle n'aura servi, en fin de compte, ma vie, ma si pure, ma si droite vie, qu'à masquer le présent ouragan de ma férocité. Ma férocité se démasque. Tout le mal que je n'ai pas fait, je vais le faire d'un seul coup.'[21]

The very last words of the play are 'Le mal court.' But if evil runs it may weary itself and fall. Alarica's cry may be either of defiance or of despair.

Audiberti, with his exuberant Southern nature, could not brook acquiescence in the presence of evil and misery. Unlike Beckett, he was not resigned to it: nor was he content, like Ionesco, to pour ridicule upon its absurdity. The passivity of *En Attendant Godot* or of *Fin de partie* was entirely foreign to his belligerent nature; he had too much pity for men and women to write plays of that mathematical satire which makes *La Leçon* or *Amédée* so remarkable. He had a taste for the bizarre, for superficially romantic costume dramas like *La Fourmi dans le corps* which have a canker at the heart, so that the spectacle of the heroine of Beckett's *Happy Days* buried first to her waist, and then to her neck, in sand would not have seemed strange to him.

But her serenity in these unpromising circumstances (one of Madeleine Renaud's most radiant performances) would have been beyond his comprehension. Audiberti was a man who

---

21. Until now my life, all things considered, my so pure and righteous life, has served only to hide the present storm of my ferocity. Now that ferocity is revealed. All the evil I have not done, I shall do now, in an instant of time.

32. Suzanne Flon and Michel Galabru in *Le Mal court* (La Bruyère 1955).
Photographs by courtesy of Lipnitzki-Viollet

demanded action, even desperate action. He was like a man on the edge of a precipice who cannot resist the temptation to fling himself over into the abyss. He anticipated Duras in desiring some act of desperate destruction, as when the Captain in *Quoat-Quoat* wishes for a catastrophe that will overwhelm his ship. That is why Alarica, frail and tense, after measuring the deplorable effects of goodness, joins the party of Creon. But, it has been asked, in admitting the incontestable supremacy of evil, can she bring out of the contagion some form of happiness and justice?

It is curious that Barrault, who is himself a practising Catholic, should appear to have taken little interest in so fundamentally Christian a dramatist as Audiberti. Nor was he responsible for the production of François Billetdoux's *Tchin-Tchin* (1959: Théâtre de Poche), the most professedly and ruthlessly Christian play of the whole period we are discussing, though he later presented Billetdoux's *Il faut passer par les nuages*. Billetdoux and his wife are people who take the Christian doctrine of poverty quite literally, and it is this that caused *Tchin-Tchin* to be so widely misunderstood. After the performance of a further play of his, *Va donc chez Torpe*, Billetdoux and Madame entertained my wife and myself to drinks in the café of the Place de l'Alma which is the scene of *La Folle de Chaillot*. Billetdoux had just published a novel, and he asked where I was staying in Paris so that he could send me a copy. When I replied that we were at the Ritz, there was a moment of terrible silence. I hastily explained that there was very convenient parking in the Place Vendôme, but it was no good. Billetdoux and Madame Billetdoux rose to their feet, said sombrely, 'We do not hold with such luxury,' and departed.

I had Billetdoux's own word for it that *Tchin-Tchin* was a play of 'Christian optimism'. Nevertheless I was subjected to a great deal of good-humoured badinage both from my colleagues and the public for maintaining that *Tchin-Tchin*, whose hero and heroine begin by behaving in a normal middle-class manner, and then descend from comparative wealth into total and deliberate poverty, and end by insulting their relations, is a Christian play.

Tchin-Tchin does in fact upset all our ordinary outlook on life. It seriously asks us to accept that a mother who finds her son drunk in the gutter, and robs him whilst he is lying helpless, has been, in so doing, touched by grace. Billetdoux's hero, a businessman whose wife has left him for a fashionable doctor, takes absolutely literally Christ's command to the rich young man to sell all that he has, and to give it to the poor. He resigns all his rights in his business, and ruins himself. He and the doctor's own wife begin at first by grieving over and resenting their betrayal; they end by accepting it, not in any spirit of sentimental forgiveness, sweetness, and light, but by the total application of the most ruthless things that Jesus ever said. Césaréo encourages Paméla Puffy-Picq to ring up his mother-in-law and call her a 'sauteuse' and a 'conasse', and I well remember the thrill of horror that swept through the audience (the tiny audience) of the Théâtre de Poche when these abominable words were uttered with remarkable vigour by the actress Katharina Renn. But they were necessary words, for did not Christ say, 'Think not that I am come to send peace on earth: I came not to send peace, but a sword . . . And a man's foes shall be they of his own household?'

When his mother-in-law replies in suitably similar terms, Mrs. Puffy-Picq hangs up the telephone, and Césaréo feels an immense relief.

> What, he asks, is there else to be done? 'Nous avons injurié les voisins, le concierge, votre époux, mon épouse, mes beaux-parents, mes frères et soeurs, le pasteur anglican, mon curé, mon adjoint, mon ancien capitaine, le commissaire du quartier,—anonymement, mais quoi!— quelques amis familiers et nos relations les plus huppées. Bon. Qui nous restes? Dites-le!'[22]

And Paméla replies, 'Bobby'.

Says Césaréo, 'You have only to turn him out into the street.' To which Paméla answers, 'I cannot. I am his mother.'

That is the last bond to be broken, the bond between mother and son, the final fulfilment of Christ's relentless words: 'The father shall be divided against the son, and the son against the father; the mother against the daughter, and the daughter

---

22. We have insulted the neighbours, the concierge, your husband, my wife, my parents-in-law, my brothers and sisters, the Anglican clergyman, my curé, my partner, the local police—anonymously, but all the same!—my former captain, some old friends, and our stuffiest relations. Good. What more is left? Tell me.
BILLETDOUX, François: *Tchin-Tchin*, La Table Ronde, Paris, 1961.

against the mother; the mother-in-law against her daughter-in-law, and the daughter-in-law against the mother-in-law.' It is fulfilled in the last scene in the play, when Paméla, now reduced to the utmost poverty, finds her drunken son asleep in the gutter, and takes his wallet from his pocket.

Equally revolted as Anouilh or Audiberti, by the spectacle the world offers him, Billetdoux is nevertheless, in spite of all appearances to the contrary, a constructive dramatist in a sense in which they are not. For he provides a remedy for the evil and distress he sees around him. This remedy is the complete abandonment of materialism, and the uncompromising adoption of Christianity as he sees it. The progress of Césaréo and Paméla Puffy-Picq is not from rags to riches, but from riches to rags: and according to Billetdoux it is a blessed progress. They begin by losing husband and wife; they end by losing everybody. That too is blessed. Freedom and salvation can be found only in the complete abandonment of all earthly ties. Most orthodox Christians would accept that stated as a simple proposition; but when Billetdoux translated it into the terms of *Tchin-Tchin* there were few who could recognise the play as Christian at all, and none who regarded it as optimistic. It is difficult for contemporary audiences instinctively to feel that a man who starts with a Rolls-Royce and finishes with broken boots has actually made an outstanding success of his life. *Tchin-Tchin* has strong claims to be looked on as the most startling, the most implacable, and the clearest play of the century.

One other dramatist of the post-war years has suggested with serenity that the world's case is not hopeless. This is Françoise Sagan, who, unlike Billetdoux, is not a Christian at all. Sagan decided at a very early age that she was an atheist. She is generally regarded, as she herself ruefully says, as a woman of pleasure, whose life is filled with fast cars and light loves, sun-drenched days and hectic nights on the Côte d'Azur. But actually the most striking feature of her work, from the delicate poetic dreaming melancholy of her first novel, *Bonjour Tristesse*, to her plays, *Château en Suède*, *Les Violons parfois* . . ., and *Le Cheval évanoui*, is its simplicity and innocence. She is too readily considered to have touched pitch; but if she has done so she has not been defiled.

Léopold, the hero of *Les Violons parfois* . . ., faces the same problem as Alarica. He is surrounded by evil. Twenty years old, an innocent from Nantes, on a walking tour, he calls on his rich uncle in Poitiers. He finds that his uncle has died, and left him sole heir to his house, his factories, and thirty million francs. Nothing has been left to Charlotte, his uncle's mistress, nor to his sister Augusta, nor to Antoine, who is Charlotte's lover. When Léopold arrives they are boiling with indignation, and are determined to rob him. Nothing in the world is easier. Within a few moments of his arrival he has signed his inheritance over to Charlotte. They are amazed, and are confident that they have a fool to deal with, a weakling.

But they are wrong. When he cares about something sufficiently Léopold exerts himself instantly. In the first battle of wits that he has with Charlotte and Antoine (over the house he has promised to buy for the elderly servant Celia) they simply stand no chance at all against the determination of his inflexible will. The reason that he does not resist robbery is simply that from the beginning, as Césaréo and Paméla succeed in doing only at the end, he has no interest in money, nor in the things that money could provide him with. Like Alarica he surrenders power to evil; unlike her he does not surrender himself.

Nor is the spirit in which he gives up his fortune in the least like that of Césaréo and Mrs. Puffy-Picq. He has no resentment, and no hostility, and no desire to cut himself off from those amongst whom he is thrown. In Ivy Compton-Burnett's *A Family and a Fortune* which Julian Mitchell adapted for the stage, the principal character, Dudley, also comes into a fortune, and also allows himself to be robbed. Also, like Léopold, he is a meek man. But he permits his possessions to go because he covets esteem; and he thinks that esteem can be purchased with money. Léopold does not think that esteem can be purchased with money. He does not think about money at all. He is simply a good man. If we ask Miss Sagan what is the remedy for all the world's ills, she replies simply this: goodness and innocence.

Léopold's goodness rebukes Charlotte, and makes her despise herself. She can appreciate the extraordinary strength of what to her companions, Antoine her lover, and Augusta the sister of her former protector, seems to be nothing more than weakness. 'Il est bon. Et ce terme est plus lourd que tous les autres, bien qu'il soit ridiculisé, usé, abaissé.'[23] But this strength leads

---

23. He is good. And this word counts more than any other, although he is mocked, swindled, humiliated.
SAGAN, Françoise: *Les Violons parfois . . .*, Julliard, Paris.

to no conventional victory. Such a victory is not what is proposed to us by Miss Sagan. Léopold's generosity with money does not make him either loved or respected. In one of the most affecting and poetic scenes in *Les Violons parfois* . . . Charlotte and Léopold stand at the window, looking at and listening to the town band of Poitiers playing amongst the plane trees in the square below, and Léopold is so happy that he says he would like to stay in Poitiers for ever. Charlotte bitterly explains that he is not liked in the household, either for himself or for the money he has given away. He is on the contrary hated. But Léopold remains serene, and his serenity angers Charlotte. She wishes that he would show some anger, some passion. But he does not. He carries his abandonment of personal rights to the extremest possible lengths. *Les Violons parfois* . . . is one of the most uncompromising plays ever written.

Léopold does not admit, the idea never even occurs to him, that he has a prior, still less an exclusive, claim on anyone or anything at all. When he proposes marriage to Charlotte, a woman twenty years older than himself, he does not expect Antoine to give her up. Antoine has over many years established rights which, he says with staggering composure, he would not dream of disturbing. It is on these terms that Antoine falls in with the proposition, with a tolerant, satisfied contempt, and the last scene of the play shows Léopold announcing his marriage amongst sniggering laughter whose note of derision he does not even notice. He is himself utterly serene, with a serenity that only Charlotte recognises, as she stands with her eyes fixed on the ground, half in shame and anger, and half in affection and admiration, as the curtain falls. The figure of Marie Bell, as she stood apart in these last moments of the play, transfixed by the presence of an incomprehensible goodness, was very memorable.

Long before the present psychological passion for playing emotional games had ever been heard of, Françoise Sagan wrote a play founded in this very perversion. It was her first play, *Château en Suède* (1960), and it has remained her most famous, though it is not in my opinion her best. It is possibly her most brilliant. It is set in a Swedish castle cut off from the world for several months by snow, and all its dialogue and its feelings are disturbingly and consummately out of the true. It is peopled by characters who appear to be eccentrics (they dress in eighteenth-century costume), but the truth dawns chillingly and slowly that they are in fact murderers. The last scene is one of domestic felicity, with all the world content and happy, the unsettling effect of the play being due to the fact that none of this happiness is deserved, and that the harmony of personal relationships ought not to exist. A discarded and incarcerated wife blissfully awaits a baby by her supplanter's brother; her husband, who has pretended to commit a murder, quietly enjoys the sister of his wife's lover; and outside in the snows is the dead body of a man they have resolved to kill, neither the first such body nor the last. Yet there is in the play, in the part of the lover, the breath of a desire for just such purity and innocence as later Miss Sagan revealed in *Les Violons parfois* . . .

Though everyone in the French theatre felt and responded to the spirit of the age the only man who systematically analysed the influence of society upon the drama was Jean Vilar (b. 1912) who when on tour with Jean-Louis Barrault and Madeleine Renaud in 1951 was recalled from London to take over the direction of the Théâtre National Populaire. As early as 1937 Vilar combated the prevalent notion that there could be no great theatre because men had ceased to be united by a common religious faith. He maintained that they were united by a calm collective despair, and that on this basis great drama could be founded: a basis on which Samuel Beckett was later to build.

For the theatre of just before and just after the war however he felt an unbounded contempt. If Audiberti could discipline himself to the strict laws of the theatre, he said, he might produce great work, and shortly afterwards Audiberti confirmed that Vilar was right by offering *Le Mal court*. Sartre and Albert Camus deserved praise for tackling the eternal problems of humanity, but their work was vitiated by the banality of their style. The only first-class living dramatist was Claudel. He thought Anouilh's *Antigone* inferior to the original. In 1942 Vilar played Synge in the provinces at a time when the theatre in Paris was in his opinion given over to baseness. This was the period that Jacques Charon considered to be a golden age. But according to Vilar, even as late as this, and despite the work of Copeau, nothing had changed since the nineteenth century. The public flocked to the plays of Cocteau, Salacrou, and Achard, who are exactly the same as Rostand, Porto-Riche and Dumas *fils*.

To Vilar the theatre was a very serious thing. It reflects the soul both of the individual and of society. The insolence of the valets in Lesage and Marivaux, the aggressivity of Figaro towards his employer, the Count Almaviva, are not far from the summoning of the States-General and the confiscation of the property of the nobility and the Church.

Anouilh, Sartre, and Giraudoux all used Greek legends as the basis for much of their work. Vilar had little patience with this classicism. The time had come, he argued, to break away from the classical tradition, to recognise that France in 1949 was nearer to the tumult of the Middle Ages than to the ordered temper of the court of Louis XIV or to the ancient Greeks. He was an atheist, but he felt nearer to a medieval mystery than to a tragedy by Racine. For this reason he praised *Sodome et Gomorrhe*, not *La Guerre de Troie n'aura pas lieu*, as Giraudoux's finest play. In *Sodome et Gomorrhe* the last melodious echo of Racine has vanished, and in its place there is a cry of terror, doubt, and anger, like the cry of Adam when he was driven out of Paradise. It was Dionysus who would revive the French theatre. This is an odd remark, for Dionysus was Greek, but not perhaps typically Greek.

By 1948 Vilar had come to the conclusion, just like Janin, Dumas *fils* and the tigers of the Royal Court, that audiences needed changing as well as what was offered to them. The thought of these new audiences roused him to great excitement. 'Le théâtre à Paris', he wrote,

> ça n'est plus qu'un musée. Il y faudra tout reprendre et refaire au moins l'architecture de la scène et l'ordonnance de la salle. Je tâcherai quelque jour de m'expliquer là-dessus. En attendant affirmons ceci:
>
> 1000 places à 100 francs valent mieux pour notre art que 300 places à 400 francs, par exemple.
>
> Une salle où l'on peut embrasser sa voisine, manger et boire, pisser n'importe où vaut mieux pour notre littérature dramatique que les théâtres pour élite ou bonbonnières bourgeoises.[24]

---

24. The theatre in Paris is no more than a museum. Everything must be re-made, both the architecture of the stage and the regulation of the audience. Some day I shall try to explain all this. In the meantime:

   1,000 seats at 100 francs are better value for our art than 300 at 400 francs.

These are rousing words, and no doubt Vilar meant them. In the course of his career he probably attracted into the Palais de Chaillot more organised trade unionists than did any other theatre in Europe. But I myself never saw any evidence that his audiences behaved with the joyous abandon that he here describes.

In the great decade of the TNP at the Palais de Chaillot Vilar had to make some modification of his principles. In particular he gave up his opposition to the classics. In his first season this was already becoming apparent. Between 17 November 1951 and 20 December 1952 he presented eight pieces: *Le Cid* (Corneille), *Mère Courage* (Brecht), *Le Prince de Hombourg* (Kleist), *L'Avare* (Molière), *Nucléa* (Pichette), *Lorenzaccio* (Musset), *Meurtre dans la cathédrale* (Eliot), and *La Nouvelle Mandragore* (Vauthier). When the TNP received its five millionth visitor in 1962 the play being performed was, ironically enough, *La Guerre de Troie n'aura pas lieu*.

What Vilar did stick rigidly to was the conviction that the theatre must reflect the struggles and contradictions of the times. He applied this principle with a meticulous conscientiousness that would surprise and shock many British directors who shared his progressive outlook. It was his belief that the director should interpret the meaning of a play, and not manhandle it so as to make it present his own views. He claimed praise for presenting both the Communist *Mère Courage* and the Nazi (his own word) *Prince de Hombourg*. Moreover he did not turn either work against itself. In playing Brecht he revealed the baseness of war, and the anarchic confusion that war breeds in the minds of ordinary people. But in *Le Prince de Hombourg* he showed the grandeur of war, its sacrifices, and its glories. He maintained that thus he was showing the dialectical struggle of the age. It is an interesting example of the devotion of the company to Vilar's principles that Gérard Philipe, who was himself a dedicated Communist, played Kleist with an enthusiasm that quickly became legendary.

This attitude naturally did not please everybody. Barrault himself protested. Jean-Paul Sartre complained that classics

---

An auditorium where you can embrace your neighbour, eat and drink, and piss where you like is worth more for our dramatic literature than theatres for the élite and the bourgeoisie.
VILAR, Jean: Oeuvres Complètes

were good in their day, but that a proletarian audience such as Vilar aimed at wanted plays written for and about itself. Vilar replied that when the TNP played at Gennevilliers, which had a Communist council, it was *Le Cid* that drew full houses, not *Mother Courage*. Rather disingenuously he refrained from adding that in *Le Cid* Philipe, then at the height of his fame as a film star, gave one of the greatest performances of his career. It was almost certainly the film star rather than Corneille who roused the enthusiasm of the people of Gennevilliers.

Vilar's prescience in foretelling as early as 1937 that great drama might result from the spiritual despair of the age was remarkable. It is unlikely however that at that date or even several years later he would have guessed that it would come from Samuel Beckett (b. 1906). For then Beckett seemed a comparatively high-spirited writer. He was not yet subdued by the events of the war, nor appalled by Nazi brutality and its devastation. It was *En attendant Godot* (1953) that made him famous, but already in 1938 he had with *Murphy*, written in English, acquired a small but enthusiastic body of readers, chiefly clustering round Iris Murdoch and Denis Healey, both on the eve of taking their brilliant Firsts in Greats at Oxford.

Murphy is a comparatively light-hearted book, about a series of adventures near the Lot's Road power station between a resolutely supine Irishman and a determined harlot. Murphy likes to tie himself up in a chair; Celia on the other hand is one of the few active characters in Beckett's work. She may agree with Vladimir and Estragon in *En attendant Godot*, and with Hamm and Clov in *Fin de partie*, that the world is an absurd place, but unlike them she has by no means given up hope of doing something about it, even if it is no more than considering the desirability of changing her pitch. She is rarely still. She fetches Murphy a horoscope. She visits her bed-ridden grandfather, whom she exasperates with her topographical exactitude about where things of trifling importance happened to her, such as meeting Murphy as she turned out of Edith Grove into Cremorne Road, with the intention of refreshing herself with a smell of the Reach. She might almost be called a woman of action, and when she finds Murphy face down on the floor, fastened and bound, with his chair on top of him, she efficiently untrusses him, and puts him to rights.

Celia belongs to a time when Beckett still felt that humanity could patronise the solar system. The opening words of the book

33. *En Attendant Godot* (Babylone 1953) with Jean Martin, L. Raimbourg, Pierre Latour and Roger Blin. Photograph by courtesy of Lipnitzki-Viollet

are 'The sun shone, having no alternative, on the nothing new,' and on page two there actually occurs the word 'pleasure', as, moreover, a thing humanly attainable. The feeling that man is capable of effective action was destroyed in Beckett by the war. Vladimir and Estragon wait an infinite time for someone who never comes. The possibility of going to meet him does not occur to them. Winnie, in *Happy Days*, is happy enough, but she sinks deeper and deeper into the ground. The powerlessness of man is in fact curiously illustrated by the way in which worldwide fame came to Beckett himself. It was the production by Peter Hall of *Waiting for Godot* at the Arts Theatre in London in 1955, rather than the French production by Roger Blin in 1953, that first made Beckett's name familiar throughout the world's theatres. Hall's was a very fine achievement, funny and at times with an imagination that took wings, but it was not what Beckett intended.

Vladimir and Estragon are clowns. The function of a clown is to fill in the intervals between those circus turns which are considered important. The *tour de force* of *En attendant Godot*, as Michel Corvin points out, is to make these intervals occupy the whole show. They symbolise Beckett's feeling that the only thing that ever happens is nothingness. But in Peter Hall's production of *Waiting for Godot* Vladimir and Estragon are not clowns, but tramps, and tramps they are now thought to be all over the world. It is in accordance with the absurdity of the universe that Beckett should have become famous through a metaphor that has gone wrong.

Beckett, in the famous antitheses of his most renowned plays, is still much influenced by the cadences of the Prayer Book with which he was familiar in his youth. Jean Genet (b. 1910) is even more influenced by the Mass. He regards the elevation of the Host as a moment of drama never equalled in the theatre, and all his plays—*Les Bonnes, Les Nègres, Les Paravents*—are demonstrations of the pomp of ritual. But of ritual used for purposes of moral revolution.

Some of the dramatists we have been considering view the evil of the world with dismay and despair; some in desperation are driven to accept it. Genet alone embraces it with joy and triumph, and clothes it in the rich panoply of incomparable prose. American schools are fond of asking pupils to draw up lists of great men of our time, expecting and often getting names like John F. Kennedy, Winston Churchill, or Charles de Gaulle. It is unlikely that any of these would be included in a list compiled by Genet.

He has in fact actually drawn up such a list: it appears in the celebrated opening pages of *Notre Dame des Fleurs*. When I read this I thought it a rather fine, even if bizarre, piece of prose. I did not realise how revolutionary and morally subversive it was until I spoke of it to John Gielgud. Gielgud is by no means a conventional member of the privileged classes, and as far as religion is concerned he is much less susceptible to its influence than Genet himself. But I have never forgotten the horror and disgust, the actual physical revulsion, with which he spoke of this celebrated passage. His face was aghast as he recalled the litany of murderers, perverts, and male prostitutes before whom Genet prostrated himself in masturbating ecstasy.

Genet exalts murder. In *Les Bonnes* (his best play, first produced in a wave of avant-gardism by Jouvet himself) the maids are sexually transported at the thought of murdering their mistress: they want at the same time to kill and to become her, as the priest turns Christ into a wafer that he eats, and His blood into wine that he drinks. The present age is inclined to be lenient with murder; it is not, as Genet is, sexually excited by it. (At least, if it is, it does not admit it.) But where Genet differs from the progressive mood of the time is that he is as exalted by the punishment of murder as by murder itself. He is thus a stange mixture of the wildly subversive and the extreme reactionary. For one of the symbols he most extravagantly reveres is the guillotine.

For all his reputation as a man implacably opposed to bourgeois philosophy he would never support the abolition of capital punishment. If he adores murderers he adores also their decapitation. His morality is completely revolutionary; it is perhaps the only truly revolutionary morality to be found in any dramatist. Like Beckett he sees the misery of the world. Unlike Beckett he is not concerned with its inevitability. Unlike Anouilh he is not concerned with protesting against it. Unlike Sagan or Audiberti he does not seek to circumvent it. He finds in it pleasure, exaltation, sexual satisfaction. When Notre-Dame at his trial explains gently how the idea had come to him of strangling M. Rogon, and the President of the court asks him why he committed the crime, he replies 'I was in a state of fabulous poverty.' When Genet wrote *Notre Dame des Fleurs* the word fabulous had not yet reached its present degradation.

Like Genet, Marguerite Duras is interested in crime, and at one period of her life wrote articles on criminal subjects for *Le Nouvel Observateur*. She was born in 1914 in what was then known as Indo-China. Both her parents were teachers. The Far East, as in her novel *The Vice-Consul*, and her play *India Song*, inspires much of her work. The desire of travel, the wish to see new places, is a theme that continually reappears in her writing, from the cruising of the rich American woman in *Le Marin de Gibraltar* to the long and weary wandering of the native girl in the opening chapters of *Le Vice-Consul*. On a smaller scale it is seen in the person of the commercial traveller in *Le Square*, who is serenely happy to move with his humble wares from town to town, from hotel to hotel, from café to café, seeing a new block of flats put up here, a new dance hall there, and children, the symbol of the coming generation, everywhere. It is about a child in a French colony in what I take to be a Far Eastern country that she has written one of her most memorable works, the remarkable short story which she calls *Le Boa* (1954).

This story is about two experiences which befell again and again a thirteen-year-old girl in a seedy boarding school in a distant, unnamed city, a school directed by the septugenarian Mlle Barbet. These experiences happened every Sunday, when all the other girls were away with their parents for the weekend. Only the young narrator remained, because her mother was too poor to take her away. Each Sunday Mlle Barbet would accompany the child to the Zoological Gardens, and there they would watch in a mixture of fascination and horror a magnificient boa, its skin shining like steel, swallow the live chicken always given to it on Sundays. This made a powerful impression on the young girl; especially the somnolent spectacle of the contented boa after his dreadful meal.

> Cette paix après le meurtre . . . Ce crime sans tache, sans trace de sang versé, sans remords. Cet ordre après la catastrophe, le paix dans la chambre du crime.[25]

This awful sight was invariably followed by another in its way not less revolting. When they returned to the pension Mlle Barbet and the girl would go to Mlle Barbet's room and drink a cup of tea with a banana. The girl then went to her own room, only a moment later to hear Mlle Barbet calling, 'Come and look.' She went back to Mlle Barbet's room. She always found Mlle Barbet in the same place, in front of the window, smiling, in pink knickers and corset, with her shoulders bare. The girl stood before her, and gazed at her, as it was understood that she had to do each Sunday after Mlle Barbet had taken her to

---

25. This peace after the murder . . . This crime without a stain, without a trace of spilt blood, without remorse. This order after the catastrophe, the peace in the room of the crime.

see the boa. 'Always have fine underwear,' this seventy-five year old woman would say. 'It is important. Learn that. I learned it too late.' She had never had the opportunity of showing herself undressed to anyone but the girl, and the girl understood every thing from the first time that the incident happened. The house was filled with death. The age-old virginity of Mlle Barbet.

'What an existence,' sighed the old woman. The girl tried to comfort her. She reminded her that she was rich, that she had fine underwear, that what Mlle Barbet had missed was perhaps not of great importance. Mlle Barbet sighed, and began to put on her clothes, and the girl knew that for a week it was finished. That for a week she would have tranquillity.

The boa devoured and digested the chicken, and regret devoured and digested Mlle Barbet, and both these devourings regularly succeeded each other, and took on for the girl a significance different from that which they would have had if they had occurred independently. Had she seen only the first sight she would always have felt for the boa a horrified hatred for making her endure in imagination the sufferings of the chicken. Had she seen only Mlle Barbet undressed, she would not only have experienced by intuition a sense of the calamities of all mankind, she would also have thought of the injustice of the social order, and of the many forms of servitude to which humanity is subject.

But she did not see them independently. She saw them one after the other, and always in the same order. Because of this succession the sight of Mlle Barbet threw her back on the memory of the boa, the splendid boa which in full sunlight and full health devoured the chicken, and took its place in an order shining with simplicity and native grandeur. In the same way, after she had seen the boa, Mlle Barbet became horror itself, a secret horror—for one did not see Mlle Barbet's virginity being devoured, one saw only its effects, and smelt its odour—a hypocritical and timid, and above all, useless horror. All this in contrast to the green paradise of the criminal boa. The boa, though it frightened her, gave her also a sense of courage and boldness. The girl thus felt real aversion only for a certain kind of horror, a hidden, unacknowledged horror; and no horror at all for murderers. On the contrary, she suffered for those in prison, not on account of the discomfort for their persons, but because their adventurous and misunderstood temperaments had been stopped in their fatal career.

34. *Le Square* with R. J. Chauffard and Kitty Albertini (Studio des Champs Elysées 1956). Photograph by courtesy of Lipnitzki-Viollet

She suffered also for prostitutes, for whom she felt an admiration equal to that she experienced for assassins. When her mother told her she thought she would never get a husband, the figure of Mlle Barbet came into her mind, and she consoled

herself with the reflection that happily, if all else failed, there
remained the brothel. For she was convinced that Mlle Barbet
was old and hideous and horrible only because she had never
had children to nourish nor a man to uncover her.

In *Le Boa* are the seeds of all Marguerite Duras's plays.

In *Le Square* there is the only symbol of placid and enduring
happiness that exists in all her work. Significantly it is a zoological garden, and what provokes and creates it is the sight of
lions, creatures which, like the boa, are deadly to mankind.
The commercial traveller whose conversation with a nursemaid
in a Paris square one spring afternoon is the substance of the
play, tells the girl how he wandered into the garden in a country
far from Paris just as the sun was setting. He had left his valise
in his room in the hotel just before dinner, and he went for a
walk round the city. He lost his way, and found himself in the
zoological garden. It was a very ordinary adventure, but as
soon as he entered the garden he felt overwhelmed with life. It
seemed to him all of a sudden that the garden had been made
for him just as much as for others.

> Comme si—je ne saurais vous dire mieux—j'avais grandi
> brusquement et que je devenais enfin à la hauteur des
> événements de ma propre vie. Je ne pouvais pas me
> décider à quitter ce jardin. La brise s'était donc levée, la
> lumière est devenue jaune de miel, et les lions eux-mêmes,
> qui flambaient de tous leurs poils, bâillaient du plaisir
> d'être là. L'air sentait à la fois le feu et les lions, et je le
> respirais comme l'odeur même d'une fraternité qui enfin me
> concernait. Tous les passants étaient attentifs les uns aux
> autres et se délassaient dans cette lumière de miel. Je me
> souviens, je trouvais qu'ils ressemblaient aux lions. J'ai été
> heureux, brusquement.[26]

---

26. As if—I don't know how else to put it—as if I'd suddenly grown taller,
and was equal at last to my own life. I couldn't bring myself to go
away. A breeze had started to blow, as I said, the light had turned the
colour of honey, and the lions, their coats all aflame, yawned with the
pleasure of being there. The air smelt of fire and lions, and I breathed
it in as if it were the incense of some secret brotherhood, a brotherhood
that I belonged to at last. All the people there were concerned with
one another, as they took their ease in the golden light. I remember
thinking that they were like lions. And I was suddenly happy.
DURAS, Marguerite: *Le Square*, NRF Gallimard, Paris.

It is a constant underlying theme, hinted at in *Le Boa*, and elaborated in the situation of the wealthy woman in *Suzanna Andler* (1968) who cannot decide whether to rent an expensive house on the Côte d'Azur, that happiness is not lastingly obtainable in society constituted as it is. The commercial traveller in *Le Square* comes nearer to achieving it than any other of her characters. He at any rate has no desire to change anything. Yet even he, when the sun goes down the sky, and the hour of closing the square approaches, feels a touch of despair. But if there ever had been any power of struggle in him, it is there no longer. He sits supinely upon the park bench, and the nursemaid urges him in vain to rise and go for a walk with her. He is an extraordinarily attractive character; one of the great charms of the play is his exquisite formal courtesy, which the girl fully returns. Duras treats him with sympathy, but in the end she despises him. He is 'un lâche' (a coward). He has nothing in him of the lion or the boa, just as the girl has no thought, even as a last resort, of prostitution. One feels that in Duras's eyes anyone is 'un lâche' who merely accepts happiness, and does not fight for it and fail, in this society, lastingly to get it.

She has a greater respect for Suzanna Andler, even though Suzanna is rich, and the commercial traveller is not. For Suzanna does not achieve happiness. Neither does the gambling son in *Des Journées entières dans les arbres*. His mother comes from a French colony (or has it been taken over by the inhabitants?) to see him for possibly the last time. She tries to persuade him to return with her to her factory, her eighty workmen, her growing wealth. Yet she hopes that he will refuse. She has had other children, and they have worked like her, and become rich like her. But the only one she cares for is Jacques, who as a boy spent whole days in the trees when other children were at school, and has been in the trees ever since. Now he is nothing more than a dancing partner in a small night club. He loves his mother; he often goes hungry; but he cannot tear himself away from his conventionally sordid life. He even takes all the old woman's jewelry, and gambles it away. Instead of being angry his mother is exalted with joy, and breaks out into a great paean of praise. She compares him with those who have apparently succeeded in life, men she despises though she has succeeded herself.

Si vous saviez, les autres, à coté, ceux des autres, à coté,

35. Madeleine Renaud and Jean Desailly in *Des Journées entières dans les arbres* (Odéon 1965). Photograph by courtesy of Lipnitzki-Viollet

des veaux, des conseilleurs, des messieurs avec . . . des
vêtements de prix . . . des chevaliers . . ., des automobiles
de prix . . ., des maisons de campagne . . ., des imbéciles . . .,
des travailleurs en un mot . . ., et des femmes, et des

appartements, et des vacances, et des enfants, des ribam-
belles d'imbéciles . . ., des exigences . . . Ça donne des
ordres à des domestiques, c'est servi à table, petit déjeuner
au lit, ça va en Italie, c'est laid, c'est laid, c'est gros,
gros . . . Regardez-le à coté, ce jeune homme, cet enfant,
ce . . . prince, oui . . . mon enfant.[27]

This is of course only a besotted old woman's view of the son
whom she loves, but in her extraordinarily tender and pathetic
performance of the part Madeleine Renaud, in Jean-Louis
Barrault's words, 'framed' the term 'ce prince'. She gave it outstanding importance, as though it were a definitive verdict and
a crown. One feels that Duras agrees with her; for Jacques, for
all his weakness, is a destroyer, like the boa. Nevertheless, there
is a great tenderness, a sympathy for the old woman's grief, in
Madame Duras' treatment of Jacques' mother, which is equalled
in the rest of her work only in her compassion for the retarded
child in *L'Après-midi de M. Andemas*.

When Madame Duras has got hold of a theme she works on
it continually. In *L'Amante anglaise* (1967) she gives an entirely
new, and improved, version of the crime she first studied in *Les
Viaducts de Seine-et-Oise*; and *Détruire, dit-elle* (1969) begins with
the same scene as her short story, *Les Chantiers*, written fifteen
years earlier. A woman is sitting in the window of the dining
room of a hotel on the edge of a wood. A man at another table
watches her. There are tennis players outside. The man and
the woman make each others' acquaintance. In *Les Chantiers*
the characters have no names, and their talking to each other
is presumably the beginning of a love story. For, as in *Le Boa*
and in the mind of the girl in *Le Square*, this was a time when
Duras believed that fulfilment might possibly save the world.

---

27. If only you knew. The others, beside him, other people's children,
compare them with him! Morons! People who give advice. Gentlemen: with . . . expensive clothes . . . signet rings . . . fast cars . . .
country houses . . . Imbeciles! In a word, people who work! With
wives and houses and holidays and children; swarms of imbecile brats.
With things they cannot be without . . . they give orders to servants,
they're waited on at table, they have breakfast in bed, they go to Italy,
they're ugly, ugly and coarse . . . Besides them, look at him, at this
young man, this child . . . this . . . prince, yes . . . my child.
DURAS, Marguerite: *Des Journées entiéres dans les arbres*, Gallimard,
Paris.

But by the time of *Détruire, dit-elle* a change has come. In it the man quickly reveals that his name is Stein, and that he is expecting his wife to join him in three days. In *Les Chantiers* the man and woman disappear together into the wood. In *Détruire, dit-elle* the woman draws back, and returns to the hotel. The partial family destruction wrought by Jacques in *Des Journées entières dans les arbres* here becomes universal and total. It is a great wind that breaks and cracks the forest and the world.

India Song (1973), which was written at the request of Peter Hall for the National Theatre, and has been filmed by Madame Duras herself, is the product of the ruptured (her own word) universe left at the end of *Détruire, dit-elle*. Two female voices tell the story of Anne-Marie Stretter and Michael Richardson, who are characters in the novels *Le Ravissement de Lol V. Stein* and *Le Vice-Consul*. The first voice is infatuated with the story of Anne-Marie Stretter; the second is infatuated with the first. Both are gentle and sweet, and neither is quite sane. Neither remembers accurately and completely, yet neither wholly forgets. Nothing is quite certain. Under these voices the story is acted as if in a dream. All the references to the geography of India, Duras insists, are false. The names of rivers and towns are purely mythical. One cannot drive in an afternoon from Calcutta to the mouth of the Ganges, nor to Nepal. The Prince of Wales hotel is not on an island of the Delta, but at Colombo, and the administrative capital of India is not Calcutta, but New Delhi.

There is a sense of dislocation, of the overthrow of order.

Whether upon these ruins will be built a better world Madame Duras does not say. Of all the dramatists who have occupied the French, or indeed any other stage, since the appearance of Beckett and Pinter, she is, in my opinion, the most arresting, the most haunting, and the most important.

This, I know, is a dangerous statement for a critic to make. Critics have not come too well out of this survey of the last hundred and fifty years of French theatre. Sarcey was wrong about *Pelléas et Mélisande* and *Antony*; Janin was right about *Antony* but dishonest about Deburau. Adolphe Brisson was excessively excited by the big scene in *Madame Colibri*, and Bordeaux misunderstood the talent of Bernstein. Léautaud failed to see any merit in *M. Trouhadec*, and Dubech chose as the man of the future someone who has never been heard of since. Pierre Brisson is said to have got a celebrated actor put into gaol, and Brasillach ended before a firing squad. Jean-Jacques Gautier was not entirely right about *Le Mal court*, and everybody was wrong about *Tchin-Tchin*. Decidedly critics have not shown up so well that the general public need have confidence in their judgments. Nevertheless, I shall say and repeat, this time without qualification, that of all the dramatists who have emerged in the French or any other theatre since the first appearance of Beckett and Pinter, incomparably the most arresting, the most haunting, and the most important is Marguerite Duras.

Index

⊕PAN AM®

The world's most experienced airline.